T5-BBX-759

Also by the Author

Competitiveness and the Kami Way
ISBN 1 85972 416 7

Competitiveness and Corporate Culture
ISBN 1 84014 559 5

Healthy Culture and Unhealthy Culture

HIDEO YAMASHITA

Ashgate

Aldershot • Burlington USA • Singapore • Sydney

Published by
Ashgate Publishing Ltd
Gower House
Croft Road
Aldershot
Hants GU11 3HR
England

Ashgate Publishing Company
131 Main Street
Burlington
Vermont 05401
USA

Ashgate website: http://www.ashgate.com

British Library Cataloguing in Publication Data
Yamashita, Hideo
    Healthy culture and unhealthy culture
    1. Corporate culture 2. Social psychology 3. Organizational
    change 4. Corporate culture - Japan - Case studies
    I. Title
    658.4'02

Library of Congress Control Number: 00-134013

ISBN 0 7546 1444 1

Printed and bound by Athenaeum Press, Ltd.,
Gateshead, Tyne & Wear.

Contents

List of Figures and Tables

Acknowledgements

I would like to express my sincere appreciation to Tan Chwee Huat, Professor, Faculty of Business Administration, National University of Singapore, Rob Goffee, Professor, London Business School, Michael West, Professor, Aston Business School, and Ed Schein, Professor, Sloan School of Management, MIT, for their support and endorsement of this book. I would also wish to thank Michael Scott Morton, Professor, Sloan School of Management, MIT, for giving me insightful comments and valuable suggestions. I am extremely grateful for the support and encouragement given to me by Ikujiro Nonaka, Professor, Japan Advanced Institute of Science and Technology, Hokuriku. Tan Thiam Soon, former Vice Dean, Faculty of Business Administration, National University of Singapore, has provided sustained support and encouragement to me over the years. Shandon Alderson and Yoshikazu Shinoda, my colleagues, were of great assistance in finalizing the chapters. I will extend my thanks to Sarah Markham, Kirstin Howgate and other editorial staff at Ashgate. Finally, thanks to Makoto Iida, Founder of Secom Group, to whom I owe much.

Whatever the weaknesses of this book, they are mine alone.

Preface

Corporate culture is the personality of a company and its identity. Just as an individual's personality develops and matures while they grow, a company's corporate culture evolves and forms as it develops. Corporate culture is said to consist of three levels in that it evolves and forms as a company develops and grows. According to Ed Schein, there are from the deepest 'Basic Assumptions', 'Values', and 'Artifacts and Creations'. Before the founding or before joining a company, every individual has learned, where they belong to, its prevailing culture. There are more than one culture in society. However, there is one leading culture which has prevailed among them. The leading culture has historically evolved and formed among people of a nation. To be precise, the leitmotif of a nation's culture formed in its early days and then has been passed down and adapted through its history by learning from generation to generation. In Japan's case, the leading culture was formed early in its history, i.e., the Kami Way. Thus the argument that corporate culture is of a four-level structure with the leading culture of the nation at its deepest level.

A corporate organization is a being acting in an environment where competition evolves constantly. Companies that win competition after competition will live long. What is significant here is for a firm to maintain its competitiveness strength for a long time. There are elements indispensable to competitiveness, and corporate culture is duly related to those elements That is, a healthy corporate culture is appropriate to the elements of competitiveness while unhealthy culture is inappropriate to them. Companies with culture unable to adapt to the elements of competitiveness are not in a position to continue to win in a competitive market. The elements of competitiveness are, in turn, to be embraced in the 3-Layer Structure of Enterprise Competitiveness. The first layer of the 3-Layer Structure can be called the Enterprise Organismic Foundation, the second layer the Enterprise Economic Base and the third layer Management System. There are also 7 Principles for the elements of competitiveness to belong to. They are creativity, righteousness, fairness, equality, sharing, self-cultivation, and learning and knowledge-accumulation. Corporate cultures which can adapt to the 7 Principles of Enterprise Competitiveness are healthy while those unable to are unhealthy.

In this context, the Kami Way is learned through tacit knowing just as in other cultures. As Michael Polanyi said, a growing young mind tacitly absorbs and interiorizes the whole conceptual framework and the rules of reasoning out of the culture they belong to. Thus, the intellectual power obtained after they mature is rooted in the knowledge tacitly absorbed in the above way. Their thoughts founded on the tacitly acquired knowledge, in turn, gives meaning to all explicit knowledge. With informal recognition obtained through tacit knowing, one can formalize relations of things and make formal theories. In that sense the basic part of culture is absorbed in the deepest level of one's mind and can have the capacity of acting as the principle of integrating. The core of the Kami Way is to practice the principles of life. It is to learn and adapt to nature. It is to learn human nature from the principles of nature. The Kami Way has only one criteria to judge things. It is to judge if things are healthy or unhealthy. Those adaptable to the principles of life and the principles of nature are taken as being healthy while those unadaptable to them are taken as being unhealthy. The Kami Way simply recognizes the state and phenomena of nature through 7 principles. The truth is always simple. In the Kami Way, one strives to understand the principles of nature as simply as possible. There is such systems thinking in the Kami Way. As will be explained later, the attributes of the Kami Way are adaptable to the 7 Principles of Enterprise Competitiveness.

Which firms can we model as one with a healthy or unhealthy corporate culture? In Chapter 6 and Chapter 7, we shall respectively explain a pair of companies, one as an example of healthy corporate culture and the other as that of an unhealthy culture. In Chapter 6, we will address the cultures of the House of Mitsui and the House of Kohnoike and search for the main causes of Mitsui's success and Kohnoike's failure by tracing historically how their cultures evolved and formed. In Chapter 7, we will take up the cultures of the House of Mitsubishi and the House of Ohkura and pursue the primary cause of the difference between Mitsubishi's success and Ohkura's failure by following their cultures' respective evolvement and development. In Chapter 8, we will address the thinking behind the Internet, explain how to interpret it, and examine how the organization of W.L. Gore & Associates, Inc. is similar to that thinking. Not surprisingly, we will find that the culture of W.L. Gore & Associates, Inc. is fully adaptable to the 3-Layer Structure of Enterprise Competitiveness and the 7 Principles of Enterprise Competitiveness.

The history of corporate culture is as old as that of corporate organization. When a firm is founded, its corporate culture originates also. Accordingly, there is much to be learned from past corporate cultures. On the other hand, the subject of corporate culture is that of the present and that of the future. Thus, it is also meaningful to examine corporate culture as associated with present information technology which may be the forerunner of the future. The author thinks that the 3-Layer Structure of Enterprise Competitiveness and the 7 Principles of Enterprise Competitiveness can be a thread uniting corporate culture of the past, the present and that of the future. Competitiveness and corporate culture are unseparably united. Understanding this relationship in a productive perspective may be a large step forward for business leaders to create a genuinely healthy and creative company in the 21st century.

1 What is Corporate Culture?

Corporate culture is to a corporate organization what personality is to an individual. Corporate culture is the personality of a company and its identity. As the individual's personality develops and forms while they grow, so the company's corporate culture evolves and forms as it develops.

The corporate organization is a living being, active in a changing environment. As such, it has to adapt itself to the changing environment. The environment here includes markets such as the product market, the materials market, the financial market, the capital market and so on, the government and the society, not to mention the natural environment. On the other hand, the company is an organization. As an organization, it has objectives with a number of people co-working for it. To render its co-working effective, it integrates the organization, which is called the internal integration. To put it another way, a company is a living being that manages its organization by adapting itself to the external environment and rendering its personnel duly co-working internally.

While the corporate organization develops and forms, it continues to cope with the issues of external adaptation and internal integration, thereby learning from them. Through its development process, the members of the company learn how to view things, how to think of them and what state of being to comply with, whereby they evolve and form corporate culture. The way of viewing things here can be alternatively said 'a view of the world' or 'a paradigm', the mode of thinking 'a view of values' and the state of being 'an ethical norm'. While the company evolves and forms, the corporate culture comes to be shared among its members. It is the shared way of viewing, the shared mode of thinking and the shared state of being among the members. It is to be noted, however, that there is not merely one culture in a company. Usually, there are more than one corporate culture in the company, i.e., one leading culture, sub cultures which follow the leading one and a small culture or cultures which have nothing in common with and independent of the leading one. To simplify the matter, we shall regard the leading culture of a company as its corporate culture from here on and proceed with our argument accordingly.

Next, there is an issue on the depth of corporate culture, i.e., how deeply it is embedded in the company. There are generally argued the three levels in its depth. According to Ed Schein, there are from the deepest 'Basic Assumptions', 'Values', and 'Artifacts and Creations'. 'Basic Assumptions' are the cultural essence, things taken for granted and invisible which are at the deepest level.

'Values' are at a greater level of awareness, and 'Artifacts and Creations' are defined as visible but often not decipherable. This is Ed Schein's three-level structure model, and his analysis based on that model is insightful indeed. However, the author argues for a four-level structure of corporate culture. The author's line of argument is as follows. Corporate culture is said to consist of three levels in that it evolves and forms as a company develops and grows. Before the foundation of the company or before joining it, however, each member of it has learnt, as an individual member of the society he (she) belongs, its prevailing culture. There are more than one culture in the society too, but there is one leading prevailing culture among them. The leading culture has historically evolved and formed among people of a nation. To be precise, the leitmotif of a nation's culture formed in its early days and then has been succeeded in its history through learning from generation to generation. In the US case, for instance, it is the leading culture originally formed in the pioneer days in its history, while in Japan's case it is the leading culture formed in its nation-creating in history, i.e., the Kami Way. The leading culture is thus embedded most deeply in the people of each nation. It is, really, at the deepest level and on that level are placed, layer by layer, those three levels as Ed Schein duly argues. Thus, corporate culture consists of four levels.

The multi-level character of corporate culture has much meaning when a corporate organization needs to be transformed. Since the external environment changes, the corporate organization has to change as well and fit it well. Yet, for the organization to be changed, its culture needs to change. Where, then, does a force that drives the culture to change come from? According to Ed Schein, the deeper levels of corporate culture can act on the shallow ones to change them. For instance, surface assumptions can be transformed by more embedded assumptions. This means that there hardly occurs any change at deeper levels. What, then, can a firm do when it is faced with a critical situation and ought to change fundamentally its ethos, values and philosophy being at deeper levels? In such a situation, what may reveal itself is the nation's culture that is implanted in the members of the firm at the deepest level. We may date back to the pioneer days to understand the ultimate thrust for change of a US firm, and the nation-forming days to know that of a Japanese firm.

We need to know, in this connection, that there are such corporate cultures as to be adaptive to the changes of the environment. Examples will be shown in Chapter 6 and Chapter 7. By those examples, we can infer that there is an unchangeable level in the multi-layer structure of corporate culture. In other words, there is something of power held at the deepest level which keeps corporate culture healthy. That level does not change at all even when the environment changes and it is absolutely needed in keeping a firm healthy. For the reasons above, the author takes the position of putting corporate culture in perspective of whether it is healthy or unhealthy, not whether it is adaptable to a strategy nor to the environment. As will be described later, a healthy corporate culture is defined as one that fits well the elements of competitiveness, while an unhealthy culture is defined as one that is unadaptable to them.

In this context, it is to be noted that there are some predecessors who followed, consciously or not, the line of thought of how a business organization can be healthy or unhealthy. Respectively, they showed insight into human nature in their own way. There was Chester I. Barnard's view on organization. His view was that an organization is a living being and made it clear that whether any command holds authority or not is up to the person who is to accept it. He also asserted that the morality level directly affects the ability of the organization to endure. That is, the company's foresight, long-term aim and lofty ideals comprise the foundation for its people's collaboration to continue. If morality is low, the leadership will not last long or it is likely that no one will be able to succeed it. Barnard showed keen insight into human nature (C.I. Barnard, 1968). Douglas McGregor believed that the conventional view on command and control is founded on the concept of power of authority and the principle of social stratum. This view assumes that one dislikes working by nature and that a normal individual prefers command. However, it is a narrow assumption due to the lack of understanding of human nature, which McGregor called the X theory. McGregor also stated that one works for a goal which they enjoy. The will to achieve their objective is dependent on their motivation. Fleeing from responsibility and their thought of safety first is not their innate nature. Most people are endowed with abilities of originality and ingenuity. They have potential capabilities to grow and develop, and to cooperate with each other. They can also control themselves. McGregor referred to this as the Y theory. With the Y theory, an organization can innovate itself and take an altogether new approach in management. He asserted further that the organization is not a pattern of relationships among individuals but that of relationships among groups. Accordingly, the management may raise its competitiveness if they realize that their success in team management is psychologically and economically advantageous to the firm (D. McGregor, 1960). Paul R. Lawrence and Jay W. Lorsh regarded business organization as a system and analyzed the organismic relations of its division and integration. They also maintained that whoever works in the organization desires, more or less, to satisfy their will to achieve their job. Therefore, they argued that such an organization is to be built as one can duly and rightfully carry out their job (P.R. Lawrence and J.W. Lorsh, 1967). Richard E. Walton tried to analyze the organization through the socio-technical approach. He made it clear that successful introduction of advanced information technology into an organization relies on the workers' desires and their frame of mind (R.E. Walton, 1989). Peter Senge, in turn, proposed the concept of a learning organization. He argued that there are five disciplines of learning which are indispensable for a firm to endure. The disciplines are

3

systems thinking, self-mastery, overcoming mental models, building up a shared vision and team learning. A firm can be either good or bad, depending on how well it puts those disciplines into practice. He also asserted that building up a learning organization is to create an organization which is in harmony with human nature (P.M. Senge, 1990). In the first half of the 18th century, in Japan, Baigan Ishida propounded the Learning of Human Nature. In his view, the truth is in one's daily life and reflective thinking. It is of significance for one to master it on their own. The Learning of Human Nature is an idea whose core concept is practical ethics for merchants to live up to. It duly argues the meaning of merchants' existence and their role in the society. It admonishes a merchant to be honest, saving-minded and diligent on the one hand, while maintaining that profit making is not unnatural. His observations were founded on keen insight into human nature (M. Shibata, 1962).

A corporate leader's role is crucial in forming corporate culture. In particular, a founder's intentions, their way of viewing the environment and their thoughts and values will be succeeded and shared, as a basic framework of corporate culture, by the existing and new members of the organization. The founder comes to grips with external adaptation issues of how to define the environment and how to survive in it, and internal integration issues of how to organize the relationship among members given the environment thus defined. By solving those issues one by one to develop the organization, the founder's intentions, their own way of viewing the environment, their thought and values and ethical norms of conduct come gradually to be reinforced, and shared among the members. In the early days of a firm, the founder struggles to reinforce their thought and tries to embed it deep in the firm so that it is shared and practiced by the members. The founder often expresses their management philosophy. In most cases, management philosophy includes values derived from successful experience in the early days of a company.

For instance, in 1954, shortly after the foundation of Honda Motor Co., Ltd., founder Honda stated his philosophy that 'the driving force in developing a company is its thought on management'. He, then, came up with 'Basic principles in running Honda' as follows.

1   Take the company as the place for one to train oneself to the fullest extent.
2   Take a wide view of the world.
3   Esteem logic in doing things.
4   Produce things in perfect concert and harmony among the members.
5   Put more priority on work and production than capital.
6   Do everything according to justice.

(H. Itami and T. Kagono, 1997, originally in Japanese)

Here are concisely stated founder Honda's ways of viewing, modes of thinking and state of being. As is the case above, it is the founder or their philosophy that is the main thrust in making corporate culture prevailed in the firm in the period of its foundation and early growth. The corporate culture thus firmly implanted is to be the source of the firm's distinctive capabilities, the object its members identify with and the force in promoting people to co-work in the organization.

A firm is composed of a group of people. The founder is powerful indeed, but the corporate culture is not only the founder's creation. The company's members are also at stake. In other words, what emerges as corporate culture reflects not merely the founder's thought but also 'the complex internal accommodation' (E. Schein, 1985) created by the members to run the organization in spite of or around the founder. It is a matter of course that the founder takes the initiative. After the firm has gone through its foundation period and grown, it naturally reaches the mid-age and maturity stages unless it creates something to revitalize itself after its growth stage. When the firm gets into the stages of mid-age and maturity, its corporate culture, which has thus far facilitated its development and growth, is not necessarily a good guide for the future. The environment may have changed. The distinctive strength of its organization may have altered due to, for instance, turnover of people, i.e., change of its members. Under those circumstances, first of all, the shallower levels of culture have to be negated and altered by the deeper levels. In so doing, leaders of revolution are needed. In the mid-age and maturity stages, most companies have a strife or discord between the conservative people that are committed to conventional practices and the progressive that intend to alter them.

As Ed Schein describes, in this connection, there are three functions that corporate culture performs, i.e., (1) survival in and adaptation to the external environment, (2) integration of its internal processes to ensure the capacity to continue to survive and adapt, and (3) anxiety reduction (Ed Schein, 1985). Out of the above functions, the conservative people focus on the function of (3) anxiety reduction and hold on to conventional practices so that they can ease their mind. The progressive party, on the other hand, pursues to renovate the corporate culture to recover the functions of (1) and (2), i.e., to survive in the external environment and to integrate internal processes. If the conservative party takes the leading part, the firm would end up taking a route to deterioration and extinction. If the progressive party takes the initiative, the organization would be renovated and brought back again to the foundation and growth stages.

In explaining how corporate culture forms and how it alters, in this context, we can draw an analogy from the dissipative structure in fluid dynamics. The dissipative structure is the opposite of the balanced structure. The balanced structure is a structure like crystal formed when there is no flow of materials and energy. The dissipative structure is, on the other hand, a dynamic structure created by the flow of materials and energy, and it is flexible enough to alter when the flow changes (K. Nishiyama, 1985). For instance, according to Bernoulli's principle, when we make a difference in temperature between the upside and the downside part of a container of liquid, the pattern of flow changes from a state of honeycomb to that of roll. And then, when we make a big difference in temperature between them, the pattern of flow turns out to be a pattern of turbulent flow. In this way, patterns of dissipative structure in a system change consecutively as the flow of materials and energy grows (K. Nishiyama, 1985). Within the system, in this context, there are small changes called 'fluctuations' which accidentally appear and disappear. A fluctuation that happens to emerge grows bigger, or some fluctuations compete with each other and one out of them wins to get to grow, whereby a dissipative structure comes into being. What makes the ecological system function is such a flow of energy whereby the system is maintained as a dissipative structure (K. Nishiyama, 1985). If a corporate organization is likened to a being acting in the ecological environment, the concept of dissipative structure can be applied. That is, corporate culture is thought to emerge out of fluctuations. A corporate organization starts when its founder and small members, who take concerted action with the founder, initiate routine-breaking and unconventional activities with the aim of attaining some ideal or objectives. Their activities here correspond to the fluctuations in an ecological system. For the 'fluctuations' to grow, it is necessary for the members to act in concert with the founder. Through the concerted action, 'a dissipative structure' appears on the stage. That structure is corporate culture formed in the early days of the firm. The dissipative structure is flexible enough to change dynamically. As a firm grows and develops, and matures, the external environment may have considerably altered. In such an environment, the firm could bring itself back into a state of instability, force 'a new fluctuation' to grow and generate 'a new dissipative structure'. That is, the firm can revive itself by creating new fluctuations. The power of reviving, in this connection, lies in the deepest level of corporate culture. In other words, the deepest level, as stated previously, is the unchangeable part of corporate culture and the last resort.

We are now in the period of technological revolution. Information technology, in particular, advances at a high speed. Under the circumstances of such phenomenal changes in technology, how is corporate culture to be taken? In the first place, the introduction of new technology into an occupation, an organization and a society can be taken as a matter of cultural transformation. Around the technology used in an occupation, for instance, there are built customs, values and images. In a similar way, there are work practices, values and technical images built around the technology used for work in a company. As the present technology is substantially transformed, or a new technology is brought into the present work, accordingly, the workers not only have to learn new work practices different from the conventional ones, but also they are forced to alter their view of values and images on their work. In other words, their corporate culture needs to be modified or altered. Here, again, it is the deepest layer of culture that can promote such modification or alteration.

In this connection, the part played by the leader and that by the corporate culture are two sides of the same coin. The leader tackles external issues of how to define the environment and how to live in it, and internal matters of how to organize the relationship among the members to survive in the environment thus defined. On the other hand, the corporate culture fulfills the part of adapting to and surviving in the external environment, that of integrating internal processes to secure such adaptation and survival. The leader is the one who represents the corporate culture of their organization. Since they really manifest it, they hold power in the organization.

Next, then, in what circumstances does a corporate culture at the deepest level reveal itself? As a firm faces a crisis, typically, its deepest culture will appear. As the leader and its members emphatically cope with the crisis, the deepest level of culture reveals itself to promote them to tackle it in quite a different way from that before. In the process of so addressing it, they come to form new ethical norms, values and new modes of doing work. In the above sense, it can be said that a crisis creates a new culture. People's emotional commitment in such a situation is intensified and their concentration on learning immensely increases. Crises are most likely to emerge from significant external adaptation problems and crucial internal integration problems. Immense decreases in sales, overstock and technological obsolescence are examples of external problems. Due to such problems, the company may have no choice but to lay off workers, which may, then, cause a critical internal problem. What can one expect to see when the company's leader grapples with such a case? In the course of addressing it, their thoughts on the importance of people and human nature gradually reveal themselves. That is, their fundamental way of viewing, mode of thinking and state of being rise to the surface from the unconscious level of their mind.

2 What is Healthy Corporate Culture?

Corporate culture is a multi-level structure. The author argues that it is a four-level structure with the leading culture of the nation being at the deepest level. The other three levels, in this context, evolve and form as a corporate organization grows and develops. Those three levels are, from the deepest, 'Basic Assumptions', 'Values', and 'Artifacts and Creations' as Ed Schein argues. Deeper levels of culture have the capacity to renovate shallower ones. Therefore, provided the deeper levels of a culture are healthy, the firm can 'metabolize' itself in an appropriate and right way. If they are unhealthy, it can not.

A corporate organization is a being acting in the environment where competition goes on incessantly. Companies that can win competition after competition can live long. What is of significance here is for a firm to maintain its competitiveness strength for a long time. There are elements indispensable to competitiveness, and corporate culture is duly related to those elements. That is, healthy corporate culture is appropriate to the elements of competitiveness while unhealthy culture is inappropriate to them. Companies with culture unadaptable to the elements of competitiveness are not in a position to continue to win on the competitive market. If it so happens that a firm can survive due to the government's protective policies and regulations for some time, such policies and regulations can not be maintained long and the firm will, in time, be thrown out of the market. Regulated markets or regulated industries, where competition is unduly restricted, spread poison over the national economy. They are the sources of rendering the national economy unhealthy. The just and fair market principle is fundamental to the healthy state of the national economy. It is for the above reason that a firm needs to form a healthy corporate culture adaptable to competitiveness strength.

What is the competitiveness, then, to which corporate culture is to be adapted? We shall next look into it in detail.

3 What is Competitiveness?

3.1 The 3-Layer Structure of Enterprise Competitiveness

Competitiveness is the power to maintain stable and long-term predominance in a just and free market economy. Accordingly, the foundation for competitiveness is an enterprise ethos originating in the establishment of an enterprise where there is a spirit of denying, spirit of negating the status quo, spirit of creativity and spirit of creating a vision. In such an enterprise, every member is willing to grapple with any situation without fear of failure, and those in the workplace freely exchange their views and opinions. Following the enterprise ethos are elements of enhancing initiative and those of norms, preparation of investment conditions, enterprise ethics and education. As a whole, they may well be considered as an 'Enterprise Organismic Foundation'. The Enterprise Organismic Foundation is a prerequisite for a firm to live and act as an organic being.

Next, the firm must prepare an economic base. One such base is generally termed the 'infrastructure', which is composed of two lines. One line consists of physical assets such as facilities, machinery, networks and the like. The other line consists of human resources such as executives, scientists, engineers, workers and the like. To build and stabilize the infrastructure, a company must continually employ human resources and procure physical assets. It also needs to invest in personnel training and their education.

Next, what is indispensable for the enterprise to continue to grow and develop is environmental improvement and conservation. This not only includes conservation of the natural environment, cooperation with and participation in a community and its activities, but also includes the environment of the workplace and attention and care to human relations in the workplace.

The final element of that base is the diffusion of new ideas, planning and others. New ideas, reforms, improvements, and intelligence about new products come into practical use only when they can be diffused, without restriction, both inside and outside an enterprise. The mechanism and the speed of diffusion are directly related to an enterprise's effective performance. Smooth lines of communication ought to be promoted. Furthermore, managers should communicate the vision, policies and the state of affairs of their enterprise to the workers. Taken together, let us name those elements of competitiveness listed above as the 'Enterprise Economic Base'. Once the Enterprise Organismic Foundation and the Enterprise Economic Base are established, competitiveness can then enter the arena. The first focus on enterprise activities is effectiveness. For example, problems which must be solved to attain effectiveness, include how to commercialize technology, how to improve cost, quality and delivery terms simultaneously, how to communicate actively both inside and outside the enterprise, how to develop, introduce and make use of technology in gaining strategic predominance, how to enhance a spirit of competitiveness and how to maintain a free market principle throughout a firm. Next, there are ethics which, in a sense, are in opposition to effectiveness. Included in this category are views such that every member of a company is a leading actor and that diligence is highly valued in their work, fair employment and appropriate post transfer, fair and just chances of promotion provided to any personnel, improvement of ethics in general and ethics of relations between management and workers. In this context, there are quite a few instances in the real world where a viable alternative can only be found in the area between effectiveness and ethics. For example, there are cases where an enterprise attempts to maintain close relations with customers to understand their real needs, or it maintains exceedingly close contact with suppliers in order to attain much higher effectiveness. In both cases, such close contact and relationship might, unexpectedly and mistakenly, deviate from the fairness of business dealings and deteriorate into compromise and protective procedures. Therefore, at all times the first priority is to be placed on the mechanism of the free market system in order for those policies not to harm effectiveness. Also, elements like the development of individual abilities and guarantee of long-term employment do not contribute to effectiveness from a short-term perspective, but do exert a positive influence from a long-term perspective. Positive influences include such qualitative factors as workers' pride and confidence in their own work which in turn, leads to the enhancement of effectiveness. In other words, the policies or elements above can be established only with a tense balance between effectiveness and ethics. This balance is tense in that those policies or elements must be severed from compromise, protectionism, unfair relations, favoritism, etc. There are also such elements of competitiveness as organizational techniques, organization whose workers are barely conscious of organizational hierarchy, recognition of quality as the end result of overall production or service activities, to generate many alternatives to a decision-making process, to demand and expect personnel to do their best and to cope with things flexibly. Taken together, these elements blend into themselves to produce the 'Management System'.

Thus, enterprise competitiveness is composed of 3-Layers which can be called the 3-Layer Structure of Enterprise Competitiveness as shown in the following figure.

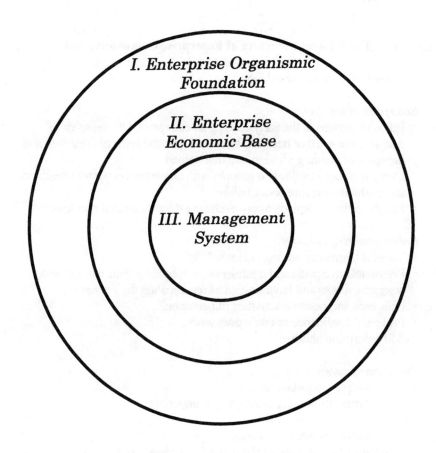

I. Enterprise Organismic Foundation

II. Enterprise Economic Base

III. Management System

Figure 3.1   The 3-Layer Structure of Enterprise Competitiveness

The Structure of Enterprise Competitiveness is composed of three layers. The first layer includes the Enterprise Organismic Foundation. It is the outermost layer, surrounding the second and the third layers. The middle layer is the Enterprise Economic Base which supports the arena for the actors, i.e. the Management System. The innermost layer the Management System. The elements of enterprise competitiveness are, in turn, grouped respectively into one of the layers as in Table 3.1.

Table 3.1   The 3-Layer Structure of Enterprise Competitiveness

I   Enterprise Organismic Foundation

Enterprise ethos
- Ethos originated in the early days of an enterprise, i.e., the spirit of denying, the spirit of negating the status quo, the spirit of creativity and the spirit of creating a vision, are maintained.
- Every member is willing to grapple with any situation without hesitation and without worrying about failure.
- People in the workplace freely exchange their views and opinions.

Enhancement of initiative
- There is teamwork among personnel.
- Personnel have pride and confidence in upholding their enterprise's competitiveness and have a sense of representing their enterprise.
- Diligence and positive activities of personnel.
- Pride and confidence in one's own work.
- Self-reforming abilities.

Provision of norms
- Law (company regulations, etc.).
- Abolishment of practices restricting competition.

Preparation of investment conditions
- Allow a sufficiently long time frame for management.
- Promotion of R&D and production-process R&D.
- Constraints on speculative purchases of enterprises or assets.

Enterprise ethics (Sense of responsibility to the society)

Education (General learning as citizen of the society)

12

II   Enterprise Economic Base

Infrastructure
- Physical assets: facilities, machinery, network.
- Human resources: executives, scientists, engineers, workers.
- Employment of human resources and procurement of physical assets to build and stabilize infrastructure.
- Investment in the training of personnel.
- Education on practical business.

Environmental improvement and conservation
- Conservation of the natural environment.
- Cooperation with and participation in a community and its activities.
- Improvement of the physical environment of the workplace.
- Attention and care to human relations in the workplace.

Diffusion of new ideas, planning and others
- Create smooth communication lines.
- Discussion on the vision, policies and the state of affairs of the enterprise from management.
- Diffuse new ideas, reforms, improvements, and intelligence on new products both inside and outside the organization.

III   Management System

Effectiveness
- Maintain a free market principle throughout the enterprise.
- Encourage competitive spirit.
- Improve cost, quality and delivery terms simultaneously.
- Development, introduction and use of technology to gain strategic predominance.
- Commercialize technology.
- Activate communication throughout.

Tense balance between effectiveness and ethics
- Have a close relationship with customers.
- Have intimate contact with suppliers.
- Organizational techniques.
- Organization whose workers are little conscious of organizational hierarchy.

13

- Recognition of quality as the end result of overall production or service activities.
- Generate many alternatives to a decision-making process.
- Demand and expect personnel to do their best.
- Cope with things flexibly.
- Develop personnel's abilities and continue their learning.
- Guarantee long-term employment.

Ethics
- Every member is a leading actor.
- A view of work in which diligence is highly esteemed.
- Improvement of ethics.
- Fair employment.
- Appropriate transfer of personnel from one post to another.
- Fair and just promotion of personnel.
- Ethics of relations between management and workers.

We have briefly described the 3-Layer Structure of Enterprise Competitiveness and the elements of competitiveness. Every element is indispensable for an enterprise to act in the environment and to attain predominance in the market. As has been explained before, corporate culture is the way of viewing things, modes of thinking and state of being which are attributable to a corporate organization. In other words, it is the view of the world, i.e., how to view the environment, the view of values and the ethical norms of conduct which are shared among people of a firm. If corporate culture is adaptable to the 3-Layer Structure of Enterprise Competitiveness, it is defined as being healthy. If it is unadaptable, it is defined as being unhealthy. A firm with healthy culture has sufficient power and capabilities to continually win in the market, and thus survives.

3.2 The 7 Principles of Enterprise Competitiveness

Probing further into competitiveness, how are the elements of competitiveness, which are embraced in the 3-Layer Structure of Enterprise Competitiveness, at work? The Competitiveness Structure is a structure or a frame of competitiveness. For the elements of competitiveness to work actively, there must be some acting principles. In our view, there are 7 principles in enterprise competitiveness. It is a matter of course that the 7 principles are closely tied with the elements of competitiveness.

Let us first explain what those principles are. We propose the following 7 principles.

14

1   Creativity
2   Righteousness
3   Fairness
4   Equality
5   Sharing
6   Self-Cultivation
7   Learning and Knowledge-Accumulation

We shall explain the above principles from 1 to 7 accordingly.

Creativity

How have companies regarded as excellent today developed and realized their present status? There is no secret about it. At every turn in their history, they did their utmost to change and innovate and produce new and original things of value. In fact, it is due to change and innovation that people mature, business organizations develop, and society makes steady progress. People are likely to desire and seek a peaceful and uneventful living. The same holds true with business firms. However, in reality, no firm can live as such. If any firm should seek to live in peace, its organization would lose vitality, could not respond with new challenges, and would simply degenerate. For a business firm today to continue to develop in the future, its organizational climate will have to remain innovative all the time. To be innovative, it is crucial for them to know, inherit and repeatedly realize to the fullest extent the spirit of denying, the spirit of negating the status quo, the spirit of creativity and the spirit of creating a vision which are present within the firm.

The spirit of denying means to deny all preconceived ideas to create new ones and continue to be innovative. If people live up to commonly accepted ideas and practices, no new and original things would be developed. To launch a new venture and to create something new, one at first must deny generally established concepts. When one tries to do new things, it is of consequence to them to set out what is justified to do and carry it through. One must first deny all that is commonly established. That denial should not be partial. One has to deny in entirety. Then, they can accept anew the things that they can certainly affirm. As an organization grows, members tend to be curbed by regulations made in the past and commonly accepted ideas in the organization. They are likely to see and judge things by precedents. If such customs prevail in the organization, the firm will be destined to follow a path to deterioration. When the firm sets out to construct a new system or venture, the spirit of denying is crucial. In this connection, S. Honda, founder of Honda Motor Co., Ltd., said as follows.

15

A person's past is the exhaust fumes of life. There is no theory but only mixed experience in those fumes. A person has to cast them away once and again. If they hold them long, they will age rapidly, and their life may stop in motion. For an aged adult to revive themselves, they had better forget things of the past soon. They ought not to show off their experienced ability in a narrowly limited area. They should, instead, understand that the truth is only the value for a person.

(S. Honda, 1992, originally in Japanese)

The spirit of negating the status quo implies to crush one's attachment to convention, accept new ideas, not to cling to the status quo, and one's will and belief in advancement and progress. Man dislikes change by nature. Without change, it is sufficient to do things customarily and mechanically just as in the past. With change however, they must cope with new challenges, which is cumbersome and demands energy. Therefore, man does not like change and tends to adopt methods and thoughts which have been used so far. Thus when one tries to do new things, they are certain to encounter disapproving attitudes toward them to keep the status quo intact. However if people adhere to conventional ways, unwilling to give their energy to progress, the organization will follow the path to misery and degeneration. It is of utmost importance for the firm that its members deny preconceived thought, break down a lazy frame of mind which wishes to live in the existing state, to spare no effort to direct their energies to bringing about new things, and to maintain their will and belief in advancement and progress.

The business organization also needs vision. If the members of a firm appropriately and correctly comprehend a vision as the future state of the firm and share it among themselves, they can duly exert their capabilities. In this sense, vision can be said the crux of collaboration. Throughout history, leaders instilled their visions into the members of their organizations.

The spirit of creativity is the essence of leadership. S. Honda believed that originality and creativity embodied Honda's philosophy. He did not like to be an imitator. He was a man with a spirit of independence and self-respect. For instance, he tenaciously committed himself to an air-cooled engine. In his view, it is very logical to cool an engine without radiator fluid. A water-cooled engine is convenient to use, but not original. It is only an imitation of the forerunners. We can also find his originality and persistence in the development of the FF, the front engine front drive system at Honda. The FF system currently can be found everywhere, but at the time of its development it was an epoch-making discovery. Honda's hit car, the Civic was a box-style car similar to a matchbox. When it was put on the market in 1972, many people were astonished and wondered if such an unusual car could be sold at all. To prevent emitting exhaust gas, Honda developed a new engine called CVCC. While other car manufacturers tried to purify exhaust gas with a catalytic agent, Honda tried to

16

do so with the development of the engine itself. Tirelessly, he devoted himself to create new technological advances. He had no intention of making money through financial techniques using stocks, paintings and real estate. He argued,

> Capital has a tendency to become frivolous and volatile. We have paid much respect to thought, time and ideas so that we could establish Honda as it is now. This management principle ought to be maintained forever. Capital should serve work and production, not the other way around.
>
> (S. Honda, 1992, originally in Japanese)

Next, let us examine the leadership of A. Morita, former chairman of Sony Corporation, as another case. Sony has pushed ahead with demand creation, i.e., creating markets where none exists. Demand creation is a venture to plan, produce and market an as yet non-existent product. There is no reason to do market research for such a product. No research is needed for newly developed products in virgin areas of the market. Things manufactured must be sold. In other words, demand creation is needed, not market research. Let us suppose that some ideal product, which some people have long dreamed of but no one has ever seen nor has ever produced, ultimately materialized somewhere. The producer would have to create the needs and desires for that product among its consumers if it is to become a real commodity. If some people have a wish for such an ideal product, it must be feasible to create needs and desires for that product among other people as well. Thus, the needs and desires for this ideal product would increase. A. Morita argued,

> A producer that plans and manufactures a product should make a market and promote sales for it on its own marketing plan.
>
> (A. Morita, 1994, originally in Japanese)

It is said that creative function is the essential property of leadership (C.I. Barnard, 1968). Most people are bestowed with a faculty of ingenuity (D. McGregor, 1960). For the members of a firm to perform creative activities, it is indispensable for them to have an enterprising spirit and courage and capabilities to reform themselves.

Righteousness

Creativity rests upon one's loyalty to the truth and the principle of righteousness. For a firm to exist, it must be beneficial and valuable to society. The firm must supply commodities and services to society so that people can obtain usefulness and benefits from them. Since it contributes to the society in such a way as above, the firm can reap profits. As a result of producing things of value, the firm can receive profits to grow. This is the right model for a firm to follow. For example, if it is highly probable for the price of a tact of land to rise in the not too distant future, the firm should not buy and hold it for reselling. Although it is certain that the firm can gain a high return if the tract of land rises in price, the rise in price is not good for society. In a society where it is necessary to purchase land to build homes, the high price of land is detrimental. Therefore, speculative purchases of land is not beneficial for society. In the recent past, many companies and people believed in the myth that real estate will necessarily increase in price. Due to the destruction of the bubble economy, they suffered a tremendous loss and huge damage. The bubble story of land is only one example. What is righteousness for a firm is to work diligently to create things of new value to the society to receive profits. The firm should not give itself up to a frivolous social climate. It should stick and keep to the principle of righteousness.

In fact the trust relationship between buyers and sellers in the free market system is founded on the principle of righteousness. In general, for a market economy and business dealings to develop, earning money must be seen as a virtue. It is to be noted however, that as precondition of this ideology, there is the principle of honesty and righteousness. To uphold the principle of righteousness, there are many laws, ethical norms and practices. Furthermore, for a firm to endure, morality is a prerequisite. Foresight, long-term objectives and lofty ideals are the foundation for its members' collaboration to endure. If the firm's morality is low, its leadership will not last and a successor will not emerge (C.I. Barnard, 1968).

As to the relationship between managers and workers, it is to be noted that trust can be established when workers come to believe in the sincerity of their managers (D. McGregor, 1960).

Fairness

Two and more people join to form an organization. When two people collaborate, they may realize a potential more than the sum of their individual potentials. This is the key of organizing. The more people there are, the more effective its organization could be. However, for such effectiveness to be realized, the organization needs to be honest, and consistently fair, and worthy of endeavoring and working for. How then, is such an organization formed? How can one build an organization which people feel is just and fair? The first priority is to make no room for compromise. In a sense, this may be an organization of obstinate and persistent people. However with compromise, the organization can not be transparent and clean. Increasing the number of cases of compromise reduces the properties of transparency and cleanness. If the members believe that a certain degree of compromise is necessary to do things smoothly and that certain shrewdness is useful, the driving force of their organization will diminish. Even if faced with difficulties, one ought to cope with them in a fair way of thinking. When every member of an organization is willing to take such a persistent attitude, it will come to be limpid in climate and worthy of working. One should build an organization where such thought permeates that there is value in striving to accomplish things wholeheartedly with a fair mind.

Sony declared in 1965 that they would discard the curriculum vitae of their personnel. In other words, academic history and the like were not to be recorded with personnel cards or whatever. A. Morita argued,

> This is a step forward to the establishment of a fair principle. That is, once the entrants are registered at Sony, the records of their school career are not to be referred to nor to be made public. They can exert their talent and ability with no restriction whatsoever, and they are to be evaluated only on their performance.
> (A. Morita, 1994, originally in Japanese)

As a matter of fact, fair treatment gives workers peace of mind (D. McGregor, 1960). Fair treatment, therefore, should start at the beginning of employment.

Fairness is the principle of the free market system. The principle of righteousness is a prerequisite for the free market system to truly function. That is, with the principle of righteousness, the fair principle of market can be at work. In such sense, fairness rests upon the principle of righteousness.

Equality

Equality is the principle of democracy. Everyone is indispensable and of value. An organization should not impair the dignity of the person whatever happens. S. Honda said,

> It is a sin to discriminate against people. Man must be treated equal anytime and anywhere. There is no difference whatsoever between one person and another.
> (S. Honda, 1992, originally in Japanese)

Factions which tend to be formed in an organization run squarely against man's equality. Honda argued,

> If an organization has factions, it means that it lacks the spirit of human equality...If people respect each other and recognize human nature as it is, there will be no factionalism whatsoever. Factionalism is the product of an old-fashioned idea that people stress incidental terms as academic career, background and home town than

man's own value. Where human relations is taken like this, there is no respect for man nor spirit of equality. It gets me angry.

(S. Honda, 1992, originally in Japanese)

In a business organization, everyone can produce change. Accordingly, everyone should get an equal opportunity for education and training, while long-term employment guarantee is to be provided to everyone. As a matter of fact, the product of people's collaboration in the organization is not the result of its leadership but that of the organization as a whole (C.I. Barnard, 1968). In this connection, Honda extremely dislikes authoritarianism. Authoritarianism does harm to originality and creativity. It is humanity's evil spirit. When authoritarianism prevails in a corporate body, it curbs free action and vitality among its members to a considerable extent, thus stagnating its business operations. It prevents its members from fully fulfilling their role. It is an illness for organization. Honda holds no esteem for the title of president. In his view, what is indispensable for an enterprise are the people, technology and the products to be made. He argued,

> I would like to be a man of free will, behaving at will either as a member of a family or of society, and at the same time be conducive to the happiness of family members and friends, and contribute to the growth and development of the society.
>
> (S. Honda, 1992, originally in Japanese)

Sharing

An organization needs a vision of its own. It must create a vision which its members can hold in common. Furthermore, the members of an organization should share knowledge and values. The sharing of knowledge and values is indispensable for them to perform in an organic manner. Without such an organic deeds, technology can not be put into practical use (L. Thurow, 1996). On the other hand, people have an internal control mechanism by which they can make any control from outside utterly useless (D. McGregor, 1960). In other words, if knowledge and values are not genuinely shared among the members of a firm, its vigor will diminish.

For knowledge and values to be held in common, communication is a necessity. Communication is an indispensable element of sharing. True sharing is also founded on the principle of equality. Thus, due consideration to human and physical environment is of great significance. Managers should have open dialogue with workers, take care of human relations and pay genuine attention to the physical environment of the workplace. This care and attention are considered to be the necessary conditions for sharing.

20

Sharing is not only needed internally. Since a business organization is a social being, it is required as corporate citizen to participate in social activities and pay attention to the natural environment (N. Iijima, 1995). It is also expected to share diverse kinds of information with society whenever necessary.

A company usually performs only a part of providing commodities or services. In terms of systems thinking, a company is in charge of a subsystem out of the whole system of business activities. It is a matter of course that it has suppliers and customers. Therefore, it is desirable for the company to share whatever necessary information with suppliers and customers in order to pursue its overall effectiveness.

Self-Cultivation

A person's natural desire is to achieve their objectives. Everyone who works in an organization wishes to gratify, to greater or lesser extent, their desire for achievement. Therefore it is of great significance to form an organization where its members can duly and rightfully carry out their job (P.R. Lawrence and J.W. Lorsh, 1967). In such an organization, a principle of equality such that everyone is indispensable may work properly coupled with a principle of fairness that one's efforts are remunerated. Thus, one's achievement of their objectives is based on the principle of equality and that of fairness prevailing in the organization.

With the base of those principles, the foundation for one to accomplish their work and cultivate themself is the will to achieve their aim. In other words, what is basic to one's self-cultivation is not to resort to petty tricks, not to make excuses. To cope with things directly, not shirking from them, is easy to say but difficult to do. When one plays petty tricks but calculates their actions, they may look intelligent in a way. But what they learn from such temporary success is to not tackle problems squarely but rather to run about to escape. When a difficult issue or an obstacle arises, one ought to grapple with it earnestly and try to solve it with genuine efforts whereby they can truly cultivate themself. As a matter of fact, an appealing and respectable person has the firm will to carry things through and the solid belief and positive thinking that one can realize things through their persistent attempts. Such firm will and solid belief may make a person cultivate themself, gain the respect of others, and assume leadership. They are the root of leading the other members and the source of accomplishing their work.

Learning and Knowledge-Accumulation

A business firm acts in an ever-changing environment. To cope with such an environment, a firm needs to learn continuously (D. McGregor, 1960). When the things learned, in turn, come to be shared among the members of a firm and accumulated in the organization, they will be of use and value. The first essential item to the firm's learning and knowledge is technology. Technology alone can not generate anything. If it is commercialized in one way or another, it brings benefit to the firm. The meaning of technology development can be found here for the firm. To gain strategic predominance, a firm ought to not only specify what technology to take and develop on its own, but also introduce technology from outside the firm. In that way, it can acquire a competitive edge. While new technologies and commodity production and development methods are indispensable for a firm to endure, it is also crucial to introduce human resources and physical assets equipped with necessary knowledge from outside the firm to synergetically make use of them. Learned knowledge is stored and embodied in the physical assets and the human resources of the organization. Therefore it is significant to get the assets and resources equipped with knowledge such that they are prepared to operate at any time.

The second item of the firm's learning and knowledge is systems thinking. What is important is not to judge matters impetuously. A long-term view and a long-range policy are required for the firm's long-term success. It is of consequence to take relations among matters or things as a whole. For a firm, precise information and the number of alternatives proposed from many different viewpoints determine the quality of decision-making. If there are few alternatives, it is probable that a many-sided deliberation is not given to the subject. It is crucially important to study as many alternatives as possible (D.A. Aaker, 1984). Also, commodities must be improved systematically. It is of consequence to improve cost, quality and delivery terms simultaneously. In trying to achieve this, new knowledge is gained, which raises the effectiveness of management (D.A. Aaker, 1984). It is also vitally important for a firm to have a positive way of thinking. Big organizations, in a negative way of thinking, tend to exclude those who have made mistakes from promotion and select those with no or few mistakes. Promoting in such manner may adversely affect the firm. Under such circumstances, people will not dare to do things to the utmost but instead, try to be as faultless and safe as possible. They will be weak in spirit and lose the meaning and value of their work. As one proverb says, failure is the turning point toward success. Success does not come if there is no failure. Success can not be without risk. As the case may be, it is necessary to give due advice to a person who has failed and ask them to reflect upon themself. It is much more important, however, to take a failure as an altogether positive element to promote that person's and company's growth in the future. Growth is only made feasible by one's positive attributes, such as not being afraid of making failures. Positive thinking is the only way for one to keep on making a daring advance. In coping with radically different matters, fixed ideas are the most detrimental. Therefore it is of significance for one to cultivate their intellectual abilities daily so as to flexibly deal with whatever matters arise. To foster such flexible intellectual abilities, one must be given opportunities to cultivate their abilities continually. The third item of the firm's learning and knowledge is human resources. A firm acts in the society. Accordingly, it is a precondition for the firm's activities that its members have general knowledge as citizens of the society. Also, investment in the training of personnel and their education on practical business are indispensable for the firm to hold and develop an effective and valid knowledge base. On the other hand, a business organization is an organic system of collaboration. For the organic system to function effectively, the organization must be adapted for human nature. What is to be noted here is that a person sets out to learn willingly and voluntarily only when they recognize that they alone can decide their future (P. Senge, 1990). In other words, the principle of equality is a precondition for learning. A company prepares itself for new technology by institutionalizing the personnel's continual learning. The foundation of people's continual learning is the principle of self-cultivation. What has been learned, in turn, turns out to be powerful and effective if it is shared among the members of the firm and accumulated within the organization (I. Nonaka and N.Konno, 1995). Learning can be of use and value with the principle of sharing being at work. As to team learning, it is crucial for the members to sense equality with their colleagues and hold common objectives. Man likes to learn by nature. Learning is the true character of man. When it comes to learning in the organization, however, one has to bear in mind the principle of equality, that of self-cultivation and that of sharing.

Summary

There are 7 Principles at work in enterprise competitiveness. They are the following.

1   Creativity
2   Righteousness
3   Fairness
4   Equality
5   Sharing
6   Self-Cultivation
7   Learning and Knowledge-Accumulation

The 7 Principles above are closely related with each other. Creativity is founded on one's loyalty to the truth and the Principle of Righteousness. The Principle of Righteousness is a precondition for the free market system to function. The fair market principle is valid only when the Principle of Righteousness is at work. In

23

that sense, fairness also rests upon the Principle of Righteousness. In a business organization, sharing of knowledge and values is indispensable, and sharing is based on the Principle of Equality. People working in an organization wish to satisfy, more or less, their desire to achieve their objectives. To gratify their desire of achievement, the organization needs a principle of equality that everyone is indispensable and a principle of fairness that every effort is rewarded. In other words, self-cultivation is based on the Principle of Equality and that of Fairness. Learning rests upon the Principle of Equality. The foundation of people's continual learning in the organization is, in turn, self-cultivation. Things learned are of use and value when they are shared among the members of the firm and accumulated within the organization. Learning can be put into practical use with the Principle of Sharing at work. Thus the 7 Principles are closely and intimately connected with each other so as to duly function.

Which Principle can be taken as the core principle among the 7 Principles of Enterprise Competitiveness? A business organization is a living being. For the organization to act and endure, it must reform itself continuously. It constantly needs to metabolize itself, fling away old values of no use, and continue to create objects of new value. On reflection, it is innovation that has made the advancement of mankind literally feasible. It is all due to change and innovation that as man grows, a firm also grows and develops and society makes progress. In such a sense, the spirit of denying, the spirit of negating the status quo, the spirit of creativity and the spirit of creating a vision are truly the most important. Thus, the Principle of Creativity is the core principle of enterprise competitiveness. Creativity is fundamental for a business firm to live as an organism. For that reason, as will be described later, the elements of competitiveness which belong to the Principle of Creativity are placed in the first layer of Enterprise Organismic Foundation in the 3-Layer Structure of Enterprise Competitiveness. Creativity is the fundamental principle prior to building the second layer of Enterprise Economic Base and the third layer of Management System.

4 The 7 Principles of Enterprise Competitiveness and the Elements of Competitiveness

We have taken two different views of enterprise competitiveness. One is the 3-Layer Structure of Enterprise Competitiveness which is a static view of competitiveness, and the other is the 7 Principles of Enterprise Competitiveness which is a dynamic view of competitiveness. The ways of viewing competitiveness are different indeed. However, there is an intimate relationship between them.

There are 50 elements of competitiveness in the 3-Layer Structure of Enterprise Competitiveness. Those elements comprise the content of the Structure. More precisely, there are 15 elements in the first layer, 12 in the second layer and 23 in the third layer. On the other hand, for the 7 Principles to function as a dynamic force, the 50 elements must play their role. Thus, each of the 50 elements belongs to one of the 7 Principles and works as the driving force for the Principle it belongs to. That is, the elements of competitiveness are statically positioned in the 3-Layer Structure of Enterprise Competitiveness while they work as promoters of the 7 Principles of Enterprise Competitiveness. By analogy, the Structure is the home where the elements reside, while the 7 Principles are the arena where those elements play their performance. The 50 elements work on the 7 Principles respectively. The 50 elements of competitiveness, which play their performance on their arena, i.e., the 7 Principles, are classified as follows.

The Principle of Creativity : 3 elements
The Principle of Righteousness : 7 elements
The Principle of Fairness : 5 elements
The Principle of Equality : 7 elements
The Principle of Sharing : 10 elements
The Principle of Self-Cultivation : 3 elements
The Principle of Learning and Knowledge-Accumulation : 15 elements

The number of elements for each Principle has no relation to its importance. The 50 elements are not a measure of quantity, but rather qualitative factors. As stated before, the Principle of Creativity is the most crucial among the 7 Principles. Therefore the elements belonging to that Principle are exceedingly significant.

To repeat, the 3-Layer Structure of Enterprise Competitiveness is the structure where the elements of competitiveness are classified according to their innate properties, while the 7 Principles of Enterprise Competitiveness are the arena for those elements to act in actual terms. The elements respectively belong to their own arena.

Now, then, let us explain the elements of competitiveness belonging to one out of the 7 Principles in order below.

4.1 Creativity

The elements of competitiveness belonging to the Principle of Creativity are the following.

- Ethos originated in the early days of an enterprise, i.e., the spirit of denying, the spirit of negating the status quo, the spirit of creativity and the spirit of creating a vision, are maintained.
- Every member is willing to grapple with any situation without hesitation and without worrying about failure.
- Self-reforming abilities.

Ethos originated in the early days of an enterprise, i.e., the spirit of denying, the spirit of negating the status quo, the spirit of creativity and the spirit of creating a vision, are maintained

How have so-called excellent companies today come to their present position? Their history may tell us what lie behind their success. Whenever they have encountered drastic changes and difficulties both inside and outside their organization, they overcame them by changing and innovating themselves, and created new and original ideas, products and services. It is due to change and innovation that people grow, business organizations develop, and society makes steady progress. Man is likely to desire and spend a steady and uneventful life. Business firms are also likely to wish such a living. However, in reality, no firm can continue to live as such. If a firm seeks to live in peace, its organization would lose strength, could not respond coming challenges, and would fall into degeneration. For a business firm today to continue to develop and endure, an organizational climate which is creative and innovative is required. To be creative and innovative, it is absolutely necessary for them to know, inherit and realize the spirit of denying, the spirit of negating the status quo, the spirit of creativity and the spirit of creating a vision which were recognized in the firm's founding days.

The spirit of denying means to deny all conventionally established ideas and concepts so as to gain newly creative ones. The spirit of negating the status quo implies to crush one's attachment to convention and the attitude of refusing new ideas, not to cling to the status quo, and keep holding one's will and belief in advancement and progress. The spirit of creativity is the essence of leadership. The business organization also needs vision. If the members of a firm appropriately and correctly comprehend a vision as the future state of the firm and share it among themselves, they can duly exert their capabilities.

Every member is willing to grapple with any situation without hesitation and without worrying about failure

For people to exhibit their talent and capabilities, the environment around them is a significant factor, but their willingness is also crucial in addressing problems set before them. An organization is empowered by a driving force to accomplish things, but an individual is not powerless either. At times, the individual can demonstrate their abilities to the fullest extent.

Self-reforming abilities

For the members of a firm to perform creative activities, it is indispensable for them to have an enterprising spirit and the courage and capabilities to reform themselves. A healthy spirit can continually renovate itself. It shows interest in many things and quite often asks a simple question 'why'. There is an attitude of mind that tries to think things anew, disregarding established concepts. The healthy spirit can abolish old customs and practices. Unlearning, a crucial attribute of healthy spirit, is absolutely necessary for one not to be overly committed to past learning. It is altogether indispensable in solving the trade-off between adaptation to the present work and that to new changes in the environment. Unlearning is to gain a new life. It is to try to destroy established concepts.

4.2 Righteousness

The following elements belong to the Principle of Righteousness.

- Law (company regulations, etc.).
- Ethics of relations between management and workers.
- Abolishment of practices restricting competition.
- Constraints on speculative purchases of enterprises or assets.
- Enterprise ethics (Sense of responsibility to the society).
- A view of work in which diligence is highly esteemed.
- Improvement in ethics.

Law (company regulations, etc.)

A firm ought to be governed by stipulated laws or regulations. It is not to be ruled in any other way such as paternalism, by-virtue principle and the like. Fundamental norms of people's conduct must be clearly stated in law.

Ethics of relations between management and workers

As to the relationship between managers and workers, trust can be established when workers come to believe in the sincerity of their managers. In fact, collaboration can only be realized with the reliable relationship between management and workers. To render the relationship dependable, ethical norms are to be established between them.

Abolishment of practices restricting competition

A firm can be evaluated by how well it acts in the competitive market. Since such a norm is of absolute necessity, anything restricting competition must be completely removed.

Constraints on speculative purchases of enterprises or assets

As an example, if a firm has an opportunity to obtain a tract of land whose price is likely to rise, the firm should not take such an opportunity. Certainly the firm can gain a high return if the tract of land bought cheap rises in price. However, the increase in price can not be good for society. When members of society plan to purchase land to build homes, this high price is likely to keep such a plan from materializing. Therefore speculative purchases of land is detrimental to the society. In the recent past, the myth that land necessarily increases in price was prevalent among many companies and people. When the bubble economy collapsed, that myth was shattered to pieces. The bubble story of land is only one example of the speculative purchases of assets. A firm should work with a true and sincere mind to create things of new value to society in order to receive due return. The firm should exercise good judgement in any situation.

Enterprise ethics (Sense of responsibility to the society)

Enterprise ethics indicates that members are prohibited from doing unjust things, such as forming conspiracies. The company must control itself. For the company to endure, morality is a prerequisite.

A view of work in which diligence is highly esteemed

The view of diligence affects how workers view their work. It is related to workers' morale and managers' ethics.

Improvement of ethics

This refers to the necessity of maintaining and upgrading ethics at all times. Here, ethics indicate how members of an organization ought to be while Enterprise ethics above refers to how a firm should be in the society.

4.3 Fairness

The elements of competitiveness which belong to the Principle of Fairness are as follows.

· Maintain a free market principle throughout an enterprise.
· Encourage competitive spirit.
· Fair employment.
· Appropriate transfer of personnel from one post to another.
· Fair and just promotion of personnel.

Maintain a free market principle throughout an enterprise

Maintaining a free market principle refers to an internal mechanism of competition. As an example of such mechanism, there is the 'functional division system'.

> A number of Japanese companies have created a unique structure of organization called the functional division system. In this system, there are two lines of divisions. One line is composed of marketing and sales divisions and the other line is those of production...In the functional division system, business dealings between the two lines are to be carried out on the basis of competition...Production divisions compete with each other for the limited resources of marketing and sales divisions. In a similar way, marketing and sales divisions compete among them for those of production divisions ...In an organization of functional division system, there is an internal market where business dealings between the two lines of divisions can be coordinated...A typical example of such an organization is Matsushita Electric Co., Ltd.
>
> (H. Itami and T. Kagono, 1997, originally in Japanese)

29

Encourage competitive spirit

To encourage one's competitive spirit, various incentives can be employed. There are generally the incentives of money and the evaluation of one's work and contribution. A corporate philosophy is another incentive since it can move people. Work itself is a high-level incentive if one is deeply interested in it. If one identifies doing their work with their worth of living, it comes to be a fairly firm incentive.

Fair employment

Fair employment means that people are to be employed without any partiality such as the 'academic' principle. In the academic career principle, people from some designated schools are exclusively employed by discriminating against those from other schools. A firm's view of values, whether it is conscious or not, is reflected in its way of employment. As a matter of course, it is extremely important that the firm's view of values can be generally accepted in the society and regarded as fair.

Appropriate transfer of personnel from one post to another

Appropriate transfer of personnel is significant in two ways. First, it has to do with the incentive of evaluation. The appropriate transfer is principally based on the result of one's work and their capabilities. Second, it is a necessary condition when metabolizing the organization or coping with changes in and out. By the transfer of personnel, the company can not only expedite information diffusion throughout the organization but also curb excessive specialization among the workers. If the workers are too specialized, they encounter many problems. For instance, they have difficulty communicating each other, they can not easily change their work position, they are not able to keep pace with new technological advances outside of their organization, and they can not adapt themselves to changes occurring in the environment. Thus, if transfers between departments are rare, the firm can not transform its organization or cope with changes outside in an appropriate manner. The transfer of personnel is essential.

Fair and just promotion of personnel

Fair and just promotion implies the fairness of personnel's management. Included here are equal opportunity and allowing second chances for those who make mistakes. Everyone can make mistakes. However, by learning from the first failure, one may succeed in a new, second challenge. Such learning turns out to be large part of the firm's assets. While opportunities are to be available to everyone, the second chance for people who make mistakes may have deep meaning.

4.4 Equality

The following elements belong to the Principle of Equality.

- People in the workplace freely exchange their views and opinions.
- There is teamwork among personnel.
- Personnel have pride and confidence in upholding their enterprise's competitiveness and have a sense of representing their enterprise.
- Organization whose workers are barely conscious of organizational hierarchy.
- Recognition of quality as the end result of overall production or service activities.
- Guarantee long-term employment.
- Every member is a leading actor.

People in the workplace freely exchange their views and opinions

When people in the workplace have the will to express their views, opinions and are allowed to discuss ideas freely, they are much more likely to be productive. For an organization to be healthy, such an environment must be formed where every member can freely express what they have in mind.

There is teamwork among personnel

The crux of management is collaboration. To promote people to co-work, teamwork is essential.

Personnel have pride and confidence in upholding their enterprise's competitiveness and have a sense of representing their enterprise

This element represents the high morale of workers. Once workers are assured that they are indispensable for their company and the company will suffer unless they perform their part, they will feel valuable and proud of the company. With such feeling of pride, workers are more willing to do their part. The following story is indicative of such a sense of indispensability.

A young salaried-man had to take a leave to attend a Buddhist service of his relative. People in the business world are usually busy. He had misgivings about taking leave since his colleagues were busy working, but realized that everyone would use vacation days in such a case. He was hesitant at first but went to his manager and asked for three days' leave. The manager smiled at him and instantly told him that it was all right for him to have 3 days or even 5 days of leave. It seemed that the manager was a man of kindness as far as this story went...However, the young man thought it over after he had been given the consent...The manager may have meant that the work could be carried out without him...Having thought it in this way, the young man was shocked. He had a sense of alienation from the company. This story is interesting as a matter of one's sense of indispensability. When the manager permitted the young man to have a leave with such an ease, the young man was shocked, which damaged his sense of being indispensable for the company.

(H. Kato, 1970, originally in Japanese)

Organization whose workers are barely conscious of organizational hierarchy

The issue here is what people feel about their organization. If they feel it a place where they can work on their own way, it is fine. If they feel forced to work from above, it is not. Generally, the smaller an organization is, the more people can show their talent. A flat organization is more appropriate than any other form for individuals to build their ideas, express and discuss them freely with others.

Recognition of quality as the end result of overall production or service activities

The recognition of quality means the necessity of overcoming functional barriers in the organization to attain the best quality of goods or services. Everyone is to be responsible for the end result of overall production or service activities. When workers receive complaints from customers about products or services, it is important for them to feel that the complaints are to them as well as to their bosses or other departments. Feeling like this is enormously significant which ultimately leads them to the correct way of dealing with customers.

Guarantee long-term employment

The economic value of one's work derives from their skill. A long-term employment guarantee can contribute to forming a worker's skill. Moreover, it is indispensable, if a worker's skill is specific only to their company. The long-

32

term employment guarantee may be a necessary condition for periodical post changes to be effective among workers, for workers to accumulate information needed for their work, for workers to go beyond functional barriers in an organization and communicate smoothly with each other. It can undoubtedly promote the interchange among workers, rendering periodic post changes effective and broaden the workers' human network. Such interchange among workers is most instrumental in facilitating their collaboration which is the essence of organizing people. The long-term employment guarantee here should not to be mistaken for the life-long employment guarantee. It can be long but not life-long. It is also wrong to take the long-term employment guarantee as paternalism. The company will have to address whatever changes in the future in the most adaptive way.

Every member is a leading actor

Being a leading actor corresponds to self-actualization, the highest level of desire in Maslow's structure of human desires. One has an innate ability and desire to act in one's own way. One also has the ability to co-operate. Accordingly, when one participates positively in an organization and can identify oneself with it, they may make an all-out effort to do work.

4.5 Sharing

The elements of competitiveness belonging to the Principle of Sharing are the following.

- Conservation of the natural environment.
- Co-operation with and participation in a community and its activities.
- Improvement of the physical environment of the workplace.
- Attention and care to human relations in the workplace.
- Create smooth communication lines.
- Discussion on the vision, policies and the state of affairs of the enterprise from management.
- Diffuse new ideas, reforms, improvements, and intelligence on new products both inside and outside the organization.
- Activate communication throughout.
- Have a close relationship with customers.
- Have intimate contact with suppliers.

A company acts in the natural environment as well as in the social environment. Therefore, it should be keenly conscious of the environment. Before the end of World War II, there were four major incidents of mining pollution involving sulfur dioxide. Out of the four mining companies concerned, Sumitomo and Hitachi are known to have earnestly tried to solve their problems in the Besshi copper mine and the Hitachi mine respectively. Their endeavors were quite unusual at that time, and thus was recorded as a remarkable performance in the history of environmental issues.

> Those two mining companies having acted before the end of World War II coped remarkably well with pollution problems, which represents good management principles and the excellent performance of individuals concerned who presumably had the ethos of 'vocation' as Max Weber implies. The House of Sumitomo and the House of Hitachi were not as big as at present. Their organizations may have been small enough for talented individuals to show their capabilities...The other pollution-generating companies lacked the sense of corporate ethics to create their solutions to the environmental problems they were responsible for...Sumitomo and Hitachi finally overcame the sulfur dioxide problem they had generated by their own endeavors. Engineers at those houses employed their full capabilities in making inroads into the problem and developing an effective facility to solve it, which in turn, contributed to the expansion and development of their businesses. These two cases show that when a company takes responsibility for its pollution problem and makes all-out efforts to solve it, it can not only lessen the problem inordinately, but ultimately develop and expand its business.
>
> (N. Iijima, 1995, originally in Japanese)

We can conjecture that the ethos of vocation prevalent at that time in Sumitomo and Hitachi have been maintained ever since to form a major source of their competitiveness.

Cooperation with and participation in a community and its activities

A firm acts in the social environment. Thus, it ought to cooperate and participate in the community's activities. In particular, it must be keenly concerned with pollution issues in the community. A corporate organization lives through continual interaction with the social environment and the natural environment. Take wastes as an example. A company performs activities such as of producing and delivering, and as a result of these activities, they produce wastes. The treatment of wastes is not only regulated by law, but also socially evaluated. Moreover, a new type of pollution problem has appeared which is different from the one above. In this new type, citizens in the community are the major polluter. The harm stems from emission and noise generated in driving a car, contaminated water drained from homes and litter. Firms are required to co-operate in addressing those issues in the community.

Improvement of the physical environment of the workplace

The workplace environment is closely related with the natural environment of a community where a company operates. For instance, occupational diseases are usually related to pollution problems. If the workers are severely injured or sickened due to a harmful workplace environment, then after a certain period of time, the pollution problems will follow in the environment outside. This relationship has been generally noticed in history (N. Iijima, 1995).

Attention and care to human relations in the workplace

The essence of organization is collaboration. Management is to adapt to changes in the external environment and make workers collaborate for it. For a successful collaboration, it is important to consider human relations in the organization.

Create smooth communication lines

The smooth flow of communication in an organization is indispensable for the speed and quality of decision-making.

Discussion on the vision, policies and the state of affairs of the enterprise from management

Such a discussion is crucial in building a reliable relationship between the management and workers and in promoting collaboration between them. By sharing management information, the management and workers can overcome their sense of boss and subordinate relationship and departmental barriers so that a constructive proposal may come out of the management and workers.

Diffuse new ideas, reforms, improvements, and intelligence on new products both inside and outside the organization

The diffusion of new ideas and the like conveys whatever information to the customers or the 'people living their own life'.

People living their own life in the society of today are likely to place more value on their way of life and watch corporate activities rather keenly since they take the position of preserving the environment, saving natural resources and proceeding

35

with normalization. It is said that a company will not survive in the 21st century unless it produces 'products gentle to the globe' and 'things amiable to people' since people living their own life expect and demand such products or things.

(M. Okuzumi, 1997, originally in Japanese)

Accordingly, firms are expected to send off information of ideas, reform and improvement which are suited to customers or people living their own life.

Activate communication throughout

For a firm to deal with abnormalities and changes in the environment with an appropriate speed and preciseness, it is vital to activate communication in and out of the organization. It may not be in a position to activate communication, if the organization is too committed to the pursuit of effectiveness in a conventional way and thus may be too late to adapt to abnormalities and changes. As D.A. Aaker pointed out, Ford in the 1920s is a case in point. Since Ford's policy of cost reduction was too powerful at that time, and the company solely focused on executing that policy, it did not prepare to transform its operation although it was direly needed to cope with the changes in the environment. Early in the 1920s, customers came to prefer a car which was pleasant to ride, weighty and closed. However, as Alfred P. Sloan, ex-president of General Motors, said, Henry Ford adhered to the concept of the T-model which was an excellent open convertible. Since the T-model was of a light chassis, it could not be converted into a weighty closed car. In less than 2 years from 1923 the closed car made the T-model obsolete. As a result, in May 1927, Ford was forced to shut down operations to create a new production line to compete in the market. To produce a new model, Ford lost $200 million, changed 15,000 devices and reassembled more than 25,000 pieces of equipment. It also laid off 60,000 workers in the Detroit district alone. This indicates that when a firm can benefit immensely by reducing the unit cost of production following its experience curve, it is inclined to keep itself from identifying and addressing critical changes in the environment (D.A. Aaker, 1984). Ford was committed so much to the experience curve that it failed to recognize the importance of balance between the effectiveness of the present work and adaptation to new changes. In other words, it entirely lacked the appropriate and vital communication with customers or people outside.

Have a close relationship with customers

Having such a close relationship is to know customers' real needs and produce goods or services which are tailored to them.

Have intimate contact with suppliers .

Having such intimate contact reflects the fact that goods or services are produced in a teamwork form with cooperation with suppliers. The cooperation with suppliers is particularly significant when differentiating a product from other similar ones. To differentiate it, specifications are likely to be complex. In such a case, the company's close contact with suppliers is crucial.

4.6 Self-Cultivation

The elements of competitiveness which belong to the Principle of Self-Cultivation are as follows.

· Diligence and positive activities of personnel.
· Pride and confidence in one's own work.
· Demand and expect personnel to do their best.

Diligence and positive activities of personnel

A crucial principle of organization is that one's efforts can pay off. If one's virtues of honesty, diligence and integrity do not pay off, the organization is in a state of illness. On the other hand, if those virtues are generally recognized, the firm is in a position to push ahead with rationalization and advancement.

Pride and confidence in one's own work

One's pride makes them an excellent worker and a good citizen. Take the following case for instance.

> American truck drivers, who carry items a long distance, call themselves 'the guardian of highways' although they have no honor to certify it. For example, if the cars following them are in a hurry, they will let them pass by. If they find a car which happens to be in trouble and is forced to be left by the side of a road, they may help repair it as a professional repairman. If they happen to discover any suspicious activities on the road, they will instantly inform the police of them. The attitude of a long-haul truck driver towards the drivers of private cars running on a highway is likened to that of a father to his immature children. The truck driver is a professional. A professional never shows reckless or unreasonable behaviors. They always watch immature laymen generously...What is concerned here is a matter of one's pride.   (H. Kato, 1970, originally in Japanese)

In this connection, S. Kobayashi, at Sony Corporation's Atsugi works, tells the story below.

> It was a few years ago now. People in the development department moved to Atsugi works from the headquarters. Those people and the persons appointed as carrier at that time were carrying together equipment and utensils into the works. When a man with a college background at Atsugi works was watching a manager from the development department carrying them, he said to the manager. 'Why not leave that kind of work to porters?' In hearing that remark, those appointed as carrier then felt indignant and got out of the place, leaving earlier than usual. When I heard about the above incident, I did not blame anyone in charge of carrying. I even felt agreeable to their behavior. I severely blamed that man with a college background for this incident. I don't say that engineers should do the work of carrying, but they should respect the dignity of others.
>
> (H. Kato, 1970, originally in Japanese)

One's pride is related to their sense of worth of working and worth of living, out of which their energy is derived for working.

Demand and expect personnel to do their best

Psychologically, personnel can devote energies to work when their leader is humanly attractive and remarkable in personality. In other words, those qualities are required for one to be a leader. Unless a leader can draw out energy from workers, the leader can not expect them to collaborate. Business management is essentially to form and maintain the conditions under which people can endeavor to collaborate.

4.7 Learning and Knowledge-Accumulation

The following elements of competitiveness belong to the Principle of Learning and Knowledge-Accumulation.

Technology
- Commercialize technology.
- Development, introduction and use of technology to gain strategic predominance.
- Promotion of R&D and production-process R&D.
- Employment of human resources and procurement of physical assets to build and stabilize infrastructure.
- Physical assets.

- Human resources.
  Systems thinking
- Allow a sufficiently long time frame for management.
- Generate many alternatives to a decision-making process.
- Improve cost, quality and delivery terms simultaneously.
- Cope with things flexibly.
- Develop personnel's abilities and continue their learning.
  People
- Education (General learning as citizen of the society).
- Investment in the training of personnel.
- Education on practical business.
- Organizational techniques.

Commercialize technology

To gain a predominant position on the market, the firm must have not only vital technology components to be used in developing products and services, but also the capability of commercializing them.

Development, introduction and use of technology to gain strategic predominance

Gaining strategic predominance means to differentiate goods from competitors'. Uniquely differentiated goods are a factor of sustainable competitive advantage just as low cost (D.A., Aaker, 1984).

Promotion of R&D and production-process R&D

A firm is recognized in society and survives by creating new products or services. To continue to create new products or services, R&D is indispensable. In particular, in the case of a manufacturing firm, innovation in its production process is crucial and comes to be a powerful competitive edge.

Employment of human resources and procurement of physical assets to build and stabilize infrastructure

To gain strategic predominance, a firm should not only specify what technology to take and develop on its own, but also introduce relevant technology from outside the firm. Technological knowledge is usually stored and embodied in the physical assets and the human resources of an organization. Therefore, it is significant to get the assets and resources equipped with such knowledge.

Physical assets

Technical knowledge is accumulated in physical assets. Thus, the technical strength of a company is usually embodied in them.

Human resources

Technical knowledge is also accumulated in human resources. Thus, the technical strength of a company is usually embodied in them.

Allow a sufficiently long time frame for management

Allowing a long time frame shows that a firm should prepare things needed from the long-term perspective while pursuing to attain short-term results. The competitiveness of a firm is the strength of winning continually in the market generation after generation. The long-term perspective is crucial in that respect.

Generate many alternatives to a decision-making process

Generating many alternatives indicates that it is crucial in business decision-making to contrive and compare more than one strategy. To work out an effective strategy, the key is to focus on the process of strategy planning and examine alternative plans (D.A. Aaker, 1984). More alternatives will lead to better choices.

Improve cost, quality and delivery terms simultaneously

Low cost is one of the conditions to sustain competitive advantage. However, the firm can not gain competitive advantage if quality and delivery terms are inferior. When cost, quality and delivery terms are simultaneously improved, then low cost becomes the decisive factor to gain strategic predominance.

Cope with things flexibly

In the workplace, there are generally two types of work. One is to carry out repetitive and monotonous jobs and the other is to work out a solution to problems. Problems include faulty goods, problems caused by changes made in products or in the production line due to an alteration in demand, changes in the composition of personnel and so forth. Workers are required to have the capacity of flexibly coping with regular problems and irregular ones caused by changes both inside and outside their organization.

Develop personnel's abilities and continue their learning

For an organization to be transformed when necessary, the continual learning of the members is an indispensable condition. The goal of their learning is not only to get new knowledge and new technology, but also to maintain an intellectually young and rejuvenated mind.

Education (General learning as citizen of the society)

A firm acts in the society. As citizen of the society, it must learn and follow good sense, manner and the like ascribed to genuine humanity.

Investment in the training of personnel

Training is not to be taken as an expense but rather that of investment. It is a productive investment conducive to the build-up of human resources. As is often said, information resources are crucial in solidifying a firm's competitiveness and fostering its capability to develop. They are the accumulation of technical knowledge. Learning through training is indispensable.

Education on practical business

Education on practical business generally indicates On the Job Training. OJT is a system where workers have opportunities of cultivating and improving their technical abilities on the job. There are basically two ways of OJT. One is to transfer a worker gradually from easy jobs to difficult ones. The other is to transfer them periodically from one workplace to another. By the latter way of OJT, a worker can gain their experience in wider areas of work.

Organizational techniques

There are many structures of organization with their respective characteristics. As to the division system, the primary reason of adopting it is to cope with diverse kinds of environment. Divisions act mostly on their own to meet changes in the environment. A matrix-form of organization is employed to reduce interdependence among departments by sharing resources, in particular, human resources. The sharing of information is also an effective factor characteristic of the matrix organization. A 'holon' management system is a system where its independent parts are loosely united to form the whole. A system whose parts are tightly combined reacts too slowly when the environment changes. On the other hand, a system with its parts loosely united can respond faster than one with its parts tightly combined. Sensitivity to changes in the environment is in proportion to the dimension of fluctuations in a system. Currently, the organizational structures described above have been proposed or put in practical use. Yet, new ones will be developed further still (I. Nonaka and N. Konno, 1995). However, whatever structure of organization is chosen, it can not be a ready solution to the trade-off between external adaptation and internal integration. A company must work out a solution to the trade-off suited for the present work and adaptable to changes. We can take a principle of personnel management at Honda Motor Co., Ltd. as a case in point. At Honda, a person is to be assigned to whatever post if they have the knowledge at least 40 percent of the job. It is a settlement to the trade-off between the thought of 'the right person in the right place' and that of 'adaptation to alterations to come in the future'. We call an organization with such a trade-off solution a 'loose organization'. In a loose organization, the present and the future coexist. It is flexible enough to cope with whatever changes occur in and outside the organization.

4.8 Summary

We have described the elements of competitiveness belonging to the 7 Principles of Enterprise Competitiveness respectively. Those elements are statically positioned in the 3-Layer Structure of Enterprise Competitiveness while they work as promoters of the 7 Principles. For the 7 Principles to function as a dynamic force, the 50 elements must play their role. By analogy, the Structure is the home where the elements reside, while the 7 Principles are the arena where those elements play their performance. The 50 elements work on the 7 Principles of Enterprise Competitiveness respectively.

Finally, let us show the 7 Principles of Enterprise Competitiveness and the elements of competitiveness ascribed to them in Table 4.1.

Table 4.1   The 7 Principles of Enterprise Competitiveness

1   Creativity
- Ethos originated in the early days of an enterprise, i.e., the spirit of denying, the spirit of negating the status quo, the spirit of creativity and the spirit of creating a vision, are maintained.
- Every member is willing to grapple with any situation without hesitation and without worrying about failure.
- Self-reforming abilities.

2   Righteousness
   · Law (company regulations, etc.).
   · Ethics of relations between management and workers.
   · Abolishment of practices restricting competition.
   · Constraints on speculative purchases of enterprises or assets.
   · Enterprise ethics (Sense of responsibility to the society).
   · A view of work in which diligence is highly esteemed.
   · Improvement of ethics.

3   Fairness
   · Maintain a free market principle throughout the enterprise.
   · Encourage competitive spirit.
   · Fair employment.
   · Appropriate transfer of personnel from one post to another.
   · Fair and just promotion of personnel.

4   Equality
   · People in the workplace freely exchange their views and opinions.
   · There is teamwork among personnel.
   · Personnel have pride and confidence in upholding their enterprise's competitiveness and have a sense of representing their enterprise.
   · Organization whose workers are barely conscious of organizational hierarchy.
   · Recognition of quality as the end result of overall production or service activities.
   · Guarantee long-term employment.
   · Every member is a leading actor.

5   Sharing
   · Conservation of the natural environment.
   · Cooperation with and participation in a community and its activities.
   · Improvement of the physical environment of the workplace.
   · Attention and care to human relations in the workplace.
   · Create smooth communication lines.
   · Discussion on the vision, policies and the state of affairs of the enterprise from management.
   · Diffuse new ideas, reforms, improvements, and intelligence on new products both inside and outside the organization.
   · Activate communication throughout.
   · Have a close relationship with customers.
   · Have intimate contact with suppliers.

6   Self-Cultivation
    · Diligence and positive activities of personnel.
    · Pride and confidence in one's own work.
    · Demand and expect personnel to do their best.

7   Learning and Knowledge-Accumulation

Technology
    · Commercialize technology.
    · Development, introduction and use of technology to gain strategic predominance.
    · Promotion of R&D and production-process R&D.
    · Employment of human resources and procurement of physical assets to build and stabilize infrastructure.
    · Physical assets.
    · Human resources.

Systems thinking
    · Allow a sufficiently long time frame for management.
    · Generate many alternatives to a decision-making process.
    · Improve cost, quality and delivery terms simultaneously.
    · Cope with things flexibly.
    · Develop personnel's abilities and continue their learning.

People
    · Education (General learning as citizen of the society).
    · Investment in the training of personnel.
    · Education on practical business.
    · Organizational techniques.

5 The Kami Way and the 7 Principles of Enterprise Competitiveness

As has been mentioned in Chapter 1, the leitmotif of culture formed in the early days of a nation is learned and inherited from that time on. In Japan's case, the Kami Way was formed in the days of its foundation. The Kami Way is implanted in the deepest level of a Japanese mind. On top of that level, the three layers of organizational culture are stacked layer by layer as Ed Schein argues. This multi-layer nature of corporate culture is vital for an organization to transform itself. To an organization, the external environment is constantly changing. The corporate culture must adapt itself continually to the changes. Where does the driving force of changing corporate culture come from? According to Ed Schein, the deeper levels act on the shallower levels to transform itself. By utilizing its deep-rooted assumptions, it changes the surface assumptions. This presumes hardly any change occurs in the deeper levels. There are cases, however, when a firm must completely metabolize itself and so bring about a revolutionary change such as the transformation of corporate climate, the turning of conventional values into new ones and the reformation of corporate philosophy. Under such circumstances, how would the firm go about it? What is expected to come out here may well be the most basic part of culture which is deeply embedded in the members of the firm, i.e., the culture inherited from the foundation days of the nation. In Japan's case, it is the Kami Way.

The basic part of the Kami Way is learned through tacit knowing just as that of other cultures. A growing young mind tacitly absorbs and interiorizes the whole conceptual framework and the rules of reasoning out of the culture they belong to (M. Polanyi, 1966). The intellectual power obtained after they grow up is rooted in the knowledge tacitly absorbed. Their thoughts founded on that tacitly acquired knowledge gives meaning to all explicit knowledge (M. Polanyi, 1996). With informal recognition obtained through tacit knowing, one can formalize relations of things and make formal theories. In that sense, the basic part of culture tacitly absorbed is in the deepest level of one's mind and can have the capacity of acting as the principle of integrating.

The core of the Kami Way is the tacit understanding of the mechanism of nature. We shall first explain the Kami Way in details and then see how the Kami Way is adaptable to the 7 Principles of Enterprise Competitiveness.

5.1 The Kami Way

In short, the Kami Way is to practice the principles of life (Y. Hamuro, 1997). It is to learn and adapt to nature. It is to learn human nature from the principles of nature. The Kami Way has only one criterion in judging things. It is to judge if things are healthy or unhealthy. Those adaptable to the principles of life and the principles of nature are taken as being healthy while those unadaptable to them are taken as being unhealthy. In the author's view, the Kami Way simply recognizes the state and phenomena of nature through 7 principles. The truth is always simple. It is human egos that make the simplicity of the truth intricate and complicated. In the Kami Way, there is such systems thinking as to understand the principles of nature as simply as possible. The 7 principles of the Kami Way are the following.

1 Energy of nature
2 Reviving of nature
3 Cleanness of nature
4 Benefit of nature
5 Coexistence of nature
6 Wave motion of nature
7 Balance of nature

Let us put forth below the above principles of nature, and the attributes of the Kami Way ascribable to those principles respectively.

Energy of nature

Four and a half billion years ago, some planets were born to revolve round the sun. The earth was one of them. One billion years after that, the initial living things appeared in the water on the earth. Hence, water is considered to have huge power to generate life. It is the origin of all life. However, if there is no mountain, a river can not flow. In that sense, the mountain can be said to be the origin of life. From time immemorial, the Japanese have worshiped nature and customarily enshrined deities in the mountains. Mountains are part of the earth formed by blowing energies from inside the earth like volcanic and seismic activities. Due to such immeasurable forces of nature and because the mountain is the place generating water indispensable for man's life, Japanese people have enshrined and worshiped deities in the mountains from olden days (Y. Hamuro, 1999).

Through tacit knowing of the vital power of nature, the Musubi, an attribute of the Kami Way, was produced.

The Musubi implies 'giving birth' and 'making and forming'. It indicates the capacity of producing, generating, and creating.

(H. Yamashita, 1998)

If one is isolated from the vital power of nature, what will become of them? In this case, one wraps themself up and conceals themself from nature. It is called 'Tsumi' in the Kami Way. Supposing that the energies absorbed from nature dried up, what will happen to them? Such exhausting of natural energies is named 'Kegare'. The Kegare refers to contaminants beyond man's consciousness such as evil acts, illness, disaster, dirtiness, egotism, greed, a deep-seated grudge and so forth. But, it originally means to drain one's stored natural energies from them (Y. Hamuro, 1997). The Tsumi and the Kegare both express one's utterly unhealthy state and can be the cause of illness and misfortune. They run counter to the principle of life. To recover from Tsumi and Kegare, the Kami Way carries out a ritual by using the power of water which is called 'Harai'. Water is thought to hold great force. Dying means that one's stored energies completely disappear.

On the contrary, then, what if one positively absorbs energies from nature? In the Kami Way, it is referred to as 'Mitama-Furi'.

The Mitama-Furi, i.e., soul-invigorating, is a spiritual exercise conducted in the Kami Way. It is an exercise to invigorate one's exhausted and waning soul and to revive life spirits. It is, also, an exercise to introduce into one's soul a clean, bright and right working of a deity soul, i.e., nature. One of the typical Mitama-Furi cases is carrying a portable shrine. In a shrine festival, people carry a portable shrine on their shoulders, which is an incantatory act for Mitama-Furi.

(H. Yamashita, 1998)

Thus, the Mitama-Furi lives up to the principles of life. It means to invigorate one's soul.

In sum, in the principle of energy of nature, there are two attributes of the Kami Way. One is Musubi meaning to generate and form life, and the other is Mitama-Furi implying to invigorate one's vital power.

Reviving of nature

Nature circulates all the time. Things and phenomena in nature are all formed through circulation and balance. For instance, water rises as vapor but falls as rain. And it returns as vapor and continues endlessly. Water holds such a mysterious power of circulation. Similarly, man's body can revive by old cells transmitting their genes to new cells which in turn hand them down to still new ones and on and on. Thus, man's life can revive. The Yomigaeri, another

47

attribute of the Kami Way, was formed through the regeneration of nature.

> The Yomigaeri holds that deities, men and all that comprises nature are reborn every year. Through incessant rebirth, one's life can be maintained perpetually. The Yomigaeri, furthermore, is to gain new life particularly when united with the Musubi. Life of everything is maintained through continuous making, forming and reviving.
>
> (H. Yamashita, 1998)

What is of consequence here is that man's life circulates endlessly. Without Yomigaeri, it will stagnate and cease to exist. In other words, unless our forefathers were to live and transmit their lives to us, we can not posibly live. Unless we are to live and rightfully hand our lives to our offspring, they will not be able to live. Thus, we are linked with both our forefathers and offspring, which is meant by circulation. The Kami Way expresses such circulation as above 'Many Deities as One Deity, One Deity as Many Deities'. That is,

> One's life and spirit were given by one's parents, whose life and spirit were, in turn, given by their parents, and on and on, so that one's life and spirit have been inherited through generations. One's ancestors were, in turn, tied with their fathers' spirits which were strung out of the deities of life and others at the beginning of Heaven and Earth. Such a relationship is briefly comprehended in the expression 'Many Deities as One Deity, One Deity as Many Deities'.
>
> (H. Yamashita, 1996)

As will be explained later, the Kami Way calls things and phenomena in the natural world 'Yaoyorozu-No-Kami', or a hundred myriad deities. The Yaoyorozu-No-Kami, in this context, includes man's ancestors as part of nature. It is thought that man can absorb energies not only from things in the natural world but also from their forefathers. The thought expressed here is of a very tenacious succession of human life.

In the principle of reviving of nature, there are two attributes of the Kami Way, i.e., the Yomigaeri expressing circulation and reviving of life, and Many Deities as One Deity, One Deity as Many Deities indicating the transmittal of life from ancestors to offspring.

Cleanness of nature

Water is the origin of life. Living things are originally born in the water. When land creatures evolved, some of the sea water was stored in their body. That is why man's body fluids are composed similarly to sea water (Y. Hamuro, 1999). Man's body is 60 to 70 percent water, and man can not possibly live unless we take in water. If clean and nutritious water is not absorbed into the body, one cannot be healthy. If the body fluids of a healthy person are examined and compared with those of an unhealthy person, it is found out that the healthy person's fluids are clean and transparent while the unhealthy person's are impure and dirty (Y. Hamuro, 1997).

In the Kami Way, in this connection, there is a thought that one can purify themself with clean water. It is called 'Misogi'.

> The Misogi, i.e., purification-making, is a spiritual exercise for people to purify themselves. In practicing Misogi, people step in an icy cold river to put the whole body in it or stand under a waterfall so that they can purify themselves, freeing them from various dirts of human egotism. Misogi represents the ethical view that purity is of the highest value.
>
> (H. Yamashita, 1996)

The thought here is that one can recover one's purity and cleanness through the power of water. In the principle of cleanness of nature, there is the Misogi, meaning purification-making to try to take away dirt of various kinds to restore purity and cleanness.

Benefit of nature

It is thought in the Kami Way that we can live with the benefit of nature and our forefathers' wisdom and knowledge. Having been surrounded by and grown up in a beneficial and invigorating natural environment, the Japanese may have tacitly accepted the idea that people owe benefits of various kinds to nature and their ancestors. The Matsuri is, in this connection, an event to express man's appreciation to deities, i.e., things and phenomena in the world of nature. People make an offering of food and sake to deities during a Matsuri, and at the end, they eat and drink the food and sake to appreciate the deities for their blessing. It is generally called 'Deities and Men Co-Dining'.

In expressing one's appreciation to deities, furthermore, one does it with their sincere and honest mind. If one is sincere and honest, their mind's wave motion is right and normal. If one's wave motion is normal, they are healthy enough in physical and mental conditions. That sincere and honest mind is named 'Akaki-Kokoro' in the Kami Way.

> The Akaki-Kokoro stands for 'sincerity' and 'a true heart'. To set a high value on a bright and clear mind forms an ethical basis of the Kami Way. The Akaki-Kokoro represents purity of mind. It indicates integrity and stainlessness.
>
> (H. Yamashita, 1998)

Akaki-Kokoro is an attribute of the Kami Way, representing the right and honest mind to express one's appreciation to the benefit of nature.

Coexistence with nature

The Kami Way takes a view that people live with nature. In the natural world, there coexist things of many and diverse kinds. Due to such coexistence, man can survive. Nature teaches us that all the things live together. The true state of man's living is found where they live with deities, other people and nature. Owing to such a way of thinking as above, 'Deities and Men Co-Working', an attribute of the Kami Way, seems to have been formed.

> The Deities and Men Co-Working represents the high value of working, diligence, and pride and confidence in one's work.
>
> (H. Yamashita, 1996)

By the same token, 'Co-Dining', another attribute of the Kami Way, can be understood.

> The Co-Dining means that men dine with deities or that men dine with others. Food is, in itself, a gift bestowed by deities. Dining is, therefore, a deed between men and others as well as one between deities and men.
>
> (H. Yamashita, 1996)

The thought of coexistence with nature is connected with the idea that one is to try to absorb whatever things from the outside and make them their own. If one should drive out things in the natural world one after another, they can not endure. Therefore, one is to take in as many things as possible. Thus, the idea of 'Kanjyo' and 'Shugo', attributes of the Kami Way came into being. The Kanjyo may have originated in having tacitly understood the fact that the seeds of trees and grasses are carried over by wind and birds from one place to others where they newly grow up. It is generally understood, however, as follows.

> The Kanjyo is taking part of a deity from an existing shrine and transferring it to a new shrine. It is also the receipt of a deity's spirit from a certain shrine, and adding it to the shrine of its receiver. The shrine that thus obtains or adds a part of a deity or its spirit is called the Masha. The Masha is, as it were, a franchisee within a franchise system. In that way, shrines have increased in number, and now there are about 81,000 shrines nationwide.
>
> (H. Yamashita, 1998)

The concept of Shugo, on the other hand, seems to have stemmed from people's learning of the blending and mixture of different species. It is, however, expanded to mean the following.

> The Shugo introduces deities and doctrines from diverse sources, joining them into one whole. If one sticks to conventional deities or doctrines and lives in peace only with them, one begins to lose an enterprising spirit and effectiveness in one's ways of viewing things and modes of thinking. In other words, everything stagnates and becomes impure unless new deities or doctrines are introduced to challenge and unite themselves with the conventional ones.
>
> (H. Yamashita, 1998)

Thus, in the principle of coexistence with nature, Deities and Men Co-Working indicates men's working with nature, Kanjyo, to accept deities as broadly as possible, and Shugo, to join deities and doctrines of different nature into a whole.

Wave motion of nature

In the Kami Way's view, behind man's verbal words there is the wave motion of nature. One's verbal words are thought to have the capacity of making things appear and creating them. If one utters good words, good things will appear. If one utters bad words, those bad will come out. Good words bring happiness and bad words bring unhappiness. There exists a spirit in man's verbal words. It is named 'Kotodama' in the Kami Way. The Kotodama indicates the vital importance of telling the truth. Why does man alone have words? There are no other animals that can speak words. Nature created man as its most advanced form and gave them words. Therefore, the words are a benefit of nature as well.

In the principle of the wave motion of nature, there is the Kotodama, or the spirit of words. It accommodates the power of making things appear and that of creating them. It indicates the significance of conveying the truth.

Balance of nature

There are diverse kinds of elements in the world of nature. Many living creatures live and any one of them can not survive alone. Every creature can live only when balanced with others. There are fish, birds, other animals, still others, and even bacteria in the world of nature. Every creature transmits its life generation after generation as in coexistence with others. Owing to such coexistence, man can hand down their life successively. If man should kill other creatures one after another, their vital power will diminish accordingly. If the living things coexisting with man should disappear, man is destined to cease to exist. There are many and diverse things coexisting in nature. The Kami Way, in this context, calls all the things and phenomena in nature 'Yaoyorozu-No-Kami'. The Yaoyorozu-No-Kami is, directly translated, eight hundred myriad deities.

> In the Kami Way, a mountain and a river can be a deity. A sword or an accessory, even a wolf may well be a deity. The deity is placed on the extended line of nature and human beings. Here, there is no one and only supreme being.
> (H. Yamashita, 1996)

Man's ancestors are part of nature. In other words, man's forefathers are taken as deities. The thought of coexistence and balance seems to be related with the formation of Japanese people. A recent investigation of their origin, using DNA, tells us that Japanese people are composed of quite a few species or races. In its 12,000 years of history, many and diverse races came over to the islands of Japan to settle and coexist with others. The Japanese have historically practiced and learned coexistence and balance.

In sum, in the principle of balance of nature, there is the Yaoyorozu-No-Kami, an attribute of the Kami Way, manifesting coexistence and balance.

Summary

The Kami Way is to practice principles of life. It is to learn and adapt to nature. It is to learn human nature from the principles of nature. The Kami Way simply recognizes the state and phenomena of nature through 7 principles. They are energy of nature, reviving of nature, cleanness of nature, benefit of nature, coexistence with nature, wave motion of nature and balance of nature. The attributes of the Kami Way, in turn, respectively manifest and belong to one out of those principles.

That is, the 7 principles and the attributes of the Kami Way manifesting them are correspondingly shown as in Table 5.1.

Table 5.1   The Kami Way's 7 Principles and Attributes

1 Energy of nature	Musubi	To create life.
	Mitama-Furi	Soul-invigorating.
2 Reviving of nature	Yomigaeri	Circulation and reviving of life.
	Many Deities as One Deity, One Deity as Many Deities	To transmit life from ancestors to offspring.

3	Cleanness of nature	Misogi	Purification-making. To recover cleanness.
4	Benefit of nature	Akaki-Kokoro	A sincere and honest mind to appreciate nature for its benefit.
5	Coexistence with nature	Deities and Men Co-Woking Kanjyo	To work with nature. To accept spirits of deities as broadly as possible.
		Shugo	To join deities or doctrines of different nature into one whole.
6	Wave motion of nautre	Kotodama	To create with the spirit of words.
7	Balance of nature	Yaoyorozu-No-Kami	To manifest coexistence and balance.

5.2 The Kami Way and the 7 Principles of Enterprise Competitiveness

How are the attributes of the Kami Way to be taken against the 7 Principles of Enterprise Competitiveness? What relationship can one recognize between them? Are they associated with each other positively, negatively or in some other way? We shall here probe into that relationship by taking up and examining each attribute of the Kami Way respectively.

Let us first take up Musubi and Yomigaeri. The Musubi expresses the immeasurable force of nature and its power of generating life. It implies 'giving birth' and 'making and forming'. It indicates the capacity of producing, the capacity of generating and the capacity of uniting. The Yomigaeri, on the other hand, indicates the mysterious power of circulation in nature. It represents the circulation and reviving of life. It holds that deities, men and all that comprises nature are reborn every year. Through incessant rebirth, one's life can be maintained perpetually. Yomigaeri, furthermore, is to gain new life particularly when united with the Musubi. Life is maintained through continuous making, forming and reviving. Thus, the Musubi, manifesting the energy of nature, and the Yomigaeri, representing the reviving of nature, express the creative force and state of nature. A business organization is a living being. To create and

53

revive its life is fundamental to its existence. The meaning of creativity for the organization resides here. Accordingly, it may well be said that the Musubi and the Yomigaeri are adaptable to the Principle of Creativity, the core principle of the 7 Principles of Enterprise Competitiveness.

Let us next take up Akaki-Kokoro. The Akaki-Kokoro is one's sincere and honest mind to appreciate nature for its benefit. A sincere and honest person can keep the wave motion of their mind in the correct state. If their wave motion of mind is correct, they are healthy in both physical and mental conditions. As previously noted, the Kami Way only judges things to be healthy or unhealthy. Things healthy are right and those unhealthy are wrong. The Akaki-Kokoro as seen in human nature is considered to be the basis for righteousness. Without such human nature, one could have no resort to righteousness. One's sincere and honest mind is a prerequisite for it. It could be said, thus, that the Akaki-Kokoro is equivalent to the Principle of Righteousness out of the 7 Principles of Enterprise Competitiveness.

What of the Misogi? The Misogi is to purify oneself in a clean water. It is purification-making, trying to clear the dirt of human egotism and recover their own purity and cleanness. It shows the state of being fair in that it eliminates things dirty and recovers those clean. What the fair spirit does first and foremost may be to remove dirt out of one's mind. Cleanness or transparency is the attribute of fairness. The Misogi adapts itself to the Principle of Fairness among the 7 Principles.

We shall next see Yaoyorozu-No-Kami. The Yaoyorozu-No-Kami is the things and phenomena in the natural world, and man's forefathers as well. It manifests the coexistence and balance among them. There is no one and supreme being. Every being can transmit life to its descendants in coexistence with others. Any living being is indispensable. Man can hand down life to their children among many and diverse things. If the living things coexisting with man should disappear, they can not live on any longer. The thought here is that all living beings are brothers and sisters with each other. Thus, the Yaoyorozu-No-Kami can adapt itself to the Principle of Equality out of the 7 Principles of Enterprise Competitiveness. It is vitally important that all beings coexist, keeping in balance.

In the Kami Way, man lives with nature. Diverse spieces coexist in the world of nature. It is due to such coexistence that man can possibly live on. The true state of man's living is that they live with deities, other people and nature. The Deities and Men Co-Working, an attribute of the Kami Way, may have been formed to indicate the sharing of work between deities and men. The Deities and Men Co-Working, thus, can be adaptable to the Principle of Sharing among the 7 Principles.

The Kami Way has an attribute of Many Deities as One Deity, One Deity as Many Deities. It is to hand over life from ancestors to offspring. To put it

54

another way, given the time axis of life, man's ancestors and offspring share life among them. Therefore, as viewed from the time axis of life, Many Deities as One Deity, One Deity as Many Deities can be adapted for the Principle of Sharing.

The Mitama-Furi is to positively take in energies from nature and recover one's vital power. It is an exercise to introduce a clean, bright and right working of a deity soul, i.e., nature into one's soul. It implies soul-invigorating. The thought is that everyone can cultivate themself and that they are equipped with capacity of developing their own abilities. One must have a willingness sufficient to cultivate and develop themself. Accordingly, the Mitama-Furi may well be adaptable to the Principle of Self-Cultivation among the 7 Principles of Enterprise Competitiveness.

Finally, the Kotodama, and Kanjyo and Shugo. The Kotodama is the spirit of words which has a power of making things appear and that of creating them. It expresses the significance of conveying the truth. To make things appear and to create them are the aim of human learning while conveying the truth is fundamental to learning. The Kotodama is, therefore, adapted for the Principle of Learning and Knowledge-Accumulation of the 7 Principles of Enterprise Competitiveness. As explained before there is the thought of absorbing whatever things necessary in the Kami Way. If things in the world of nature should be eliminated, man can not live at all. It is man's wisdom, therefore, to accept as many things as possible. The Kanjyo and the Shugo both manifest that wisdom. Kanjyo is to accept things and phenomena in the natural world, i.e., spirits of deities, as broadly as possible. Shugo is to join deities or doctrines of varied nature into one whole. Those concepts, thus, may well be adaptable to the Principle of Learning and Knowledge-Accumulation.

Taken together, the attributes of the Kami Way are respectively considered to be adaptable to the 7 Principles of Enterprise Competitiveness. We shall show the adaptability of the Kami Way's attributes to the 7 Principles of Enterprise Competitiveness in Table 5.2.

Table 5.2   The 7 Principles of Enterprise Competitiveness and the Kami Way's Attributes

The 7 Principles of Enterprise Competitiveness	The Kami Way's attributes
Creativity	Musubi	To create life.
	Yomigaeri	Circulation and Reviving of life.

Righteousness	Akaki-Kokoro	A Sincere and honest mind to appreciate nature for its benefit.
Fairness	Misogi	Purification-making. To recover cleanness.
Equality	Yaoyorozu-No-Kami	Things and phenomena in the natural world.
Sharing	Deities and Men Co-Working Many Deities as One Deity, One Deity as Many Deities	To work with nature. To transmit life from ancestors to offspring.
Self-Cultivation	Mitama-Furi	Soul-invigorating.
Learning and Knowledge-Accumulation	Kotodama	To create with the spirit of words.
	Kanjyo	To accept spirits of deities as broadly as possible.
	Shugo	To join deities or doctrines of different nature into one whole.

The basics of culture is learned through tacit knowing. As put forth before, a young and growing mind tacitly absorbs and interiorizes the whole conceptual framework and all the rules of reasoning out of the culture to which they belong. Their intellectual power after they grow up is rooted in the tactly acquired knowledge while their thought based on that knowledge gives meaning to all explicit knowledge (M. Polanyi, 1966). With informal recognition through tacit knowing at work, formalizing relations among matters becomes feasible and formal theories can be formed. In that sense, the basic part of culture which is obtained through tacit knowing has the power of working as the principle of integration. The core of the Kami Way is absorbed by tacitly recognizing the mechanism of nature. It is the principles tacitly learned from nature.

To repeat, the Kami Way is to practice principles of life. Its criterion of judgment is to see if things are healthy or unhealthy. Those adaptable to the principles of life and the principles of nature are taken as being healthy while those unadaptable to them are taken as being unhealthy. The Kami Way simply recognizes the force and state of nature through the 7 principles. The truth is always simple. It is human egos, in the Kami Way's view, that get the simplicity complicated and intricate. The Kami offers simple ways to grasp the principles acting in nature.

The Kami Way dates back to the Jomon period that started about 12,000 years ago. It has been formed, developed and inherited from that time on. It is the wisdom and knowledge with which the Japanese have long lived. It is human intelligence. If that is so, it seems to be natural that the Kami Way is adaptable to the 7 Principles of Enterprise Competitiveness.

The Kami Way, as the basic layer of culture, forms the deepest level of corporate culture. It can not possibly be said, however, that the Kami Way reveals itself in every corporate culture to play its due part. Man has egos. It is their egos that prevent them from simply understanding the truth. The egos make things utterly complicated. They hinder the basic layer of culture from acting in the correct way. The ego that prefers the state of stability, dislikes change and sticks to conventionalism is sure to shorten the life of a company. Even If the human intelligence is there, how to recognize and understand it duly and rightfully is on the people's and the company's side.

Now, then, what firm, in reality, can we take up as a firm with healthy corporate culture or one with unhealthy corporate culture? In the following Chapter 6 and Chapter 7, we shall respectively take up a pair of companies, one as an example of healthy corporate culture and the other as that of unhealthy culture. We shall, then, see how the pair of companies' corporate culture historically evolved and formed while they were created and developed, and trace how one company could sustain its corporate culture in a healthy state and how the other could not keep it healthy, having left it degraded into an unhealthy state.

6 Case Study: The House of Mitsui and the House of Kohnoike

The House of Mitsui and the House of Kohnoike were both representative commercial concerns of the Tokugawa times (1603-1867). Mitsui first set up Echigoya draper and later Mitsui money exchange house and thus laid the foundation of Mitsui Zaibatsu later on. Kohnoike started a business of money exchange in the period of the first master, Masanari Kohnoike. It was succeeded and developed by the second master, having been appointed as one of the ten authorized exchangers from 1661 to 1673. Since then, Kohnoike had often occupied one of the key positions of ten authorized exchangers through the Tokugawa era up to the last days of its regime. The House of Mitsui and the House of Kohnoike both evolved and developed in the Tokugawa times (1603-1867), having employed many workers and notably thrived. However, with the arrival of a new era, i.e., the Meiji era, when a revolution of industrialization and modernization occurred, these two houses were respectively destined to follow quite a different route. That is, Mitsui managed well to get over this period of change, succeeded and developed further ever since while Kohnoike failed to pass that critical period and fell into obscurity in the end. Where, then, is found the primary cause of the difference between Mitsui's success and Kohnoike's failure? We think that it is found in the difference between the corporate culture of Mitsui and that of Kohnoike in the closing days of the Tokugawa shogunate regime. At that time, Mitsui's culture was healthy enough while Kohnoike's was just the opposite. That difference was truly revealed at the dawn of the Meiji Restoration, whereby Mitsui and Kohnoike could not but take altogether a different route. How, then, had the corporate culture of Mitsui and that of Kohnoike evolved and formed from their foundation? And in what state were those cultures in the closing days of the Tokugawa regime respectively? Let us first take up the corporate culture of Mitsui and then that of Kohnoike.

6.1 The House of Mitsui

The ethos of Matsuzaka

Mitsui family originated in Matsuzaka, Ise, southeast of Kyoto. The place of Matsuzaka was a castle town developed by Ujisato Gamoh, a powerful clan from Ohmi in the late 16th century. When the clan of Gamoh moved to Matsuzaka, many people came from Ohmi and settled there, among whom there were a number of Ohmi merchants. These Ohmi merchants, then, turned out to be a good rival to Ise merchants who had been acting in the area of Ise from a long time before. The father of Takatoshi Mitsui, founder of the House of Mitsui, was a merchant from Ohmi. He moved to Matsuzaka and dealt in sake, Japanese wine, and miso, soybean paste for soup, as well as running a pawnshop. Takatoshi's mother named Shuhoh had eight children, four sons and four daughters, of which Takatoshi was the youngest son. His mother Shuhoh disciplined herself in daily life and took good care of the employees. She was truly pious to deities in the Kami Way and 'tathagatas' in Buddhism. She made it a practice to get up 4 a.m. every day and pour water over herself even in midwinter to clean herself, and then give her prayers to the deities and tathagatas. We can see in such a practice the Misogi and the Value of Cleanness, attributes of the Kami Way. It is not difficult to imagine, therefore, that Shuhoh may have deeply influenced Takatoshi through her self-disciplined way of life.

Matsuzaka was in the center of fertile field in the southern part of Ise. It was near a good harbor so that it was a convenient place for marine transport. In addition, Gamoh, the lord of Matsuzaka, planned and executed a policy of creating the free market. Thus, the commercial business developed and notedly thrived there. Matsuzaka also came to be a key land transport center after Gamoh had remade the conventional route to the Ise Shrine in order to pass through the castle town of Matsuzaka. Many merchants came over to settle in this place from all over the country. Matsuzaka, therefore, markedly prospered as the main commercial center of southern Ise. Merchants in Matsuzaka had many opportunities of getting in contact with people from all over the country who came to visit the Great Shrines of Ise. They were, accordingly, well informed of various kinds of affairs in many parts of the country. Since they were in a position to acquire information of diverse kinds and endowed with the free market, many of them were rich in enterprising spirit. For this reason, many merchants at first accumulated money through commerce in Matsuzaka and then went to Edo (modern Tokyo) to start their business. It is said that in the early 17th century there were a number of merchants from Matsuzaka in Edo who were called the 'Ise merchants' since Matsuzaka was part of the greater area of Ise. In Matsuzaka, in this connection, its cotton cloth was very popular among visitors to the Shrines as a souvenir. The Matsuzaka cotton cloth was locally produced in the town of Matsuzaka and its neighboring villages which Ise merchants in the beginning carried to Edo for trade. It is in this environment where such a free market was available and many merchants had a highly enterprising spirit that Takatoshoi Mitsui, founder of the House of Mitsui, grew up. Takatoshi may have been deeply imbued with the ethos of Matsuzaka described above when he was growing.

Now, it was Toshitsugu, the eldest brother of Takatoshi, that went to Edo to get into business for the first time from Mitsui family. He had stayed in his relative's shop in Edo for a while to work as an apprentice and then, in 1627, at the age of 20, he opened a fancy goods shop with a small capital in Honcho 4th street, Edo. A little afterwards, then, he came to deal in drapery. In those days, drapery was a promising business in Edo. Thus, Shigetoshi, the elder brother of Takatoshi, went to the eldest brother's shop from Matsuzaka to assist him. Trade at the shop gradually grew and increased so much that they had to purchase and stock plenty of Nishijin textile from Kyoto. The eldest brother Toshitsugu, then, determined to have a shop of purchasing and stocking in Kyoto, and went down there to open and run it himself. The elder brother Shigetoshi was, therefore, commissioned to take charge of the Edo shop. It is around that time that Takatoshi, at the age of 14, entered the Edo shop as a salesclerk. After he had worked for it for some time, the elder brother Shigetoshi was to return to Matsuzaka to take care of the mother Shuhoh due to the state of her health. As a result, Takatoshi was placed in charge of the Edo shop. While he took charge of it, he emphasized a principle of customer-orientedness to the clerks, having thus shown his commercial talent. While he dealt with vendors who went down to sell, for instance, in the northeastern region of the country, he never sold goods at an inordinately high price because they were countrymen having little knowledge of the quality and price of those goods. On the contrary, he carefully treated the vendors so that they would be certain to come to Toshitsugu's shop the next year on. 'If one would sell goods at an unreasonable price to vendors with dealings in provincial areas of the country', Takatoshi told the salesclerks, 'they could hardly sell them there because of the high price and therefore would not come again to one's shop which, as a result, would suffer a loss'. He, thus, criticized the evil practice of selling goods at an inordinately high price which prevailed among the other merchants at that time. We can see in Takatoshi's admonishment above the view of value that one ought not to deal in a dirty business, i.e., Value of Cleanness, an attribute of the Kami Way. It seems to us that he was so deeply influenced by his mother Shuhoh in this respect who had practically embodied Value of Cleanliness. Takatoshi was, in those days, determined to be a 'Kyoto merchant with a shop in Edo' and make preparations for it. However, in 1649 the elder brother Shigetsugu who had taken care of Shuhoh suddenly died at the age of 36 in Matsuzaka. As a result, there was no one now to look after the mother. A little later, Shuhoh and the eldest brother asked Takatoshi to come back to Matsuzaka. He accepted without reluctance. He was 28 years old at that time. Before he went back to Matsuzaka, he recommended to the eldest brother a man named Shohbei, who had been in charge of cooking rice in the kitchen at the shop, as chief clerk since Takatoshi recognized good personal character in him. Shohbei undertook the charge of running Toshitsugu's Edo shop and sustained his role well after Takatoshi had gone back home.

Now, having been back home, Takatoshi settled down and married Kane, the eldest daughter of Kiyoemon Nakagawa in 1649. After that, they had the first son Takahei in 1653, the second son Takatomi the next year, the third son Takaharu in 1657 and so on. They were thus blessed with ten sons and five daughters during their life. In 1652, in this connection, Takatoshi purchased a lot for residence and built his shop and private house there, and set out to run a business of finance and that of commerce. These two lines of business were to form the base of his undertaking later. Takatoshi gave his due consideration to the training of clerks. For instance, he sent such employees as Tokuemon and Kiemon to the eldest brother Toshitsugu's shop in Edo for learning business in practice. What he had in mind is to nurture personnel from the long-term standpoint so that they would be conducive to his business in the future. In 1667 when the first son Takahei became 15 years old, Takatoshi sent him to the Edo shop of Toshitsugu's for practicing himself in trade. The next year, in 1668, the second son Takatomi was also sent to the shop there for the same purpose. Time passed, and in 1672 when the first son Takahei returned to Matsuzaka for a temporary stay, he earnestly proposed that Takatoshi should have his own store in Edo. Takatoshi agreed to that proposal and set out to prepare for it. It is, just then, in July 1673 that the eldest brother Toshitsugu died of illness in Kyoto. The old mother Shuhoh, on that occasion, gave a positive support to the opening of Takatoshi's store in Edo. The first son Takahei, 21 years of age then, had had seven years of experience in business and the second son Takatomi, 20 years old, had experienced business in practice for 6 years. Also, some clerks had already been nurtured in Edo.

New business way

Time at last came. The first son Takahei at first found and rented a small building with a frontage of 2.7 meters to open a new store in Honcho 1st street, Edo. Then, in August 1673 the same year, Takatoshi and Takahei went to Kyoto, found a shut-down shop with a frontage of 2.4 meters and rented it to open a new shop for the purchase and stock of textile from Kyoto. In those days there were no textile manufacturers in Edo. The center of textile manufacturing was at Nishijin in Kyoto so that it was a general way for drapers in Edo to have shops in Kyoto specific to the purchase and stock of Nishijin textile. After having opened the shop in Kyoto, the first son Takahei put up a store sign curtain of 'Echigoya Hachiroemon' at the front of the sales store in Edo. The first son Takahei, then, went up to Kyoto to run the purchasing shop there, while the second son Takatomi was put in charge of the sales store at Honcho 1st street in Edo. Headquarters in their drapery business was placed in Matsuzaka

61

and thus Takatoshi was to stay in Matsuzaka as before. In 1673 when the House of Mitsui was founded, therefore, there were one sales store of drapery with 15 employees in Edo and one purchasing shop in Kyoto in all.

Edo was the place of the Tokugawa shogunate government where many samurai warriors resided not only of the Tokugawa but also of other lords since the lords were then regulated by the government to come and stay in Edo periodically away from their domain. To meet the demand of those samurai warriors' consumption, a number of craftsmen and merchants had moved to Edo from other parts of the country, whereby Edo had become a big city. There were purveyors to the Tokugawa government, in this connection, who had so intimate and unfair relation to it as to have other competitors disadvantaged. Bunzaemon Kinokuniya and Mozaemon Naraya were good examples. Now as to drapery business, the business center of Edo was in the streets of Honcho, and the 1st through 4th streets were lined with about 20 to 30 drapery stores among which the large ones had a frontage of 6 meters. Takatoshi's drapery store of 'Echigoya' was opened in such an environment. Thus, a severe competition would lie in its way. It was a customary way of business, then, that drapers carried goods out to customers' place where the customers chose out of them. Sales on credit was also a practice prevailed where payment was usually made once a year, i.e., in December or twice a year, i.e., in June and December of the year. Most dealings were with feudal lords, their retainers and big merchants. Under those circumstances, the people of Echigoya, at first, carried a small amount of textile fabrics on their shoulders to peddle around in Edo. Therefore, sales were in the beginning small and limited. With everyone's concerted efforts, however, they gradually established a good relation to customers. Furthermore, Takatoshi contrived a new way of business, overcoming such a limitation in sales above. The first contrivance was to sell goods to merchants who had dealings in provincial parts of the country. That is, Echigoya set out to sell goods to the provincial merchants at wholesale. In drapery business, few attempts had been made thus far of wholesaling goods to those merchants since sales direct to end customers were bigger in profit in view of a single transaction. Takatoshi, however, pursued to attain the advantage of such trade by increasing turnover of sales and rendering inventory small although margins were small because it was dealings with merchants. Sales to those merchants contributed greatly to Echigoya's business, having increased its profits. The second one was 'sales at the store'. It was to conduct business at the store on a cash basis. As stated above, it was a prevailing practice, then, for a draper to carry goods to customers' premises where the customers chose out of them to buy, its payment being made on credit once or twice a year. The sales at the store on a cash basis, therefore, was a 180-degree turn from the old customs of business, showing a spirit of denying the status quo. In this new way of business, Echigoya could reduce cost of sales since the expenses incurred in selling goods to customers at the store were far smaller than those in carrying them over to the customers' place to sell. Yet, many and diverse goods were shown at the store all the time. In addition, since its sales were in cash, it could increase the turnover of capital. The payment to suppliers, in this context, was made twice a year on a deferred basis so that the cash available from the time of selling to that of payment could be used to bring in new designs of textile to display at the store. With the new business way, also, Echigoya could set goods at lower prices than at other stores and sell a large amount while the customers enjoyed choosing among the commodities of many kinds and of cheap prices to suit their taste. Sales at the store was, in particular, appropriate to meet the demands of craftsmen and merchants who were increasing in population at that time, i.e., the mass market. Through this way of business, Takatoshi came to believe that a store can prosper by providing customers convenience and service. Sales at the store on a cash basis only work with a practice of honest trade. Customers can not easily tell which textiles are of good quality just by looking at them. In other words, when the store wins the confidence among people that it provides textiles of high quality at a reasonable price, then, it would be accepted by the public. It is sincere and honest trade, therefore, that was the secret of success of the sales at the store.

Taken together, we can see here the corporate culture of Echigoya, i.e., the House of Mitsui's culture that formed in the days of its formation. By denying the status quo, the way of sales at the store was newly devised and formed. The spirit of denying the present state and that of creating new things shown here were firmly implanted in the personnel's mind at the House of Mitsui to form the deepest layer of its culture. Here, we can recognize Musubi, an attribute of the Kami Way. Behind the way of selling at the store, there was a spirit of sincere and honest business. Sincerity and honesty represent Akaki-kokoro, another significant attribute of the Kami Way. Moreover, Takatoshi's belief may have been deeply imprinted in him that the prosperity of a business house can only be achieved by offering sincere services to customers. The ethos above in the foundation days of the House of Mitsui, it is thought, turned out to be a valuable prototype of its culture which would evolve and develop from then on.

Rules and directions

Early enough, in August 1673 when Echigoya was set up, Takatoshi devised rules and directions for it while he was in Matsuzaka. These rules and directions are said to be among the oldest of this kind in history. The following are an excerpt of them.

· Clerks must not do whatever kind of gamble.
· Clerks who are cautious about and diligent in their work are to be known to

everyone after half a year. If they continue to work cautiously and diligently for a year or two, they are to be rewarded.

- Clerks must not sell goods on credit to their relatives and acquaintances without permission.
- Clerks must not quarrel with each other. Those who like to seek a quarrel with somebody are to be dismissed since it does harm to business. It is not necessary for clerks to carry money, even a penny, with him. Clerks' money ought to be put in the store manager's keeping so that interest may accrue to it. If anyone carries money with him, he is to be dismissed since it shows his selfish desire.
- Clerks must not hire a prostitute or have relations with bad friends.
- Clerks must not receive anything from others to keep it in custody.
- Clerks must not sell goods on credit in customers' premises.
- Clerks must wear nothing but cotton clothes and cotton belt.
- Clerks must not borrow and use money from their acquaintances.
- Clerks must not do gambling or hire a prostitute to entertain customers and win their favor. Even if transactions can not be concluded without it, they must not do so.
- Clerks must not deal in goods of dubious nature even with a testifier.

(Y. Nakata, 1959)

All the clerks at Echigoya pledged themselves to abide by the store's rules and directions above by giving their signature. These ethical norms seem to have played a large role in the formation of Mitsui's culture in its days of foundation. In August 1675, Takatoshi added to the original rules and directions such as that clerks ought to take care of their health; that a half-yearly settlement of accounts is to be made; that a dead stock ought to be judged quickly and timely and sold at a bargain to a secondhand clothes store; that clerks support each other in their work; and so forth. Among the newly added clauses, the dead stock's quick disposal clause shows the consideration that the store ought to be always filled up and arranged with new and fresh goods. The clause of collaboration reminds us of Matsuri, an attribute of the Kami Way (II. Yamashita, 1996), that other clerks around the clerk in charge ought to cheer him up as if by beating a drum and playing on the flute.

Echigoya's new way of business gained an extremely favorable acceptance among the public. Its second store was thus opened in 1676 at Honcho 2nd street, Edo. In July 1676, Takatoshi newly wrote the store's 27 clauses of rule and sent it to the Edo stores. The following are its excerpt.

- Clerks ought to find out and put aside whatever stained goods and consult with each other to dispose of them even at a bargain price.
- Clerks must not take customers to a teahouse to entertain them and catch their

64

fancy without permission. If the customer is a very important person so that it is necessary to entertain them in some way, clerks can consult with each other to offer them a simple and light entertainment only once or twice a year. Such an entertainment is preferably to be given within the store. If a teahouse is to be used, houses in the areas in Tenjin and Asakusa are all right to use but in others areas are not. Do not use the same teahouse two and more times a year.

· Clerks ought to take care of customers coming to the store and other customers as well so that competitors may not easily attract their attention...

· Clerks who are ardent in whatever affairs of business are to be promoted whether they are new clerks or senior ones.

(Y. Nakata, 1959)

It is stipulated here that deteriorated goods are to be sold at a discount; that entertainment to customers is in principle prohibited; that if necessary it is to be inexpensively given but not to be offered customarily; that cautious attention and sincere service are to be provided to customers so that they may not be attracted by other stores; that ardent clerks are to be promoted whether their service with the store is long or not; and so on. Later in 1695, this rule of 27 clauses was systematically developed and arranged by the second son Takatomi which ended up in a rule book named 'House of Mitsui Rule Book'.

The ethos in the early days of Mitsui

Takatoshi, on the other hand, instructed the store managers to make clerks' performance appraisal. Based on that appraisal, the clerks at Echigoya were rewarded. His thought was that when the criteria are made clear of rewarding a good performer and punishing a bad performer, all the clerks would take such criteria as a guide to their daily work. The thought of such a reward system, i.e., promoting good performers to higher ranks, became part of Echigoya's culture in its early days. At the stores of Echigoya, in this context, there was held a meeting of clerks every month. In the meeting they freely discussed whatever measures to take in order to attain the store's development and prosperity as well as reflecting upon their day-to-day business work. Such free discussion among the clerks also turned out to be part of Echigoya's culture. Behind the practice of a meeting with free discussion among the clerks, there was Takatoshi's basic management principle of producing many merchants of talent. He tried to talk to every clerk, it is said, without favor or partiality, and cultivate senior clerks' abilities. According to his endeavor, such excellent merchants were brought out as Shichizaemon Ishiwara, Tohemon Wakita in Echigoya, Edo and Sohsuke Nakanishi in the purchasing shop in Kyoto, and further, after entering the business of money exchange, Jihei Matsuno in the Kyoto shop of

65

money exchange. In the recognition of their outstanding contribution to Mitsui's business, Takatoshi later helped them to set up a subsidiary house or to found an independent house by providing them capital in the same line of business as Mitsui. Their stores were called 'the stores of grandchildren'. To keep those contributors in memory for long, furthermore, it was made a practice that a newly appointed general manager of each store was to bear the contributor's name of his store, i.e., Tohemon, Sohsuke, Jihei and so on generation after generation. Cultivating one's talent was, thus, a matter of great significance to Mitsui, and that way of thinking came to be firmly rooted as part of its culture.

In the ethos as above in the early days of Mitsui, the clerks identified themselves with Takatoshi's thought, freely offered their views and opinions, and proposed their own plans on business affairs, which turned out to be greatly conducive to the development of Mitsui. Developing clerks' talent was, in this connection, tied with the reward system, i.e., a way of selecting capable persons for promotion at Mitsui where an internal mechanism of competition worked well. At the House of Mitsui, boys aged 11 to 13 were periodically employed and they were screened out by a selection test conducted every seven to eight years, three times in total. The first selection test determined who could stay as an employee. If one could pass that test, he was appointed as a clerk with no title. Then, the second test was conducted to see if applicants have an ability of holding a responsible position. If they were recognized to have such an ability, they could be promoted to such senior clerks as an assistant manager or a manager. In the third test of selection, those clerks were selected that had so high managerial capabilities as to be able to run a store as general manager. The clerks who had passed the selection test three times consecutively were further promoted to a director named Myohdai and Motojime depending on their abilities. In this context, there was a second chance system at Mitsui. That is, it provided capital of initiation and the right of using its store name, i.e., Echigoya, and its trademark to the retiring clerks who had passed only the first test and served a long time since passing the 1st test and the senior clerks retiring halfway after having passed the second test. As to the most capable persons having gotten through the third test of selection, Mitsui made an all-out effort to retain them by rewarding them for their position and contribution. That is, it took various measures for men of remarkable talent to work for it long time (A. Chimoto, 1998).

Having negatived the conventional practices of business and creating the new way of sales at the store, then, Takatoshi evolved and developed his business to succeed greatly. As a result, such a reputation came to pervade among the public that Echigoya offered inexpensive commodities and their services were good as well. It so happened that a key retainer, in charge of purchasing, of the lord of Echizen Matsudaira, heard such a reputation. He had thus far purchased textiles from the House of Matsuya, a purveyor to Echizen

Matsudaira. The retainer at once came to Echigoya to find its textiles cheaper than at Matsuya, and so purchased a large amount of crepe of many kinds from Echigoya. It made Matsuya enormously resentful, however, since it had enjoyed its position of purveyor with no interference. Matsuya tried to ostracize Echigoya from the circle of drapers by co-working with fellow drapers in the streets of Honcho and Kokucho in a guild-like way and making a plot with them. That is, they concluded a trade boycott to Echigoya and stopped dealing with it. However, that boycott turned out to be little harm to Echigoya since wholesalers in Kyoto continued to deal with it in a friendly way as before. Then, later, all the drapers in Edo conspired with each other, trying to prevent the wholesalers in Kyoto from supplying goods to Echigoya. But those merchants in Kyoto were well acquainted with the cause of this strife and thus continued to have dealings with Echigoya. Later still, the drapers in Edo contrived varied plots, making an attempt to estrange the clerks from Echigoya. As described before, however, in the early days of Echigoya there were formed such cultural traits as ethical norms, a spirit of sincerity and honesty, a fundamental principle of serving customers, a monthly meeting and free discussion among the clerks, and the clerks' firm sense of identity with founder Takatoshi. Accordingly, the clerks were not upset by the above sort of contrivance. In addition, the general manager Shichizaemon then coped admirably well with the difficulties, instructing and leading the clerks appropriately. The drapers in the streets of Honcho and Kokucho, as a last resort, brought in a lawsuit against Echigoya at the magistrate's office. Their argument was that Echigoya redyed secondhand textiles to sell them as if they were new ones; that it was selling goods of inferior quality as if they were of good quality; that it extended its business, having intimate relation to all the lords in Edo. Due to those unlawful activities, they maintained, all the other drapers in Edo suffered. The ill-willed argument above pervaded as a rumor in the city of Edo for a time so that Echigoya's business was adversely affected. However, Echigoya's daily trade proved its business of sincerity and honesty, and thus such a wrong rumor came to vanish in the end. As described above, what was tested in this crisis was Echigoya's corporate culture, among others, its clerks' sincerity and honesty, i.e., Akaki-kokoro, an attribute of the Kami Way. That crux of corporate culture was firmly consolidated by having gotten through such critical circumstances as mentioned above and rooted deeply with other attributes in the personnel at the House of Mitsui.

Now, Echigoya's Kyoto shop had purchased textiles from Nishijin out of which the amount of thin silk fabrics like habutae, a soft lightweight Japanese silk in plain weave, were the largest. As to the thin silk fabrics, in this context, the Kyoto shop had bought them in a conventional way, i.e., through a broker. In 1681, however, it so happened that Kiemon Tamiya, a broker there, came to ask Mitsui to buy out his brokerage house, i.e., his right of a broker. His house had been one of the brokers dealing in the thin fabrics at Nishijin, and then it had financial difficulties. Mitsui accepted his request and from then on was to buy the fabrics directly from suppliers at Nishijin. Kiemon Tamiya, whose name was changed to Kiemon Mitsui afterwards, was put in charge of purchasing textiles from Nishijin because of his experience in such dealings. The direct purchase from Nishijin came out to help promoting Takatoshi's 'quick sales at small profits' and 'bargain sales' although, as a result, Echigoya suffered a strong opposition from fellow wholesalers in Kyoto.

In winter 1682, on the other hand, a big fire occurred in Edo when the strife, as stated previously, with those merchants in the streets of Honcho had not yet been settled. Because the fire spread out to all the streets of Honcho, Echigoya's stores on the 1st street and the 2nd street were both reduced to ashes. On this occasion, Takatoshi determined to move out to the streets of Surugacho, and opened stores there in spring 1683. This transfer of his stores meant that the strife with the merchants in Honcho and Kokucho came to a settlement. At the outset of business in the streets of Surugacho, Takatoshi delivered a public notice of Echigoya's fair, fixed-price sales with no overcharge broadly in the city of Edo. As has been explained, textile goods were of so many kinds that laymen could not easily tell which ones were of good quality and which ones were of reasonable price. Therefore, there were wicked traders then who misused such customers' weakness, making undue profits. There was correspondingly an evil practice common to customers of beating down prices at first before buying. Takatoshi endeavored to break down such profiteering and evil practices, and render the fixed-price sales with no overcharge prevailed in the market. So, he always tried to purchase textiles from Kyoto as cheap as possible. In other words, he pushed ahead with the quick sales at small profits, which was designed to attract as many customers as possible, by rationalizing the way of business. In addition to the fixed-price sales with no overcharge, he pioneered in cutting a unit of textile into small pieces to sell and tailoring clothes instantly at the store which turned out to be enormously popular among the public. By expanding the kinds of textile and service as above, Echigoya succeeded in making the craftsmen and the farmers in the outskirts of the city of Edo their new customers. Their economic life was virtually rising at that time.

Money exchange business

On the occasion that Echigoya moved out to Surugacho, Takatoshi also opened a house of money exchange just next to the Echigoya store. As the sales in drapery in Edo had grown rapidly, the money remitted to the purchasing shop in Kyoto amounted to much. Yet, as Echigoya had entrusted money exchangers to remit the money to the Kyoto shop, the amount of commission had increased greatly. Furthermore, at that time, people in Edo used gold money and those in

68

Kyoto and Osaka used silver money. Thus, people who did business between Edo and Kyoto or Edo and Osaka had to have relationships with money exchangers, watching carefully an exchange quotation between gold and silver. In that sense, it meant much if such a big draper as Echigoya ran a house of money exchange as well. Fortunately enough, there were a group of money exchangers located in Surugacho so that a money exchange house had an easy access to whatever information available from fellow exchangers. For the reasons above, Takatoshi decided to start a money exchange business. Mitsui's money exchange house was, therefore, set up as an auxiliary organ to Echigoya's business. Sales at Echigoya increasingly expanded due to the new way of business and its sincere trade, while the shop in Kyoto was accordingly enlarged. Such an expansion in business, in turn, made it necessary to replenish capital so that Takatoshi decided to invest all his assets he had in Matsuzaka in that line of business and move the headquarters from Matsuzaka to Kyoto in 1686 when he was 65 years old. In the same year, he newly opened a money exchange shop in Kyoto since the Edo exchange house had successfully operated. Echigoya's business was always busy and filled with a large number of customers. Its good reputation, therefore, may have reached officials in charge of purchasing at the Tokugawa shogunate government.

In 1687, one year after Mitsui's headquarters had been moved to Kyoto, the message was transmitted by a Tokugawa official to the fourth son Takatomo that Echigoya was to be a purveyor on textiles to it. Many houses of drapery then desired to be a purveyor to the Tokugawa, but it was exceedingly difficult for any house to be appointed as its purveyor. Therefore, they endeavored to contact with the officials in charge, sending them presents of various kinds, and try to win the position of its purveyor. Generally, however, it was only the merchant houses with a long history of business and having direct or indirect relation to the Tokugawa family that were qualified to be appointed as its purveyor. Thus, the appointment of Echigoya as a purveyor of the Tokugawa had two meanings. One is that during the period from 1688 to 1707, which was usually called 'Genroku' period, craftsmen and merchants gradually rose in the society with the advancement of economy and one's real capability and talent were, accordingly, more evaluated than their family status or lineage. The time came, therefore, that Takatoshi Mitsui was recognized as such since he had caught up with and even surpassed in business such privileged merchants as Nuinosuke Gotoh and Shirojiro Chaya who had a special connection to the first shogun Ieyasu. The other is that by being chosen as the purveyor, Echigoya could soften the strife with the other drapers in Edo and prevent them from making wicked plots. Although it had the advantages above, the purveyor's business cost much with little profit. Moreover, Takatoshi was disgusted at doing business with vested rights or a privilege. He recognized them as opposed to the right way of business. He thought that the right business way was for merchants to compete on a just and fair market without any connection with a person in feudal power to disadvantage other competitors. Based on such thought, he separated the purveyor's business from the main business of Echigoya and set up another shop in Hongincho 2nd street, Nihonbashi, as the Edo service shop for the government. Similarly, in 1691, he separated the purveyor's business from the Kyoto purchasing shop to open another one as the Kyoto service shop for the government. From then on, Mitsui's purveyor service continued 31 years up to 1718 when it terminated due to the Tokugawa 8th shogun Yoshimune's feudal reactionary policy that the position of textiles was to be held only by those merchants related directly or indirectly to the Tokugawa family. In 1716, two years before its termination, in this context, the 9th son Takahisa, who had charge of the service shops for the government, had already considered how to decline its service because the customary gifts sent to the officials and other related expenses were much too costly. Therefore, as Mitsui was dismissed from that service in 1718, he at once wrote an admonition to his offspring that one ought not to wish for a purveyor's business.

In 1687 when its business was increasingly expanding, Echigoya decided to separate the sales function of cotton cloth and cotton and the Kanto silk fabrics, whose suppliers were in the areas around Edo, from that of the main line of Nishijin silk fabrics to set up an independent Edo cotton shop. The new cotton shop was suited more for the masses. Later, more stores and shops were established to meet a new, rising demand. As in 1688, the House of Mitsui owned 11 stores and shops in total comprising those of drapery, money exchange and others in Edo, Kyoto, Osaka and Matsuzaka. The house of money exchange in Edo, in this connection, had multiplied its business since 1683. In 1689, it was permitted to enter the authorized money exchange circle and further in 1691 appointed as an agent of the Tokugawa government treasury's money exchange in Osaka, when Takatoshi was 70 years of age. In the private sector, at that time, the amount of remittance from Edo to Kyoto and Osaka was always more than that from Kyoto and Osaka to Edo, and thus the money exchange was in a one-sided state. In this connection, the Tokugawa shogunate government had collected taxes in gold and silver money in its own territory in the western part of Japan and sent the money to its treasury in Osaka to transport it to Edo by horses and carriers. Such a way of transporting gold and silver money, however, had run a great risk and an immense cost as well. So, the Tokugawa government came to consider remitting it by money exchange. They contrived a plan that the remittance from Edo to Osaka in the private sector was to be offset by that of their collected taxes from Osaka to Edo through exchange transactions. That plan was called the Tokugawa government treasury's money exchange in Osaka. In the plan, the Tokugawa government was to hand an amount of gold and silver money from the treasury over to money exchangers in Osaka who, in turn, purchased bills of exchange with that amount of money from wholesalers in Kyoto and Osaka. The money exchangers in Osaka then sent the bills to the exchangers in Edo who collected money by those bills from merchants in Edo and pay that money to the Tokugawa government. When Mitsui was appointed as an agent of the Tokugawa government treasury's money exchange, Takatoshi opened at once the Osaka shop of money exchange in Kohraibashi, 1st street, Osaka as a branch of the money exchange house in Edo. He knew well that a purveyor to the Tokugawa shogunate government was quite risky to take, but recognized at the same time that it was of great significance for Mitui to deal in official money exchange in view of all its lines of business. Since then, Mitsui continued to hold that agent role up to the closing days of the Tokugawa regime. Mitsui's money exchange business was later developed into broader financial trade in the three cities of Kyoto, Osaka and Edo. The main line of its financial business was, however, commercial finance. Mitsui had a business principle of conducting many financial dealings with small profits, which corresponded to the way of business at the Echigoya drapery stores, i.e., 'quick sales in cash at small profits with no overcharge'. Thus, Echigoya drapery stores and Mitsui money exchange shops came to be the two largest lines of business of which Takatoshi had control. By having combined to operate them, the House of Mitsui developed more and more.

Takatoshi's thought and belief

In the early days of Mitsui, Takatoshi had carried out business with his own thought and belief. His ways of viewing, modes of thinking and state of being were, in turn, succeeded by his children and the leading executive managers of the House of Mitsui. Later, his children collected his words and followed the thought behind his deeds to create the precepts and the constitution of the House of Mitsui, whereby Mitsui's culture was firmly consolidated. The crux of Mitsui's constitution was the 'Sohjiku's Testament' compiled by the first son Takahei in 1722. It comprises Takatoshi's thought and his last injunctions. 'Sohjiku' was the name of Takahei after his retirement from business. Next, there was the 'History of Mitsui' recounting the origin of the House of Mitsui as well as the biography of Takatoshi. The 'Book of Trade' was written by the third son Takaharu to record Takatoshi's words and deeds on the way of business. There was also the 'Records of A Merchant's Observance' describing merchants who had succeeded and those who had failed in the commercial society to allow others to learn out of the successes or failures. Further, there was the 'House of Mitsui's Rule Book' written by the second son Takatomi.

Out of the writings by the children of Takatoshi, we can draw Takatoshi's basic thought and belief to list them concisely as follows.

71

1   Thought of stoicism
2   Honesty of a merchant
3   Sincere trade
4   A spirit of service
5   Rationalizing management
6   View of work
7   View of saving

(Y. Nakata, 1959)

1   Thought of stoicism

Takatoshi thought that one's pleasure in daily life lies in doing business. It is obviously an indiscreet act for a merchant to indulge in pleasures with his earned money. What is the best for him is to live a healthy, long life and rise to a wealthy, honorable merchant at the same time. To that end, a merchant is to live prudently, pray to deities at a household shrine for his offspring's healthy and long life, and then for his wealth and prosperity. The foundation of one's business, he thought, lies in his care of health.

2   Honesty of a merchant

The honesty of a merchant means that a merchant lives his sincere vocational life. In other words, there is a merchant's own way of life behind his business activities that is to be called the merchant's honesty. Underlying Takatoshi's new way of business of 'quick sales in cash at small profits with no overcharge' there was a merchant's honesty, i.e., a fundamental principle of Echigoya's store management. In this context, in 'Tohi Mondo'(Questions and Answers between City People and Country People) written by Baigan Ishida, who constituted a theory on merchant way in the Tokugawa times, there was a phrase as follows. 'It is a merchant's honesty to derive a profit from the sale'(M. Shibata, 1962). Takatoshi had expressed the same way of thinking as above and put it in practice before the Learning of Human Nature was established and instructed by Baigan Ishida.

3   Sincere trade

The way of sales at a fixed price with no overcharge gained broad public acceptance and succeeded greatly. It was founded on the thought that a merchant is to seek and purchase things of good quality, sell them at a small profit to benefit customers and gain their confidence accordingly. Mitsui's agent business of the Tokugawa government treasury's money exchange, in this context, facilitated its way of sales at small profits still further. There were 2 to 5 months of grace period between the time it received gold and silver money in trust from the government's treasury in Osaka and when paying its equivalent money to the Tokugawa government in Edo. Yet, there was no interest charged on the money during the period of grace. Accordingly, that fund with no interest could be used to purchase many kinds of textile fabrics to sell them at a much smaller profit. Excessive profits were, thus, curbed and fair prices maintained. As a result, Mitsui gained more and more public confidence.

4 A spirit of service

Takatoshi emphasized the value of offering a good service to customers. He set out to provide new services such as cutting a unit of textile into small pieces and tailoring clothes instantly at the store for sale. Conventionally, drapers had sold textile fabrics by the unit of Tan, which was 1 meter times 34 centimeters. That is, they had not sold fabrics in less than that unit. However, the new public customers wanted to buy textiles by a much smaller unit, to which Echigoya quickly responded. Also, it started to employ a number of craftsmen to offer the service of tailoring clothes instantly at the store which was to address a new, rising demand.

5 Rationalizing management

Echigoya drapery stores adopted a division of work called the 'one clerk charged with one line'. They also devised a double entry system of accounting, hanged up a wall clock in front of their stores and so on. Those ways of management were basically to attain the justice of exchange and that of distribution, thereby benefiting both the stores and the customers. When recognizing the importance of the bottom line and following the thought of honest commerce, people would not enter into speculation. Such speculative lines of business were, in reality, shuned at Mitsui as quotation with excessive risk, mining, reclaiming of a new field for rice, civil engineering works and hoarding. A spirit of gambling was thus curbed. On the other hand, Takatoshi was considerably cautious of his purveyor service to the Tokugawa and other lords. He feared that a purveyor would likely be blinded with vested rights and undue advantages and, as a result, deviate from the main stream of commerce. In Sohjiku's Testament, there is a phrase saying that 'a purveyor's service is to be considered an aftertaste (a residue) of business'. That is, it says that a purveyor's business is not the real business. Takatoshi said that if the Tokugawa or other lords asked Mitsui to lend money for official use, it ought not to lend the amount money required, but instead, to give them a small amount of money for nothing. There were some cases, however, that Mitsui could not but lend money to them. As to those cases, he made it a rule to separate both the principal and interest of the money lent to them from the ordinary trade books and manage them as a different account so that they might not affect the business assets of Mitsui adversely. Takatoshi also set a limit to the money lent to lords, and when the amount unpaid reached that limit he disposed of it as a bad debt. He avoided having too intimate a relation to the Tokugawa and other

73

lords on the one hand, while he made an effective use of the agent role of the Tokugawa government treasury's money exchange on the other hand. He thus pushed ahead with Mitsui's rationalizing management.

6   View of work

Takatoshi truly despised an upstart who made a fortune by fraudulent deeds. He thought that the money gained without any hardship does more harm than good to its gainer. A merchant is able to harvest fruits only by working steadily and tenaciously day and night. Wealth is not given a priori by heaven. It is endowed by heaven as the result of one's work. Hard work is the original source of a successful business. For the drapery business, it is literally necessary for a master himself to work. Among the Kyoto merchants, there were those who had succeeded in their business to a certain extent, entrusted it then altogether to their employees to free themselves from work and indulge in pleasures, thereby having rendered their house going bankrupt. Takatoshi admonished that if a merchant forgot working even a while, he would go to ruin in the end. Here, morality of working is clearly expressed.

7   View of saving

Takatoshi was thoroughly a saving person and did not waste any money, even a penny. It seems to be only natural in view of his way of business. In the money exchange business, dealings with negligible interest were transacted in a large enough amount to derive a profit while in the business of drapery, goods with small profits were sold in a large quantity sufficient to be paying. Every penny was valuable. Accordingly, merchants of Mitsui were generally saving-minded in their daily life. As stated before, Takatoshi's thought and belief were succeeded by his children and the leading managers of the House of Mitsui whereby Mitsui's culture was further solidified. Such attributes of its culture, in this connection, as hard working, discretion, honesty and saving came out to influence Baigan Ishida's Learning of Human Nature later on.

A principle of no division of property

Now, in 1694, three years after the House of Mitsui was appointed as an agent of the Tokugawa government treasury's money exchange, Takatoshi Mitsui died at the age of 73. In 1693, the previous year, Takatoshi had already gathered the main persons out of his children to consult and draw up a will on the succession of Mitsui's property. The undertaking of Takatoshi was virtually a joint enterprise among his children where, as stated previously, the purchasing shops in Kyoto were run by the first son Takahei, the drapery sales stores in Edo by the second son Takatomi and the fourth son Takatomo, the money exchange shop in Kyoto by the third son Takaharu, and so on while Takatoshi himself

74

was in the headquarters in Kyoto. In deciding to allocate his property among his children, accordingly, it may have been considered how much each of them had been committed to the joint undertaking. According to Takatoshi's will, Mitsui's property was decided to be passed to the seven sons out of his family, the first daughter's family, the fifth son who had once been adopted into another family but returned then, and the fifth son's daughter, which came out to be ten inheritors. As to each one's share of interest in the property, a little more than 40 percent of the interest went to the first son Takahei, about 18 percent to the second son Takatomi, a little less than 13 percent to the third son Takaharu, a little more than 10 percent to the fourth son Takatomo, and shares in the range between a little more than 6 percent and a little more than 1 percent to the others. The way of sharing Mitsui's property above seems to have shown Takatoshi's intention that the inheritors were to be united to run Mitsui's undertaking with the first son Takahei as its leader. By this allocation, however, the interest of the property was not really divided among the inheritors. When Takatoshi's will was drawn up, the seven sons and the first daughter out of the inheritors promised the first son Takahei that all the assets of Mitsui were to be employed with a principle of no division of property in their lifetime. They further pledged that if any one of them asked for a division of the property, the first son Takahei could punish him or her in his judgement. The stores and shops of Mitsui were, in reality, functionally interdependent on each other. For instance, the drapery shops in Kyoto did purchasing activities while the stores of drapery in Edo conducted sales. The two functions of purchasing and selling were performed separately between Kyoto and Edo. In the money exchange line of business, also, the Kyoto shop functioned as headquarters, the shop in Osaka kept in trust gold and silver money from the Tokugawa government treasury and used it for short-term finance, and the Edo money exchange house exercised the financial part of the drapery stores in Edo whereby the drapery line of business and the money exchange line of business were practically combined to run. It was actually, therefore, difficult to divide Mitsui's business. Since 1694 when Takatoshi passed away, thus, Mitsui's business was to be run as the second generation's joint undertaking. The joint undertaking was, in this context, founded on the principle of no division of property which was forming a new layer, overlying the first layer of Mitsui's culture formed in the days of its foundation and in its early days. That is, the second layer of culture was gradually evolving then.

After the death of Takatoshi, Mitsui continued to show a flourishing business as before and set up more stores and shops. In 1697, it opened a thread-and-yarn store in Kyoto. In 1704, the first son Takahei undertook a drapery store run by the house of his wife's parents and renamed it the Edo Onoda store to operate. In the same year, Mitsui also opened a new shop named the Edo Onagawa shop to purchase kitchen utensils and retail hemp cloth and tobacco.

In this way, the House of Mitsui's organization expanded further still so that it became increasingly difficult for Takahei, his brothers and the executive managers of Mitsui to manage its business uniformly. While the number of stores and shops was on the increase, they were not independent as profit centers. They were interdependent on each other functionally so that it was all the more difficult to appraise each store's or shop's performance objectively. On the other hand, the members of Mitsui family gradually kept themselves from running the stores and shops, and in 1703, moreover, it was made a rule for the general managers to run them, acting as deputy for the family members. It was specified in the Articles of General Managers' Work at Mitsui. Thus, general managers such as Sohsuke Nakanishi, Tohemon Wakita, Zenjiroh Kobayashi and Jihei Matsuno who had worked for the House of Mitsui since its foundation became influential, displaying their managerial abilities to the fullest. Yet, they operated their stores and shops in a more independent and self-supporting way. Under those circumstances, Mitsui truly needed to reform its conventional organization to effectively compete with other rival stores. It was Sohsuke Nakanishi that took the initiative in pushing ahead with reorganization. Nakanishi proposed that the drapery purchasing shops in Kyoto should be united with the drapery sales stores in Edo to form a single enterprise; that the Edo money exchange house should be deprived of its substitute role of performing the drapery stores' financial function; and that the drapery stores thus conduct their financial part on their own so that the money exchange line of business be managerially separated from the drapery line. His proposal above was accepted. The purchasing shops of drapery were, at first, merged with the sales stores in Edo, and later the Osaka drapery store. Then, the Kyoto brokerage house and the Edo Onoda store were absorbed into this enterprise. It was the first stage of Mitsui's reorganization. In this stage, while the drapery line of business was united as a single enterprise with the function of its purchasing in Kyoto, the cotton shop, the shop for service to the government and the money exchange shops were left as they had been. Also the issue of how the stores and shops each ought to bear the household expenses of the Mitsui family was unsettled.

In 1709, the second son Takatomi and Sohsuke Nakanishi each proposed their plans, which turned out to be the second stage of reorganization. Takatomi's plan was that separate headquarters be set up for the drapery business, the cotton cloth business and money exchanges; that each store or shop reports to its corresponding headquarters; that the leading managers from Mitsui's foundation are positioned as chief officer at each headquarters; and that each headquarters settles accounts every three years and pays its profits to the Mitsui family. He proposed that Mitsui's business should be divided into three lines; that the members of Mitsui family be separated into three groups to govern each of the three lines of business which are to be run by the leading

76

executive managers. That is, it was a proposal to divide Mitsui's organization (M. Miyamoto, 1998). In contrast, Nakanishi proposed that a single general headquarters should be set up to exercise control over all business; that its stores and shops directly report to the general headquarters; and that all the property be managed by the headquarters. It was a plan of a divisional system of organization (M. Miyamoto, 1998). In 1710, after Takatomi passed away in 1709, Mitsui adopted Nakanishi's divisional system of organization plan but included parts of Takatomi's as well. By this reorganization, an organization named 'the Capitalist Union' was formed which comprised the nine Mitsui families, i.e., the first son's family, the second son's, the third son's and so forth. The Capitalist Union was similar to an unlimited partnership where the nine Mitsui families held shares of the property as partners (M. Miyamoto, 1998). The Union was, then, to function as the general headquarters of the House of Mitsui to which nine divisions belonged. The nine divisions were as follows.

1   The line of drapery business with its suppliers in Kyoto which comprised Kyoto head store, Edo sales head store and its 4 sales branch stores.
2   The line of drapery business with its suppliers in the Kanto area which consisted of Edo cloth store, one branch store in Kyoto and one branch store in Osaka.
3   The line of service to the Tokugawa and other lords which included Kyoto service shop and Edo service shop as its branch.
4   The Kyoto thread-and-yarn store
5   The Kyoto money exchange shop
6   The Edo money exchange house
7   The Osaka money exchange shop
8   The Edo Onagawa shop
9   The Matsuzaka store

The Capitalist Union of Mitsui was to invest capital in the nine divisions which was, in turn, to pay a fixed amount of dividend to the Union every fiscal year. When profits greater than the fixed dividend were earned, such costs were subtracted from that surplus as accrued interest on loans and real property leased from the Union, a house rent, a bad debt loss, retirement allowance, house repairing expenses and so on. The balance derived from the above subtraction was kept as internal reserves at each division. In the reorganization in 1710, the two divisions of the drapery business, one with its suppliers in Kyoto and the other in the Kanto area, became profit centers. On the other hand, six divisions out of the remaining seven divisions (excluding Matsuzaka store), were not in a position to be independent profit centers. Later, however, these six divisions were integrated either into the drapery business or money exchanges. For instance, in 1718, the Kyoto and Edo service shops for the Tokugawa and lords, which had consecutively shown a deficit, was integrated into the Kyoto head store in drapery business, and in 1719, the money exchange shops in Edo and Osaka were united with the Kyoto money exchange shop to form a profit center with its head shop in Kyoto. This consolidation continued until Mitsui became an organization of three divisions. As a result, the Capitalist Union was no longer involved with day-to-day business. Instead, a meeting was to be held every month with members of the nine Mitsui families and the leading executive managers. Thus, the Capitalist Union was turned into the highest decision-making body at Mitsui (M. Miyamoto, 1998). As for the nine Mitsui families' expenses, the money exchange shops had been thus far paying them. However, at this time, the payer changed to the Capitalist Union. In the days of the foundation of the Capitalist Union, moreover, each store or shop had only paid dividends on its invested capital and interest on its loans. According to the reorganization above, the stores and shops were to keep back 10 percent to 12 percent of their internal reserve for bonus funds to clerks and transfer the remainder to the investment account, i.e., the Capitalist Union's account. The assets of the Capitalist Union had quadrupled during the 8 years from 1710 to 1718. At the time of its foundation, it had a large amount of loans from the money exchange shops, but all the loans had been paid back by 1712 and since then, its assets were composed only of its own capital (M. Miyamoto, 1998).

What played a significant part in solidifying the Capitalist Union, in this connection, was Sohjiku's Testament written in 1722 by the first son Takahei. As set forth previously, the inheritors of the founder Takatoshi swore that they abide by the principle of no division of property. It was, however, limited only to their lifetime. For the principle to be observed generation after generation, therefore, it needed to be written into a constitution of the House of Mitsui. It was Sohjiku's Testament, which literally came to be the House of Mitsui's constitution. The Capitalist Union, thus, became a joint ownership among the nine Mitsui families who had their right of interest in the property of the House of Mitsui but not the right of its disposal. In other words, the nine Mitsui families were only to get a share of earnings out of the property but forbidden to exercise the right of its disposition forever. It is said that Sohjiku's Testament was referred to and its articles were recited in a meeting in the early days of January every year and in a conference held urgently. The Capitalist Union was a partnership of the nine Mitsui families where Mitsui's business was assumed to go on forever and their private right of ownership was kept from freely being exercised. In a conference of the Union, the basic policies of management were decided, but the management itself was entrusted to the general managers of each division, i.e., the drapery division, the money exchange division and the Matsuzaka store. To repeat, the fundamental principle of no division of property had been succeeded in the form of the Capitalist Union following Nakanishi's plan in 1710, and it was later codified in Sohjiku's Testament. Thus, the thought of no division of property, i.e., the second layer of Mitsui's culture, was reinforced further with the Capitalist Union and Sohjiku's Testament.

Division of Property in the Annei times

Mitsui's business, from that time, progressed satisfactorily until around 1750. In the case of the drapery line, its sales rapidly expanded from 1736 to 1741. According to the settlement of accounts made every three years, its profit in 1739 was 1.9 times as much as in 1724 and, that in 1748, which was the highest recorded all through the Tokugawa times, was 1.18 times as much as in 1739. In the line of money exchange, on the other hand, the net profit had shown a rapid increase up to the year of 1740. Into the latter half of 1773, however, sales of drapery business started to decline and in 1773, it fell down to half the amount of the peak year with its profit down to 40 percent of the highest. The net profit at the money exchange division also went down from 1741 to 1744 but the rate of decrease was smaller than at the division of drapery. While the drapery line of business showed a downturn in the latter half of the 1740s, its bad and uncollectable bills increased. In 1722 when Sohjiku's Tetament was drawn up, the Capitalist Union's assets were constituted as follows:

* Commerce section: 54%
* Finance section: 26%
* Others: 20%

(Y. Nakata, 1959)

It was quite a healthy constitution. After the 1740s, however, this healthiness badly deteriorated due to the increase of loans to the Tokugawa and other lords and the Mitsui families. As in 1772, the assets of the Capitalist Union were composed of the following.

* Commerce section: 25%
* Finance section: 18%
* Others:
  loans to the Tokugawa
  and other lords: 24%
  loans to the Mitsui
  families: 13%
  others: 20%

(Y. Nakata, 1959)

Out of the above, loans to the Mitsui families were those that they borrowed on the pretext of purchasing new houses, paying repair expenses and so on, but that

79

in reality they borrowed to sustain their increasingly showy and gorgeous life.

In addition, the Mitsui families had a strife among them. At the time of the foundation of the Capitalist Union, the nine Mitsui families were each granted their share of the property which totaled to 95.5 percent. The remaining 4.5 percent share was reserved for someone in the Mitsui families to gain in the future. That is, Sohjiku's Testament had stipulated that the nine Mitsui families hold 95.5 percent share of interest in the property of Mitsui and the remaining 4.5 percent be reserved for the future. Later on, Takafusa, who was three generations down from the first son Takahei, provided of his own will the reserved 4.5 percent share to his daughter's husband and his fourth son. That, in turn, caused a strife among the nine Mitsui families. Furthermore, the renowned name of 'Hachiroemon Mitsui' had been conventionally used by the second son's family, but Takafusa, the first son's 3rd generation, maintained that its name was to be used by the first son's family. Thus, the second son's second generation Takakatsu decided to retire from his post in the Capitalist Union and quit attending the Union's meetings. Further still, out of the loans to the nine Mitsui families, the largest was those to the first son's 3rd generation Takafusa, the third son's family, which had been succeeded by Takafusa's child, and Takafusa's son-in-law's family. Under those circumstances, in 1774, a plan of dividing Mitsui's business into three enterprises was proposed by the second son's, the 4th son's and the ninth son's families which had small debt to the Capitalist Union among the families. The leading executive managers at the House of Mitsui showed a strong opposition at first, but the strife among the families was in such a state that no one could possibly settle it. In October 1774, at last, Mitsui's property was divided into three groups.

This division of Mitsui's property was called 'Division of Property in the Annei times' because it occurred in the 3rd year of Annei by the Japanese calendar. Just before the division of the property, the Capitalist Union's total assets were about 58,471 kan of silver (nearly 220 tons of silver money), out of which 45 percent was bad and uncollectable debt. The largest of the debt was the loans to the lord of Kishu, in the domain of which the Matsuzaka store was located. After having subtracted the bad and uncollectable debt above, the net property was around 32,000 kan of silver out of which 37 percent was kept back in the Capitalist Union and 63 percent was divided as follows.

9,075 kan of silver	(45%) :	the first son's family and its relatives.
9,141 kan of silver	(45%) :	the second son's, the fourth son's, the ninth son's and the tenth son's families.
1,996 kan of silver	(10%):	the first daughter's family and others.
Total 20,212 kan of silver	(100%)	

According to the division of Mitsui's assets above, the first group including the first son's family and its relatives took charge of the drapery line of business, the second group comprising the second son's, the fourth son's, the ninth son's and the tenth son's families took charge of the money exchange line of business and the third group of the first daughter's family and others took charge of the Matsuzaka store. In this connection, the contents of the 11,869 kan of silver left at the Capitalist Union were as follows.

- real estate
- loans to lords
- money lent to the Tokugawa shogunate government
- money lent to the stores and shops of Mitsui for building expenses
- money lent to the stores and shops of Mitsui to take over their uncollectable loans

As can be seen, the Capitalist Union had little assets of real business and no investment in Mitsui's stores and shops (M. Miyamoto, 1998). After the 'Division of property in the Annei times', the drapery line of organization, the money exchange line of organization and the organization of Matsuzaka store were run respectively with their own capital. The Capitalist Union was thus deprived of the function of headquarters. As to the household expenses of the Mitsui families, the three organizations each undertook the part of disbursing them. As a result, the relationship between each organization and the families in charge was solidified. However, meetings at the Capitalist Union continued to be held and the Union was understood as an organ representing the House of Mitsui to the outside people. The assets remaining at the Capitalist Union were also recognized as jointly owned by the Mitsui families. As described above, the 'Division of Property in the Annei times' can be looked on as the reorganization from a divisional system of organization to a division of the organization into three enterprises (M. Miyamoto, 1998). The objectives of this reorganization were to moderate the discord among the Mitsui families, to recover the performance of each store or shop and to dispose of bad and uncollectable debt. It was unanimously agreed, therefore, that they would revert to 'the principle of no division of property' after having attained the objects. In the 'Items of agreement' exchanged among the Mitsui families in 1774, the following were the main items provided for.

- We are not to forget the principle of no division of property.
- We are, in time, to revert to the single control of accounts as in the past.
- We are to try to save, work hard and endeavor to keep our stores and shops from incurring a loss.
- If any store or shop would suffer a loss during the period of 'Division of Property', the families in charge of its store or shop are to be punished by

reducing their share of the property when coming back to the single organization of Mitsui.

Agreement in the Kansei times

It took a little more than 20 years, however, for Mitsui to revert to the single form of organization. The first persons, who positively argued for the integration of the three divided enterprises, were the ninth son's family's 4th generation Takagoh and the executive managers at the Edo stores in the organization of drapery business. However, the second son's family's 3rd generation Takatoh and the leading managers in the organization of money exchange business were opposed to the integration because the drapery business was still in a bad state, and not yet recovered; the loans to the Mitsui families were not fully disposed of and so forth. It just so happened, however, that from 1793 to 1795, many members of the Mitsui family were summoned to the Tokugawa shogunate government and the lord of Kishu for examination since they had been in troubles with each other about how to perform a funeral service after the death of the second son's family's 3rd generation Takatoh and the issue of Takatoh's eldest son's succession to the second son's family. By this incident, people outside of the House of Mitsui came to know that Mitsui's principle of no division of property was just a pretense and in reality it had a strife within. Mitsui was, thus, officially reprimanded. It was Takagoh, the ninth son's family's 4th generation, that accepted the reprimand alone. He incurred a punishment of dismissal from his place of residence, which literally meant a great crisis for the House of Mitsui. Through this crisis, the thought of integrating the three lines of business had been gradually forming among the Mitsui families, and in 1797 the 'Letter of Firm Agreement' was concluded among 15 members of the Mitsui family including retired persons and 38 executive managers of the House of Mitsui. The single organization of Mitsui was, thus, reestablished.

It was called the 'Agreement in the Kansei times' since the year 1797 corresponded to the 9th year of Kansei by the Japanese calendar. In this way, Mitsui was able to integrate its organization while having faced with a huge crisis. It meant that the second layer of Mitsui's culture, i.e., the thought of no division of property, had been deeply rooted in the people of Mitsui. Although the property, which had been divided and allocated into the three lines of organization, was united again in the Capitalist Union and invested anew in those organizations, the returns to the Union came out to be a fixed amount paid biannually by each organization. Moreover, profits calculated by the settlement of accounts every three years were to be accumulated in the respective organizations. Accordingly, what remained at the Capitalist Union was only the assets which were likely to be uncollectable such as loans to the Tokugawa and other lords and those to the Mitsui families with some investment in each organization as at the time of the 'Agreement in the Kansei times'. That is, the Capitalist Union was not in a position any more to increase capital in the respective organizations. Its function of capital allocation died down. While each organization became more and more free and independent, it was confirmed that the capital of the Mitsui families were to be collectively administered and a claim to a division of interest in the capital was not to be allowed. The spirit of no division of property was maintained and at the same time the executive managers had more leeway to run their enterprises in a self-supporting way. The Capitalist Union was deprived of the function of managing and the Mitsui families were kept from exercising their ownership right freely and individually (M. Miyamoto, 1998). In that sense, the second layer of the House of Mitsui's culture may have been transformed considerably. What promoted that transformation then seems to have been the spirit of denying the existing state and that of creativity of the first (basic) layer of its culture. Just as the new business practice had been established by denying the conventional ways of the drapery business, now the original form of the Capitalist Union was negated to create its new form. Here, also, such attributes as honesty, sincerity and a spirit of rationality seen in the early days of Mitsui's undertaking may have contributed to the rebirth of the Capitalist Union. With the revised principle of no division of property above, Mitsui was to manage its business up to the historic turn of the Meiji Restoration in 1868.

The business of Mitsui after the 'Agreement in the Kansei times' was never in a state of full sail with a favorable wind. It suffered a fire more than once. It also could not but make loans to the Tokugawa shogunate government and other lords, most of which turned out to be bad and uncollectable debts. Its drapery sales decreased from 1818 to 1844. During that time, the drapery line of the organization occasionally had to borrow money from the money exchange line of organization via the Capitalist Union. Into the latter half of the 1840s, the money exchange line of business fell off in profits. In the closing days of the Tokugawa regime, moreover, Mitsui had to face the critical issue of whether it was to continue to have dealings with the Tokugawa shogunate regime or not. At the turning point in history from the Tokugawa times to the Meiji era, therefore, the leaders of Mitsui had immense difficulties deciding how to steer their house in the right direction. On this occasion, Takaaki Mitsui in Kyoto then co-worked well with the highest executive manager Rizaemon Minomura who was in Edo to collect whatever crucial information on political and economic affairs. While Takaaki had access to the Imperial Court and kept communicating with the key retainers of the lord of Satsuma, the lord of Chohshu and others who were later to establish the Meiji government, Rizaemon Minomura continued to be in contact with the Tokugawa shogunate government. In other words, Mitsui had taken a neutral attitude toward the

Imperial Court's side and the Tokugawa government's side for a while, but ultimately took the part of the Imperial Court's, providing financial support to them. Thus, Mitsui turned out to be a contributor to the new Meiji government.

Reorganization after the Meiji Restoration

After the Meiji Restoration, Rizaemon Minomura came to grips with the reform of Mitsui's organization. In 1874, he drew up the 'Amendments of the Capitalist Union' in which it was stipulated that the Capitalist Union was not to be controlled by the Mitsui families; that the property of Mitsui was not to be owned by the Mitsui families but to be owned by the organization of the House of Mitsui. The above thought was soon materialized by the foundation of Mitsui Bank which was to be the headquarters for all lines of business. When Mitsui Bank was founded with its capital fixed at two million yen, the former Capitalist Union invested one million yen, the Mitsui families 0.5 million yen and the leading executive managers and other workers of the House of Mitsui 0.5 million yen. According to Minomura's thought, here, the investment by the Mitsui families was only 25 percent of the total since the property of the Capitalist Union was the 'fortune jointly owned by the employer and the employees'. Minomura's reform meant that the executive managers and other workers of the House of Mitsui were granted a right of share of the Capitalist Union's property from which they had conventionally been excluded. It was, therefore, a great turn from what it had been and a substantial change in the principle of no division of property, i.e., the second layer of Mitsui's culture. It was a solid fact that the executive managers and other employees had contributed much to the creation of the Capitalist Union's property. It could be said, therefore, that the property was, in effect, the 'fortune jointly owned by the employer and the employees'. In the new era of Meiji, also, the executive managers and others at the House of Mitsui took the initiative in running its business. Thus, the second layer of Mitsui's culture as it had been, was negated and replaced with a newly formed principle of the 'fortune jointly owned by the employer and the employees'. At the time of the foundation of Mitsui Bank in 1876, Rizaemon Minomura modernized its employment relations by changing the conventional system of domestic employment to a new modern employment system. That is, by denying the relationship of a master and a domestic employee, he defined that the Mitsui family members and the employees of the House of Mitsui were 'equal partners'(A. Chimoto, 1998).

Following Minomura, Hikojiroh Nakagamigawa took leadership in reforming Mitsui. He set up the department of industrial finance at Mitsui Bank, invested in such manufacturers as Tomioka Filature, Oji Paper Manufacturing, Kanegafuchi Spinning, Shibaura Works and so on, and pioneered the manufacturing sector for finace. In addition, he developed a new employment system to hire many highly educated persons at Mitsui Bank, and promoted them to higher positions whereby he tried to renovate the ethos of Mitsui at that time. For a private bank to employ highly educated persons, it was absolutely necessary then to offer fairly good conditions since most of them desired to enter and actually got into government, educational and legal circles. Therefore, Mitsui Bank increased the salary of its bank clerks to surpass that of the government officials. It also tried to raise the clerks' morale. It further adopted the merit system in personnel management and promoted clerks to higher posts according to their achievements (A. Chimoto, 1998). Nakagamigawa emphasized that a businessman must not be a purveyor; that he can accomplish his work by helping himself and abiding by a way of justice. Here, we can see that such attributes were active in an unbroken way at the House of Mitsui as the spirit of denying the existing state, that of creativity, honesty, integrity, internal competition, evaluation of personnel by their achievements and so forth which were evidently of the first layer of Mitsui's culture.

In 1893 when the Commercial Code was in effect, Mitsui decided to divide its business into four unlimited partnerships, i.e., Mitsui Bank, Mitsui Trading, Mitsui Mining and Mitsukoshi Drapery Store. The 11 families of Mitsui then became a partner in each one of those partnerships. It did not mean, however, that the property of Mitsui was divided into the 11 families. With the establishment of the four partnerships, a new organization called the 'Mitsui Family Club' was formed which was to own the shares of those partnerships. That is, the 'Mitsui Family Club' duly took over the faculty of the Capitalist Union. Furthermore, in 1905 when the Corporation Tax Act was amended, Mitsui changed the partnerships into joint-stock companies, and in 1909 it set up a new Mitsui partnership which was collectively to own the shares of those joint-stock companies. Mitsui's business, thereafter, went on successfully.

We can point out here, in this connection, that behind the thought of no division of property at Mitsui, there is recognized the way of viewing and thinking of 'Many Deities as One Deity, One Deity as Many Deities' in the Kami Way. The thought of no division of property, thus, may have been a unifying principle at Mitsui. As well as this attribute, furthermore, such attributes as the mind of Musubi and Akaki-kokoro were found existing in the first (basic) layer of Mitsui's culture as previously noted. In that sense, the culture of Mitsui seems to have had the basic national culture of the Kami Way at the deepest level.

Mitsui's culture

Now, we have traced historically how the culture of Mitsui formed and developed. How does, then, Mitsui's culture adapt itself to the Competitiveness as shown in Chapter 3 and Chapter 4?

In retrospect, the first layer of Mitsui's culture formed in the days of its foundation and in its early days when founder Takatoshi Mitsui was actively engaged in business. This basic layer helped to form and evolve the second layer later, and deny it later still to form the new second layer. The original second layer appeared when Takatoshi's will was drawn up and the eight inheritors promised the first son Takahei to observe the principle of no division of property. That is, when Mitsui's business was succeeded as a joint undertaking by the second generation, the second layer of its culture started to evolve. The second layer was consolidated, afterwards, when the Capitalist Union was founded according to the proposal of Sohsuke Nakanishi, the highest executive manager of the House of Mitsui then. It possessed the property of Mitsui whose ownership shares were jointly held by the nine Mitsui families. Moreover, with the Sohjiku's Testament written in 1722 by Takahei, founder Takatoshi's first son, which turned out to be the constitution of the House of Mitsui, the second layer was further imprinted in the mind of people at Mitsui. Into the latter half of the 1740s, however, they divided Mitsui into three organizations because the drapery line of business had fallen into a slump, the assets of the Capitalist Union had deteriorated in quality, the loans to the Tokugawa and other lords had greatly increased, the loans to the Mitsui families had expanded, and further a grave discord had arisen among the families of Mitsui. It was called the 'Division of Property in the Annei times', and the principle of no division of property was in great danger. In 1797, however, the Mitsui families and the executive managers of the House of Mitsui united and agreed to integrate its business, which was called the 'Agreement in the Kansei times', whereby the principle of not dividing property was restored. Although that principle was revived, it was not in its previous form, but in a transformed one. What helped to transform it was mainly the spirit of denying the existing state and that of creativity ascribed to the first (basic) layer of Mitsui's culture. Next, in the transition from the Tokugawa times to the Meiji era, Mitsui's second layer of culture was again compelled to make a big change. It was Rizaemon Minomura's reform that promoted its change. He denied the conventional thought on the property of the Capitalist Union and defined it as the 'fortune jointly owned by the employer and the employees'. He also stated clearly that the Mitsui family members and the employees of the House of Mitsui were equal partners. Accordingly, the principle of no division of property was sustained but transformed in form. It was Hikojiro Nakagamigawa, then, that followed Rizaemon Minomura in making a reform of Mitsui. He argued emphatically that a businessperson ought not to be a purveyor and can only accomplish their work through the ways of independence and justice. Here, we can confirm that the attributes of the first layer of Mitsui's culture were active still. In other words, the first layer, i.e., the basic layer, of Mitsui's culture had lived all through the history of Mitsui without a break to the Meiji era.

Let us next see, therefore, how the first layer of Mitsui's culture fits in well with the 3-Layer Structure of Enterprise Competitiveness and the 7 Principles of Enterprise Competitiveness shown in Chapter 3 and Chapter 4. We shall first look into its adaptability competitiveness element by competitiveness element.

Ethos originated in the early days of an enterprise, i.e., the spirit of denying, the spirit of negating the status quo, the spirit of creativity and the spirit of creating a vision, are maintained The first element of the ethos originated in the days of the House of Mitsui's foundation was a spirit of denying the existing state as recognized in the new ways of commerce of 'sales at the store' and 'sales in cash'. In the past, it had been a common way of business for a draper to take goods over to customers for sale. Mitsui eliminated that approach and established sales at the store. It further denied the conventional way of sales on credit to create the new way of sales in cash. Behind the spirit of denying the status quo and that of creativity above, we can see the mind of Musubi, an attribute of the Kami Way. The second element of the ethos originated at the time of Mitsui's foundation was the value of cleanness. While founder Takatoshi Mitsui worked for the first time in his life at his eldest brother's shop in Edo, he detected and severely criticized the common way of business of selling goods at an inordinate and unreasonable price to peddlers who were, in turn, going to sell them in the provincial areas of the country. He had a firm will to never do such a dirty trade. His value of cleanness reminds us of his mother's way of life. She made it a daily practice to rise at four in the morning every day, pour water over herself even in the middle of winter to clean her mind and body, and then pray to deities and fathagatas. We can see here Misogi and Value of Cleanness, attributes of the Kami Way, which may have formed the foundation of Takatoshi's value of cleanness. The thought of stoicism he later argued for may be founded on his value of cleanness. He thought that it was the best way for a merchant to lead a healthy and long life and thereby gain wealth and prosperity. He also thought that it was altogether imprudent for a merchant to indulge in worldly pleasures. The third element of the ethos generated in the days of the foundation of Mitsui was that a free market is the real arena for merchants. Matsuzaka, Takatoshi's birthplace, was where the free market was kept in order and many merchants were rich in enterprising spirit. It was not the right way for him, accordingly, to do business with the Tokugawa shogunate government and other lords by having so intimate relation to them as to disadvantage other competitors. Out of here, in reality, his way of thinking arose that a purveyor's business is an aftertaste.

The ethos described above, which formed in the days of its Mitsui's foundation, had been succeeded consecutively ever since, having helped Mitsui continue to advance and develop after the Meiji Restoration.

Every member is willing to grapple with any situation without hesitation and without worrying about failure Takatoshi Mitsui opened the Echigoya in the line of drapery business in Edo. As its business showed a successful achievement, the conventional drapers there employed harassing tactics to damage its stores. They, at last, contrived a scheme to pursuade the clerks of Echigoya to break away from it. On that occasion, Shichizaemon, general manager at Echigoya, led and worked well with the clerks to break down that wicked scheme.

People in the workplace freely exchange their views and opinions In the Echigoya drapery stores, there were held regular meetings among the clerks. On those occasions, they freely discussed what means and measures were conceivable and applicable for their business to go on prospering while they looked back and reflected their daily business activities.

There is teamwork among personnel As stated above, general manager Shichizaemon and the clerks at Echigoya collaborated well to go through the crisis.

Diligence and positive activities of personnel Takatoshi's view of work transferred to the clerks that merchants can harvest benefits by working steadily and tenaciously day and night, i.e., sowing the seeds of hard working. What promoted and embodied this view of work was a competitive mechanism of the internal promotion system at Mitsui.

Self-reforming abilities Around the time when Takatoshi opened the first store of Echigoya, it was a general way of business for drapers to carry goods over to customers for sale. In the beginning, therefore, Echigoya followed that common way to peddle a small amount of textile to lords and their retainers and big merchants. It was also the time, however, that craftsmen and merchants came to gain economic strength. Mitsui perceived that change in the market and altered its way of business into that more appropriate to it.

Law (company regulations, etc.) In 1673 when Takatoshi Mitsui opened the store of Echigoya, he duly laid down the store rules. Later, in 1676, he added 27 articles to it in which entertaining customers was, in principle, prohibited. The store rules were, later still, compiled by the second son Takatomi into House of Mitsui's Rule Book. It was Sohjiku's Testament, in this connection, drawn up

88

by founder Takatoshi's first son Takahei, that turned out to be the norm and the constitution of the House of Mitsui for the following generations. Sohjiku's Testament bolstered the principle of no division of property, the thought of which formed the second layer of Mitsui's culture.

Abolishment of practices restricting competition Founder Takatoshi Mitsui thought that it is the right way for a merchant to do business on a free market. Accordingly, he tried to avoid having so unfair relations with the Tokugawa and other lords as to disadvantage others. He even said that a purveyor's business is an aftertaste of the real business. That is, in his thought, a purveyor's business is not the real business. He understood that it was his own way to compete just and fair to the bitter end on the market, keeping himself from holding any relation to the feudal powers in an unfair manner.

Constraints on speculative purchases of enterprises or assets Takatoshi evaded entering risky speculations, mining, reclaiming of new fields of rice, civil engineering, hoarding and the like.

Enterprise ethics (Sense of responsibility to the society) In such ways of business as 'sales at the store', 'quick sales at small profits' and 'sales in cash with no overcharge', it was vitally important to gain customers' confidence. That is, the new ways of business were effected only on the foundation of Mitsui's sincere and honest trade, offering customers goods of good quality at a reasonable and inexpensive price. That is why Takatoshi repeatedly argued for honesty and sincere trade. We can see Akaki-kokoro, an attribute of the Kami Way, behind this thought.

Human resources There were a number of men of talent and ability at Mitsui. For instance, there were such able personnel as Shichizaemon Ishiwara, Tohemon Wakita, Sohsuke Nakanishi and Jihei Matsuno who turned out to be the high executive managers.

Investment in the training of personnel Takatoshi endeavored to cultivate men of talent. Even before the foundation of his store in Edo, he had already sent Tokuemon and Riemon, his employees, to his eldest son Toshitsugu's Edo shop to learn business practically. He had such a long-term standpoint as to foster the able personnel who would be of use in his business in the future.

Education on practical business At Mitsui, the employed people gradually learnt necessary skill for business in doing their job. That is, OJT was exercised, and those who had mastered it within a predetermined time were promoted.

Discussion on the vision, policies and the state of affairs of the enterprise from management As has been explained previously, there was a regular monthly meeting held among the clerks at Echigoya. They had a free discussion there on what steps they could take to improve their business as well as reflecting on their day-to-day business.

Diffuse new ideas, reforms, improvements, and intelligence on new products both inside and outside the organization In the prevailing ethos of the early days of the House of Mitsui, the clerks had a sense of identity with founder Takatoshi Mitsui, talking freely with anyone, and offering suggestions and proposals, not a few of which were taken up and employed at Echigoya.

Maintain a free market principle throughout the enterprise Men of talent were cultivated through the reward system and the way of selecting the elite at Mitsui. The elite were selected by an internal mechanism of competition, i.e., the internal promotion system. Boys of 11 to 13 years of age were first employed and thereafter the selection tests were conducted for them every 7 to 8 years. The first test was to determine which employees could stay to work as a clerk at Mitsui. The second one was to examine which clerks had talent and ability to be senior clerks such as managers and assistant managers. The third and final test was to decide who was to rise to the top management of Mitsui.

Improve cost, quality and delivery terms simultaneously Echigoya pushed ahead with rationalizing commerce by the way of 'quick sales with small profits and no overcharge'. Behind this rationalizing commerce, there was the view of saving that even a penny was not to be wasted. It also rendered such services as of cutting a unit of textile in small pieces for sale and tailoring clothes instantly at the store, thus having met the new, rising demand.

Organizing techniques Echigoya employed a division of work by commodities called the 'one clerk for one line'. It was a policy of rationalizing management.

Guarantee long-term employment As explained before, in the internal promotion system at Mitsui, the tests were conducted in the three stages of selection. The test in the 3rd stage was the most difficult of all determining who was to rise to the top management. For those having passed the 3rd test, various measures were devised to keep them work at Mitsui.

Fair and just promotion of personnel Founder Takatoshi Mitsui instructed each store and shop to exercise a worker's performance appraisal like that of today. On the basis of that appraisal, good performers were duly rewarded. His thought was that if the management made clear a principle of punishment and reward, and rewarded good performers by promoting them to higher ranks, then all the clerks would understand that they ought to follow that criteria and use it as a guiding principle for their daily work.

In sum, the first layer of Mitsui's culture was, as a whole, adapted to the 3-Layer Structure of Enterprise Competitiveness and the 7 Principles of Enterprise Competitiveness. We can show it in a table form as in Table 6.1 and Table 6.2.

Table 6.1   The 3-Layer Structure of Enterprise Competitiveness

I   Enterprise Organismic Foundation

Enterprise ethos
- Ethos originated in the early days of an enterprise,   Adaptable
  i.e., the spirit of denying, the spirit of negating
  the status quo, the spirit of creativity and the spirit
  of creating a vision, are maintained.
- Every member is willing to grapple with any   Adaptable
  situation without hesitation and without worrying
  about failure.
- People in the workplace freely exchange   Adaptable
  their views and opinions.

Enhancement of initiative
- There is teamwork among personnel.   Adaptable
- Personnel have pride and confidence in
  upholding their enterprise's competitiveness
  and have a sense of representing
  their enterprise.
- Diligence and positive activities of personnel.   Adaptable
- Pride and confidence in one's own work.
- Self-reforming abilities.   Adaptable

Provision of norms
- Law (company regulations, etc.).   Adaptable
- Abolishment of practices restricting competition.   Adaptable

Preparation of investment conditions
- Allow a sufficiently long time frame
  for management.
- Promotion of R&D and production-process R&D.

91

• Constraints on speculative purchases of enterprises or assets.	Adaptable
Enterprise ethics (Sense of responsibility to the society)	Adaptable

Education
(General learning as citizen of the society)

II   Enterprise Economic Base

Infrastructure

• Physical assets	facilities, machinery, network.	
• Human resources	executives, scientists, engineers, workers.	Adaptable
• Employment of human resources and procurement of physical assets to build and stabilize infrastructure.		
• Investment in the training of personnel.		Adaptable
• Education on practical business.		Adaptable

Environmental improvement and conservation
• Conservation of the natural environment.
• Cooperation with and participation in
  a community and its activities.
• Improvement of the physical environment of
  the workplace.
• Attention and care to human relations in
  the workplace.

Diffusion of new ideas, planning and others

• Create smooth communication lines.	
• Discussion on the vision, policies and the state of affairs of the enterprise from management.	Adaptable
• Diffuse new ideas, reforms, improvements, and intelligence on new products both inside and outside the organization.	Adaptable

Effectiveness
- Maintain a free market principle throughout   Adaptable
  the enterprise.
- Encourage competitive spirit.
- Improve cost, quality and delivery terms   Adaptable
  simultaneously.
- Development, introduction and use of technology
  to gain strategic predominance.
- Commercialize technology.
- Activate communication throughout.

Tense balance between effectiveness and ethics
- Have a close relationship with customers.
- Have intimate contact with suppliers.
- Organizational techniques.   Adaptable
- Organization whose workers are barely
  conscious of organizational hierarchy.
- Recognition of quality as the end result
  of overall production and service activities.
- Generate many alternatives to
  a decision-making process.
- Demand and expect personnel to do their best.
- Cope with things flexibly.
- Develop personnel's abilities and
  continue their learning.
- Guarantee long-term employment.   Adaptable

Ethics
- Every member is a leading actor.
- A view of work in which diligence is
  highly esteemed.
- Improvement of ethics.
- Fair employment
- Appropriate transfer of personnel from one
  post to another.
- Fair and just promotion of personnel.   Adaptable
- Ethics of relations between management and
  workers.

Table 6.2   The 7 Principles of Enterprise Competitiveness

1 Creativity
- Ethos originated in the early days of an enterprise,   Adaptable
  i.e., the spirit of nying, the spirit of negating
  the status quo, the spirit of creativity and the spirit
  of creating a vision, are maintained.
- Every member is willing to grapple with any   Adaptable
  situation without hesitation and without worrying
  about failure.
- Self-reforming abilities.   Adaptable

2   Righteousness
- Law (company regulations, etc.).   Adaptable
- Ethics of relations between management and workers.
- Abolishment of practices restricting competition.   Adaptable
- Constraints on speculative purchases of   Adaptable
  enterprises or assets.
- Enterprise ethics   Adaptable
  (Sense of responsibility to the society).
- A view of work in which diligence is highly esteemed.
- Improvement of ethics.

3   Fairness
- Maintain a free market principle throughout   Adaptable
  the enterprise.
- Encourage competitive spirit.
- Fair employment.
- Appropriate transfer of personnel from one
  post to another.
- Fair and just promotion of personnel.   Adaptable

4   Equality
- People in the workplace freely exchange   Adaptable
  their views and opinions.
- There is teamwork among personnel.   Adaptable
- Personnel have pride and confidence in
  upholding their enterprise's competitiveness
  and have a sense of representing their enterprise.
- Organization whose workers are barely
  conscious of organizational hierarchy.

- Recognition of quality as the end result
of overall production or service activities.
- Guarantee long-term employment.   Adaptable
- Every member is a leading actor.

5   Sharing
- Conservation of the natural environment.
- Cooperation with and participation in
a community and its activities.
- Improvement of the physical environment of
the workplace.
- Attention and care to human relations in
the workplace.
- Create smooth communication lines.
- Discussion on the vision, policies and the state of   Adaptable
affairs of the enterprise from management.
- Diffuse new ideas, reforms, improvements, and   Adaptable
intelligence on new products both inside and
outside the organization.
- Activate communication throughout.
- Have a close relationship with customers.
- Have intimate contact with suppliers.

6   Self-Cultivation
- Diligence and positive activities of personnel.   Adaptable
- Pride and confidence in one's own work.
- Demand and expect personnel to do their best.

7   Learning and Knowledge-Accumulation

Technology
- Commercialize technology.
- Development, introduction and use of technology
to gain strategic predominance.
- Promotion of R&D and production-process R&D.
- Employment of human resources and
procurement of physical assets to build
and stabilize infrastructure.
- Physical assets.
- Human resources.   Adaptable

Systems thinking
- Allow a sufficiently long time frame
  for management.
- Generate many alternatives to
  a decision-making process.
- Improve cost, quality and delivery terms   Adaptable
  simultaneously.
- Cope with things flexibly.
- Develop personnel's abilities and
  continue their learning.

People
- Education
  (General learning as citizen of the society).
- Investment in the training of personnel.   Adaptable
- Education on practical business.   Adaptable
- Organizational techniques.   Adaptable

6.2 The House of Kohnoike

As shown in the previous section, the House of Mitsui had evolved and developed in the Tokugawa times and managed to steer through the transition of the Meiji Restoration, and continued to develop thereafter. Mitsui came across a number of difficult phases or turning points in history. Each time, however, the first layer of its culture revealed itself to let Mitsui go through such a crisis and back it up to adapt to a new environment. At the arrival of the Meiji era, not to mention, the culture of Mitsui was duly active just as it had been and its ways of viewing, modes of thinking and state of being helped Mitsui to fit in well with this new era. In other words, as previously stated, its culture was fully healthy sufficient to be adaptive to the 3-Layer Structure of Enterprise Competitiveness and the 7 Principles of Enterprise Competitiveness.

Now, then, what was the case of the House of Kohnoike taken which had similarly evolved and developed as a wealthy merchant in the Tokugawa times? The House of Kohnoike, in contrast to the House of Mitsui, failed to steer through the transition of Meiji and fell into obscurity in the end. There may have been a difference between the culture of Mitsui and that of Kohnoike. Accordingly, let us next see how the culture of Kohnoike had evolved and developed in history and in what state it was in the closing days of the Tokugawa shogunate regime.

It was Shinroku Yukimoto Kohnoike that laid the foundation of the House of Kohnoike as its originator. In 1570, he was born in the Kohnoike village, Itami, Settsu (Osaka, now). He started a sake brewing business there and in its early days he not only peddled it in the vicinity of his village but also carried it far up to Edo for sale. Sake was, then, not like the refined sake of transparent color now, but unrefined and opaque in color. In 1600, Shinroku Yukimoto established for the first time the technology of refining the opaque sake into the transparent one, and set out to sell that perfectly clear sake. The new sake was accepted by many people whereby his business flourished. As a matter of course, it was transported by land to Edo, and the House of Kohnoike was the first to sell such refined sake to people in Edo. It was the time when the Tokugawa shogunate family had just fixed Edo as the new capital city of Japan. Edo was, therefore, still a newly opened district and far behind the city of Kyoto or that of Osaka in such necessities of life as food, clothes and housing. Thus, what people in Edo had acquired was usually the opaque sake. Shinroku often made a trip between his village and Edo on the Tokaido highway (a highway from Kyoto to Edo), carrying the tasty sake of transparent color. Soon, it became popular among people in Edo and sold well. With such an increasing demand, he decided to send it by sea since its transport by a horse was no longer sufficient. In this connection, the Tokugawa shogunate government had already established the 'alternate-year dwelling system' where feudal lords all over the country would periodically come to Edo to live for a fixed period of time and then return to their domains. There were, therefore, many lords and their retainers dwelling in their residences in Edo, where they had the opportunity to taste Kohnoike's sake. When they returned to their domain, they told the story of their enjoying such a refined and transparent sake in Edo, which later spread to every corner of their domain. Thus, the name of Kohnoike's sake turned out to be well known all through the country. As Shinroku's House increasingly developed, he decided to open a new store in 1619 at Uchikyuhoji-cho, Osaka to brew and sell sake, while in 1608 Masanari, founder of the House of Kohnoike, had been born. In this context, the fact was of vital importance that Shinroku was called the originator and Masanari was recognized as founder of the House of Kohnoike. As will be seen later, when the ownership changed from Shinroku to Masanari, the culture of Kohnoike altered immensely.

As mentioned above, Shinroku started to ship sake to Edo since the transport by a horse load could not really satisfy the rising demand there. As time went on, however, he considered taking one step further to aim at the business of marine transport itself. In 1625 when the House of Kohnoike initiated the business of marine transport, Shinroku was 56 years of age and founder Masanari 18 years old. A cargo-vessel business between Osaka and

Edo had been originally set out by shipping agents of Sakai, a city next to Osaka city. After 1624, however, many agents of shipping appeared in Osaka, competing well and overwhelming those in Sakai. It was around that time when Kohnoike found its way into the marine transport business. Kohnoike took sake of its own brewing on board its boat to send it to Edo and in returning it was commissioned by lords staying in Edo to carry goods over to Osaka. Kohnoike's shipping business developed further with founder Masanari's endeavor. He set up the center of its business in Kujyoto, Osaka, dealing with many lords to expand it. He transported, in particular, the rice collected as tax by lords in the western part of Japan to the markets of Osaka and Edo. Through that transportation business, founder Masanari Kohnoike became intimate with key retainers of many lords, whereby the House of Kohnoike grew to make a loan to the lords which was generally called the 'loans to lords'. In the beginning, however, Kohnoike did not lend money directly to lords but transferred it to them through the House of Gohei Tenhnojiya who had been engaged in the 'loans to lords' as its own occupation. It was to minimize the risk of incurring bad debt. Masanari was pretty scrupulous in that respect. In 1643, Masanari's first son Yukimune was born as the second generation at the House of Kohnoike when it was running three lines of business, i.e., brewing, marine transportation and money lending to lords.

Alteration of business

In 1650, however, originator Shinroku Yukimoto passed away and, thereafter, the House of Kohnoike's business was to alter immensely. The alteration of its business began in 1656 when Masanari entered into the money exchange line of business. With the money exchange as its main business, Kohnoike accumulated more and more wealth, while Masanari discontinued its brewing business which had been initiated by originator Shinroku. Thus, in the times of founder Masanari and the second generation Yukimune, the House of Kohnoike was engaged in two lines of business, i.e., the line of marine transportation and that of money exchange including the loans to lords. In 1662, money exchangers were officially recognized by the Tokugawa shogunate government. Money exchangers in Osaka were, then, classified into a full-line money exchanger, a limited-line money exchanger or a small-coin money exchanger by size and kind of business. The full-line money exchanger performed like banks of today, fulfilling such functions as of exchanging money, making loans, drawing a bill, buying and selling a money order, deposit and so forth. The small-coin exchanger with little capital was in great numbers in the city of Osaka, exchanging small coins. The limited-line money exchanger was just in-between. Out of the above three kinds, the House of Kohnoike was a full-line money exchanger. The Tokugawa shogunate government, then, elected ten houses as a money exchange service agent of the government out of the full-line money exchangers which were called the 'ten exchange service agents'. In 1670 when founder Masanari was 63 years of age and the second generation Yukimune 28 years old, the House of Kohnoike was elected as one of the ten exchange service agents. The ten exchange agents were provided various kinds of privileges by the Tokugawa government.

Among the full-line money exchangers, in this connection, those of great means filled the post of 'kuramoto' or 'kakeya' as a financial agent for the Tokugawa or other lords as well as serving as one of the ten exchange agents. 'Kuramoto' and 'kakeya' were both a name of office at the 'warehouse residence'. The owners of a warehouse residence were lords around the country and their key retainers, shrines and temples, the Tokugawa government and its direct retainers, and so forth. They collected and sent rice and other articles paid in kind to their warehouse residence for sale which were located in Osaka, Edo and other big cities with convenient means for finance. The kuramoto was an officer who had charge of the revenue and expenditure accounts in selling articles kept in custody at a warehouse residence. After having sold the articles, then, it was the kakeya, an officer, who took charge of collecting money, keeping and remitting it to the owner. Kohnoike at first acted as an agent of kakeya for the lord of Okayama, and in 1689 the second generation Yukimune and his son, the third generation Munetoshi, served as an agent of kakeya for the lord of Hiroshima, whose agency relationship continued to the closing days of the Tokugawa shogunate government.

Loans to lords

Among the full-line money exchanger's business, the loans to lords were guaranteed by rice which would be harvested in the lords' territory the next fall. In other words, the money exchangers made a loan to lords by taking the rice scheduled to be harvested and arrive at their warehouse residence as its security. There was a problem, however, in such a loan since the financial conditions of lords were generally not good. Due to the alternate-year dwelling system, in particular, lords had two residences and had to incur not only living expenses during their stay in Edo but also traveling expenses of going to Edo and returning to their domain. Those expenses were really immense. Moreover, harvest of rice was influenced by weather, and in a poor crop year they could not get the money scheduled to come in. Among the lords, there were those who indulged in luxury and fell into spendthrift habits. Yet, it was those luxurious lords that asked for loans and broke promise to pay it back. Some lords were deprived of their territory by the government due to their misconduct. In such deprivation, it was usually the case that the money the lords had borrowed was treated as a bad debt. Thus, the loans to lords were very high in risk, likely to be uncollectable. On the other hand, the rate of interest on loans to lords was also high. It was so high that the cumulative amount of interest would get to the amount of its principal in less than 10 years. It is said, therefore, that the money exchangers in Osaka aimed to earn interest on loans, not expecting so much the repayment of its principal. Earnings of interest was the largest benefit of loans to lords for them. In addition, the money exchangers, who acted as an agent of kuramoto or kakeya like Kohnoike, were yearly provided an official remuneration of rice from the lords. They were also given privileges having a surname and wearing a sword which the lord usually provided only to retainers, i.e., the samurai class.

On the other hand, the House of Kohnoike made a loan to merchants. It lent money to merchants, with whom it had daily dealings, according to their credit ratings. In 1670, loans to merchants were 59.3 percent of its assets and those to lords 19 percent. After the founder Masanari passed away in 1693 and the second generation Yukimune followed him in 1696, the third generation Munetoshi took charge of running the House of Kohnoike. In 1704 during Munetoshi's times, the composition of its assets was inordinately different from that in 1670. The loans to lords occupied 73.5 percent of the total with those to merchants falling off drastically. In contrast to the House of Kohnoike, at Mitsui it was stipulated in Sohjiku's Testament that 'loans to lords were to be prohibited since the grandfather's time'. In reality, Mitsui had a small amount of loans to lords, but sustained its principle of not making it. Kohnoike, on the other hand, took the loans to lords as its main business and since 1716 onward, it gradually cut down the line of marine transport and later abandoned it.

The single line of money exchange business

The House of Kohnoike originally started the marine transportation business for the purpose of carrying sake of its own brewing over to Edo. After 1656 when founder Masanari initiated the money exchange line of business, it discontinued its brewing business so that the original purpose of marine transport had terminated. From 1688 to 1703, however, it endeavored to expand the marine line by setting up a branch office at Gofuku-cho, Edo and actively operated its business with more than 100 boats of its own. Later, the transition arrived from private carrier to common carrier (public carrier). On this occasion, Kohnoike dared not to adapt to it, cutting down its marine line and abandoned it. That is, it narrowed its business down to and concentrated on the single line of money exchange business. Since 1736 when the third generation Munetoshi passed away, the House of Kohnoike was to continue to be a money-lending merchant with loans to lords being its main business, not developing any new kind of business, until the closing days of the Tokugawa regime.

Seniority system

At Kohnoike, personnel were given an allowance for the first time when they were promoted to the position of a clerk after having been employed. Both the probationary employees and clerks were disciplined sternly and scolded all day. When scolding them, the managers of Kohnoike are said to have used force. There is the thought, here, that one ought to do what is ordered without question. Therefore, there may not have been any attempt for managers to have meetings or free discussion with clerks. In about 20 months after having been appointed as clerks, they were to become a probationary manager. In another 2 to 3 years, they were to be a manager. In 2 to 3 years still further, they would become 'bekke'. The bekke was a general manager who came to work from his own residence outside of the store. It was a general manager residing outside while all the other managers and clerks lived within the store. The bekke was a manager of seniority post at Kohnoike whose role was to propose how to run Kohnoike's stores and determine what policies of business to take. The managers of seniority post gave detailed instructions to clerks, for instance, even when the clerks went to a warehouse residence of a lord for their dealings. In the seniority system, they hardly instituted a practice of electing capable persons for promotion. Those personnel that worked long for the stores and were well acquainted with the traditional way of business were highly esteemed. Tenacious classicism and conservative ethos are recognized here.

Kohnoike's culture

As has been stated, the House of Kohnoike was gradually evolved and formed by originator Shinroku, founder Masanari, the second generation Yukimune and the third generation Munetoshi. Since the times of Munetoshi, in this context, the essence of Kohnoike's business came out to be the line of loans to lords, having had intimate relation to a number of lords to develop it. Since the third generation Munetoshi's time onward, it is thought, its management adhered to the status quo and it only endeavored to save the honor of a wealthy merchant. The name of Zennemon Kohnoike, its house name, remained the same although the house owner consecutively changed to the next generation. They tried to maintain the status of their patrimonial house, and, therefore, what was individualistic of the house owners was only their posthumous Buddhist name. No remarkable men of talent came out of Kohnoike's employees, which seems to be principally due to its culture of seniority system. In the seniority system, a way of classicism system, there was no arena for capable persons; a spirit of independence and self-support was curbed; and the exchange and diffusion of information were vitally lacking among the clerks although there was a command transmission from seniors to subordinates. In its early days, however,

101

Kohnoike's culture was not of classicism nor so conservative. When originator Shinroku started with the line of brewing business, there was such an ethos as of creating new things and introducing novel things. It was rich in enterprising spirit. That is why Kohnoike created sake, i.e., refined sake, for the first time in history. Afterwards, it entered into the line of marine transportation to expand further the brewing business. Still later, however, when originator Shinroku passed away, founder Masanari closed the brewing. His closing of Kohnoike's brewing line had an immense influence on its culture since the original culture had been tightly united with the business of brewing. After having stopped producing sake, its original culture became weak and fragile. It is generally the case that a culture of a business house comes to settle firmly by surmounting one or more critical situations. In Kohnoike's case, however, they had not gone through any crisis in business and abandoned its brewing line of business before confronting such a crisis. In addition, in the times of the third generation Munetoshi, Kohnoike retired from the line of marine transport business as well. It had conducted the marine transportation line as united with the line of brewing, and actively operated it after having discontinued its brewing business. At a crucial turning in history, however, from private carrier to common carrier, Kohnoike dared not take a chance of challenging that conversion and retired from it. As a result, the original culture of Kohnoike completely vanished. In other words, they discarded their vitally important culture formed in the early days because they got 'the goose that lays golden eggs', i.e., the money exchange line of business. Accordingly, the culture of conventionalism, as seen in its seniority system, came out to form the first layer of Kohnoike's culture.

A traditional money lender

Then, what changes did Kohnoike come across at the Meiji Restoration? How did it cope with them? What turned out to be a great blow to Kohnoike was the abolishment of feudal domains of lords and the establishment of prefectures enacted by the new government in 1871. According to this act, the feudal domains were deprived of their lords and changed into prefectures, i.e., divisions of the country to which governors were elected by and dispatched from the central government. Loans which had been made thus far to each lord, in this context, was to be disposed of as follows. The debentures issued before 1843 were to be discarded and those issued between 1844 and 1867 were to be redeemed in installments covering 50 years with no interest. Also, the bonds issued from 1868 to 1872 were to be a public debt with 5 percent redeemed in installments covering 25 years. Thus, the loss to Kohnoike was inordinately heavy since it had dealings with 76 lords at that time. Its biased business policy of making loans to lords betrayed its weakness. In 1877, the House of Kohnoike filed an application with the government for the foundation of the 13th national bank according to the new law of national banking. Its promoters were the House of Kohnoike's tenth generation Yukitomi and a few members of the Kohnoike family. The new national bank was opened in 1877 as the first one in Osaka. With the capital of 200 thousand yen, Yukitomi took the post of its president. In 1897, Kohnoike set up a private bank named the Kohnoike Bank which took over the business of the 13th national bank. The 13th national bank was thus closed in the same year. In 1900, moreover, the Kohnoike Bank was transformed into a partnership bank, and in 1919, a joint-stock company. During the years between 1897 and 1906, however, the Kohnoike Bank had already been surpassed in business dealings even by provincial banks in Osaka. The main reason was that it lacked the faculty and function of an industrial or commercial bank since it had been almost solely engaged in money-lending to lords.

In sum, the new government's act of disposing the debentures of lords was a tremendous blow to the House of Kohnoike since it had invested almost all its capital in those debentures. It had paid little regard to the diversification of risks in investment. Kohnoike was, next, lacking of the faculty and function of industrial and commercial banking because it had been exclusively engaged in the line of money lending to lords. Furthermore, when faced with the turning point in industrial structure, i.e., the Meiji Restoration, it was altogether deficient in the thought and will of creating new things and introducing whatever things of value. Principally due to its conservative ethos, Kohnoike had not turned out men of talent and ability, while it had adhered to the way of thinking of a traditional money lender. It can be imagined that there was a solid classicism in the ethos of Kohnoike as at the beginning of Meiji era. That classicism may have prevented it from daring to devise, try, introduce and make whatever new things and whatever new values at the time when reforms were truly needed in all the fields in the society. In the environment of classicism, men of talent needed in a transition can not be fostered since it only recognizes the value of conforming to conventional ways and customary practices. In that respect, the House of Kohnoike was the same as the houses of traditional, custom-oriented, distinguished families. At the beginning of the new era, in fact, all but those houses remained conservative, did not venture into any new business and clung to the status quo. Yet, they were inclined to make little account of new education and new knowledge. In contrast, at Mitsui there were a number of men of the new education working for it. Such men of talent were actively engaged in the transformation and development of Mitsui as Rizaemon Minomura, Takashi Masuda and Hikojiro Nakagamigawa. In the case of Kohnoike, on the contrary, it did not develop such talent and could not but perform its conservative management. There was no talent among the managers of seniority post who could adequately employ its assets and develop it into a new banking concern in place of the Kohnoike family. Therefore, Kohnoike's business gradually declined. That is, the House of Kohnoike remained as it had been, could not transform itself into a modern banking firm and gradually fell into obscurity.

Kohnoike's culture and the competitiveness elements

Now, then, let us see how Kohnoike's culture was unadaptable to the 3-Layer Structure of Enterprise Competitiveness and the 7 Principles of Enterprise Competitiveness. We shall look into its unadaptability competitiveness element by competitiveness element.

Ethos originated in the early days of an enterprise, i.e., the spirit of denying, the spirit of negating the status quo, the spirit of creativity and the spirit of creating a vision, are maintained As has been described, the House of Kohnoike was a merchant house where originator Shinroku started with a brewing line of business and developed sake, i.e., refined sake as it is today, for the first time in history. Later, it entered into the line of marine transport for the shipment of sake. The original culture was, thus, tightly united with the manufacturing business of brewing and its related shipping business. In the early days of the House of Kohnoike, however, when founder Masanari was its owner, he abolished the line of brewing business. By this abolishment, the culture formed in the days of the foundation of Kohnoike became weak and fragile. In addition, when the third generation Munetoshi ran its business, he decided to retire from the line of marine transportation. In other words, the House of Kohnoike simply abolished the lines of brewing and shipping without having experienced any crisis or critical situation in those business and thus had no opportunity of learning from them. Accordingly, the original culture entirely went out of existence. On reflection, they called Shinroku originator and Masanari founder, which may have meant that Kohnoike's business was virtually started by Masanari. In fact, the original culture of Kohnoike was not alive as at the closing days of the Tokugawa regime.

Every member is willing to grapple with any situation without hesitation and without worrying about failure As was previously stated, personnel that worked long time for Kohnoike and were proficient in the conventional ways of business were respected. There were solid classicism and conservative ethos where the employees were inclined to adhere to the status quo.

People in the workplace freely exchange their views and opinions No meetings may have been held and no views and opinions may have been exchanged between the managers and the clerks.

104

Self-reforming abilities Such a way of thinking prevailed at Kohnoike as of conducting what was ordered to do in an instructed way to an instructed extent. It was lacking in the thought and will of creating new things and bringing in whatever things of value.

Abolishment of practices restricting competition The essence of Kohnoike's business was its loans to lords where it had so intimate relation to many lords as to disadvantage other houses. Kohnoike was provided various privileges by the lords. Such a way of business squarely ran counter to the principle of free market.

Human resources In classicism, no talent can be expected to emerge since such personnel are highly esteemed that follow traditional and customary ways. As a matter of fact, there appeared no remarkable talent at Kohnoike.

Investment in the training of personnel At Kohnoike, they made little account of new education and new knowledge.

Discussion on the vision, policies and the state of affairs of the enterprise As stated before, there was no collegial talking between seniors and clerks although there was a vertical line of command from seniors to subordinates.

Diffuse new ideas, reforms, improvements, and intelligence on new products both inside and outside the organization In the seniority system of Kohnoike, which is typical of classicism, people's spirit of self-support and self-determination was severely curbed. Their spontaneous diffusion of information and intelligence was also lacking although there was a senior-subordinate command line. It is thought that no suggestion or proposal came out of employees.

Maintain a free market principle throughout the enterprise In the seniority system, they hardly chose to promote people on their performance.

Organization whose workers are barely conscious of organizational hierarchy With the seniority system, the organization of Kohnoike was a rigid one so that every member was pretty much conscious of its stratum.

Develop personnel's abilities and continue their learning At Kohnoike, they could not turn out men of talent, which may have meant that they had no firm policy of fostering able personnel.

Every member is a leading actor The leading actors were only the master of Kohnoike and the managers of seniority post while the other managers and clerks were merely their messenger boys.

Fair and just promotion of personnel There was no management principle of electing and promoting personnel on the basis of their performance and capability. It can not be thought, therefore, that just and fair promotion was secured for the personnel.

Taken together, the culture of Kohnoike was, as a whole, unadapted to the 3-Layer Structure of Enterprise Competitiveness and the 7 Principles of Enterprise Competitiveness. It is shown in Table 6.3 and Table 6.4.

Table 6.3   The 3-Layer Structure of Enterprise Competitiveness

I   Enterprise Organismic Foundation

Enterprise ethos
- Ethos originated in the early days of an enterprise,   Unadaptable
  i.e., the spirit of denying, the spirit of negating
  the status quo, the spirit of creativity and the spirit
  of creating a vision, are maintained.
- Every member is willing to grapple with any   Unadaptable
  situation without hesitation and without worrying
  about failure.
- People in the workplace freely exchange   Unadaptable
  their views and opinions.

Enhancement of initiative
- There is teamwork among personnel.
- Personnel have pride and confidence in
  upholding their enterprise's competitiveness
  and have a sense of representing their enterprise.
- Diligence and positive activities of personnel.
- Pride and confidence in one's own work.
- Self-reforming abilities.   Unadaptable

Provision of norms
- Law (company regulations, etc.).
- Abolishment of practices restricting competition.   Unadaptable

106

Preparation of investment conditions
- Allow a sufficiently long time frame for management.
- Promotion of R&D and production-process R&D.
- Constraints on speculative purchases of enterprises or assets.

Enterprise ethics
(Sense of responsibility to the society)

Education
(General learning as citizen of the society)

II   Enterprise Economic Base

Infrastructure
- Physical assets   facilities, machinery, network.
- Human resources   executives, scientists,   Unadaptable
engineers, workers.
- Employment of human resources and procurement of physical assets to build and stabilize infrastructure.
- Investment in the training of personnel.   Unadaptable
- Education on practical business.

Environmental improvement and conservation
- Conservation of the natural environment.
- Cooperation with and participation in a community and its activities.
- Improvement of the physical environment of the workplace.
- Attention and care to human relations in the workplace.

Diffusion of new ideas, planning and others
- Create smooth communication lines.
- Discussion on the vision, policies and the state of   Unadaptable
affairs of the enterprise from management.

- Diffuse new ideas, reforms, improvements, and intelligence on new products both inside and outside the organization.   Unadaptable

III   Management System

Effectiveness
  - Maintain a free market principle throughout   Unadaptable
    the enterprise.
  - Encourage competitive spirit.
  - Improve cost, quality and delivery terms
    simultaneously.
  - Development, introduction and use of technology
    to gain strategic predominance.
  - Commercialize technology.
  - Activate communication throughout.

Tense balance between effectiveness and ethics
  - Have a close relationship with customers.
  - Have intimate contact with suppliers.
  - Organizational techniques.
  - Organization whose workers are barely   Unadaptable
    conscious of organizational hierarchy.
  - Recognition of quality as the end result
    of overall production and service activities.
  - Generate many alternatives to
    a decision-making process.
  - Demand and expect personnel to do their best.
  - Cope with things flexibly.
  - Develop personnel's abilities and   Unadaptable
    continue their learning.
  - Guarantee long-term employment.

Ethics
  - Every member is a leading actor.   Unadaptable
  - A view of work in which diligence is
    highly esteemed.
  - Improvement of ethics.
  - Fair employment.
  - Appropriate transfer of personnel from one
    post to another.

108

- Fair and just promotion of personnel.   Unadaptable
- Ethics of relations between management and
  workers.

Table 6.4   The 7 Principles of Enterprise Competitiveness

1   Creativity
- Ethos originated in the early days of an enterprise,   Unadaptable
  i.e., the spirit of denying, the spirit of negating
  the status quo, the spirit of creativity and the spirit
  of creating a vision, are maintained.
- Every member is willing to grapple with any   Unadaptable
  situation without hesitation and without worrying
  about failure.
- Self-reforming abilities.   Unadaptable

2   Righteousness
- Law (company regulations, etc.).
- Ethics of relations between management and
  workers.
- Abolishment of practices restricting competition.   Unadaptable
- Constraints on speculative purchases of
  enterprises or assets.
- Enterprise ethics
  (Sense of responsibility to the society).
- A view of work in which diligence is
  highly esteemed.
- Improvement of ethics.

3   Fairness
- Maintain a free market principle throughout   Unadaptable
  the enterprise.
- Encourage competitive spirit.
- Fair employment.
- Appropriate transfer of personnel from one
  post to another.
- Fair and just promotion of personnel.   Unadaptable

4   Equality
- People in the workplace freely exchange   Unadaptable
  their views and opinions.

- There is teamwork among personnel.
- Personnel have pride and confidence in upholding their enterprise's competitiveness and have a sense of representing their enterprise.
- Organization whose workers are barely   Unadaptable conscious of organizational hierarchy.
- Recognition of quality as the end result of overall production or service activities.
- Guarantee long-term employment.
- Every member is a leading actor.   Unadaptable

5   Sharing
- Conservation of the natural environment.
- Cooperation with and participation in a community and its activities.
- Improvement of the physical environment of the workplace.
- Attention and care to human relations in the workplace.
- Create smooth communication lines.
- Discussion on the vision, policies and the state of   Unadaptable affairs of the enterprise from management.
- Diffuse new ideas, reforms, improvements, and   Unadaptable intelligence on new products both inside and outside the organization.
- Activate communication throughout.
- Have a close relationship with customers.
- Have intimate contact with suppliers.

6   Self-Cultivation
- Diligence and positive activities of personnel.
- Pride and confidence in one's own work.
- Demand and expect personnel to do their best.

7   Learning and Knowledge-Accumulation

Technology
- Commercialize technology.
- Development, introduction and use of technology to gain strategic predominance.
- Promotion of R&D and production-process R&D.

- Employment of human resources and
  procurement of physical assets to build
  and stabilize infrastructure.
- Physical assets.
- Human resources.   Unadaptable

Systems thinking
- Allow a sufficiently long time frame
  for management.
- Generate many alternatives to
  a decision-making process.
- Improve cost, quality and delivery terms
  simultaneously.
- Cope with things flexibly.
- Develop personnel's abilities and   Unadaptable
  continue their learning.

People
- Education
  (General learning as citizen of the society).
- Investment in the training of personnel.   Unadaptable
- Education on practical business.
- Organizational techniques.

6.3 Summary

The House of Mitsui and the House of Kohnoike were both representative
merchant houses of the Tokugawa era (1603-1867). Mitsui founded Echigoya
drapery stores and Mitsui money exchange shops and laid the foundation of the
Mitsui zaibatsu later on. Kohnoike started at first with the business of brewing
sake and later the shipping line. When founder Masanari became its owner,
furthermore, it initiated the money exchange line of business and afterwards
closed its business of brewing. Later still, at the time of the third generation
Munetoshi, it abolished the line of marine transport and narrowed its business to
the single line of money exchange. Mitsui and Kohnoike both evolved and
developed in the Tokugawa times (1603-1867), having employed a number of
employees and thrived remarkably. At the arrival of the Meiji Restoration, i.e.,
that of industrialization and modernization, however, they followed quite a
different path respectively. That is, Mitsui successfully overcame the difficulties
in this transition to develop further while Kohnoike failed to get them through
and fell into obscurity in the end.

To search for the main causes of Mitsui's success and Kohnoike's failure, we have traced historically how their cultures evolved and formed. And we came to understand that Mitsui's culture was, practically, fully adaptable to the 3-Layer Structure of Enterprise Competitiveness and the 7 Principles of Enterprise Competitiveness as at the beginning of Meiji era while Kohnoike's was altogether unadaptable to them.

In the culture of Mitsui, there were found the ways of thought similar to Baigan Ishida's. For instance, such thought was in common as of hard working, prudence, honesty and saving. Mitsui learnd from the public what they demanded as Baigan Ishida learnd from Yaoyorozu-no-kami. It tried to expand sales of its silk fabrics to the general public, i.e., craftsmen, merchants and farmers although their selling had been conventionally limited to the samurai class and big merchant houses. In the latter half of the 17th century, the capital of Edo had a population of about one million. Out of the one million, 500,000 were samurai warriors since, as well as direct retainers of the Tokugawa, lords around the country periodically lived in Edo with their retainers due to the alternate-year dwelling system. The remainder 500,000 were thus craftsmen and merchants. Into the 18th century, the population of craftsmen and merchants showed a rapid increase with that of samurai unchanged. The economic strength also grew of craftsmen and merchants as well as farmers in the vicinity of Edo. It is understood that to learn from the public was vitally important. Moreover, the Tokugawa shogunate government and the lords adopted Confucianism as an official thought whereas the general public's ways of viewing, modes of thinking and state of being were of the Kami Way. At times, merchant houses used the 'filial piety', a word from Confucianism. However, the way of 'filial piety' was generally meant for merchants to maintain customers' confidence, cultivate such virtues as saving, endurance and honesty and thereby become a wealthy merchant. That is, they utterly remodeled Confucian thought in their own way (S. Hayashi, 1984). It was Baigan Ishida that systematized those merchants' ways of viewing, modes of thinking and state of being as his thought. The House of Mitsui was, in this context, a typical performer of the merchant way advocated by Baigan Ishida.

On the other hand, the culture of Kohnoike was of the seniority system where classicism and the rule-by-virtue principle, i.e., attributes of the thought of Confucianism, were apparently recognized. Kohnoike's culture may have formed through its long acquaintance with lords as its business was mainly in the line of loans to them. The House of Kohnoike was permitted to use a surname and wear a sword like samurai, whereby they may also have been influenced by the thought of Confucianism. To put it another way, Kohnoike did not learn from the public, but learnd from the samurai to whom it had so intimate relations to run business as to disadvantage other competitors. It is in the above fact that the seeds of Kohnoike's misfortune lay.

112

7 Case Study: The House of Mitsubishi and the House of Ohkura

The House of Mitsubishi and the House of Ohkura both started their business in the Meiji era. They were among the large zaibatsu up to the end of World War II in 1945. While Mitsubishi continued to develop its business after the war, Ohkura literally dissolved, falling into obscurity in the end. Where was the primary cause of the difference between Mitsubishi's success and Ohkura's failure, then? We would think that it lay in the difference between the culture of Mitsubishi and that of Ohkura at the end of the war in 1945. It seems that Mitsubishi had a healthy culture and Ohkura had an unhealthy culture at that time. That difference, in turn, may have decided their respective fate in the transition after the war. How, then, had the cultures of Mitsubishi and Ohkura evolved and developed from their foundation, and in what state were they at the end of the war? We shall first take up the culture of Mitsubishi, and then that of Ohkura.

7.1 The House of Mitsubishi

The House of Tosa

Yataro Iwasaki, founder of the House of Mitsubishi, was born in 1834 as the eldest son of a retainer in the lower echelon of the Tosa clan, one of the clans in the southeast region of the country which were to bring about the Meiji Restoration. His father Yajiro and mother Miwa had four children. Among them, later, the first son Yataro and the second son Yanosuke succeeded and came to fame, having built a palatial mansion in Tokyo. The mother Miwa then moved to it and lived with Yataro's family. She lived a plain life in that mansion, having set a spinning wheel in the living room to spin yarn and weave sackings which she took delight in presenting to her acquaintances in Tosa.

Yataro helped his father to do farming at home. In 1854, at the age of 20, he gained an opportunity to study in Edo (modern Tokyo). Since Yataro's study in Edo was at private expense, his father Yajiro decided to sell off his patrimonial mountains and forests to raise funds for it. In 1855, Yataro entered a school named 'Shoheikoh' and had Ryosai Azumi's lessons. In December the same year, however, he was informed that his father Yajiro had had an accident, so he decided to discontinue his study and went back home to Tosa. Although

113

he was thus forced to suspend his study, he may have seen in Edo an enormous change of the times. In particular, he may have perceived that the Tokugawa shogunate regime had come up against snags. After having been back home, he entered a private school called 'Shohrinjuku' run by Toyo Yoshida. In this school, there were many of Yoshida's followers such as Shojiro Goto, Toji Fukuoka, Satae Kamiyama and others who were to be elected later to run the Tosa clan and become prominent. Yataro's intimate relation with them would come to decide the fate of his life later on.

In 1866, the Tosa clan founded a trading house named 'Kaiseikan' which was to be operated under its direct management. Its object was to make the Tosa clan's finance more solid. Shojiro Goto was then appointed as president of Kaiseikan. To carry out its trading work more smoothly, the Tosa clan set up the House of Tosa, Osaka and the House of Tosa, Nagasaki as branch organs of the Kaiseikan. At first, Shoroku Yamazaki was dispatched to the House of Tosa, Nagasaki as its head. In those days, the Tosa clan had a strong sense of coastal defense so that they continued to purchase warships and arms in large quantity from merchants in and out of the country. Therefore, the House of Tosa soon turned out to be heavily in debt and its management became in a difficult state. Under those circumstances, Toji Fukuoka, who had been promoted to one of the key retainers, came to request Yataro Iwasaki to undertake the position of head at the House of Tosa, Nagasaki. In 1867, Yataro accepted his request and left for his new post in Nagasaki accompanied by Toji Fukuoka. His mission in Nagasaki was first to sell the articles transported from Tosa which were locally produced, and second to purchase warships and firearms from abroad for the Tosa clan. The time was, then, just before the transition from the Tokugawa times to the Meiji era so that the social conditions were in considerable turmoil. The clans with the intention of overthrowing the Tokugawa shogunate had become powerful indeed and their key retainers had come to gather in Kyoto and Osaka which had thus become the center of national politics and economy. Under those circumstances the Tosa clan made a decision to close the House of Tosa, Nagasaki and transfer its operations to the House of Tosa, Osaka. In October 1867, Yataro Iwasaki was to take office at the House of Tosa, Osaka, backed by the recommendation of Shojiro Goto, one of the key retainers then at Tosa.

Yataro as a businessman

The year 1868 showed a big historic turnabout. Due to the movement of overthrowing the Tokugawa by the clans of Satsuma, Chohshu, Tosa and others in the southeast region of the country, the Tokugawa shogunate at last decided to turn over the reins of government to Imperial Court and its supporters, i.e., the clans of Satsuma, Chohshu, Tosa and others. The Tokugawa shogunate

114

regime thus came to an end and the new Meiji era arrived. In 1869, Yataro assumed office as head at the House of Tosa, Osaka, but it was dissolved following the Meiji government's policy of banning clan-managed trading houses. In the same year, instead, a new house named 'House of Tsukumo' was set up and Yataro was placed in charge. The House of Tsukumo was, however, virtually Tosa clan's commercial department. Yataro ran the house with 3 ships from the Tosa clan. In 1871, however, the government enacted an act of abolition of clans and establishment of prefectures whereby the conventional lords' territories were abolished and the prefectures were, instead, set up. As a result, the Tosa clan had to dispose of the House of Tsukumo, its trading department. The new Meiji government authorities then urged the Tosa clan to have it undertaken by Yataro Iwasaki. The clan of Tosa decided to transfer all the assets of the House of Tsukumo to him. In such a way as above, Yataro turned from a retainer in charge of the commercial department at the Tosa clan to an independent businessman. As to his turnover above, such leading government officials backed him up as Shojiro Goto from the clan of Tosa, Toshimichi Ohkubo from the clan of Satsuma and Shigenobu Ohkuma from the Saga clan. The leading government officials at that time were generally called the clans-led government officials. With the backup of those clans-led government officials, Yataro obtained a transfer of two steamships from the government on the condition that he undertook a bond of 40,000 ryo issued by the government. It was an extremely inexpensive transfer.

In January 1873, Yataro changed the name of 'House of Tsukumo' to 'House of Mitsukawa', and in March of the same year, he further renamed it 'House of Mitsubishi' whereby the original form of Mitsubishi group was created. Immediately after having renamed it, he gathered all the employees of the House of Mitsubishi and told them that he decided to abandon his plan to enter the government service, establishing himself as a businessman instead, and made up his mind to engage in the shipping business. At the time of its foundation, the House of Mitsubishi had an intellectual from the best school whose name was Renpei Kondoh. In those days, the headoffice of the House of Mitsubishi was located in Osaka and Yataro's private residence was also there. He decided to open an English school within the estate of his residence and appointed Renpei Kondoh as the first director of that school. The English school turned out to play a significant role in training Mitsubishi's personnel and such men of talent as Ryohei Toyokawa, Tatsukichi Kawada and Kawaaki Hayashi, who later became the leading members of Mitsubishi. As Yukichi Fukuzawa stated in his writings the Theory of Business (1893), Yataro excelled in employing university graduates and drawing capabilities out of them. He, in fact, paid a special regard to introducing and fostering men of ability. Yataro, next, tried to remove the characteristics of samurai ascribed to the House of Tosa out of the House of Mitsubishi, and push ahead with becoming a merchant. Since the executive members of Mitsubishi were samurai, their samurai way of thinking was urged to change. They were instructed to take off a hakama, a divided skirt for samurai's formal wear, and put on an apron that merchants usually wore. When they went on their rounds of their customers, they wore a workman's 'livery' coat. In dealing with a person at a customer firm, they were instructed to politely bow their head and show him or her every courtesy whatever rank he or she was. It was emphasized that 'an apron is a merchant's formal dress', and the distinction of classes, characteristic of the feudal society, was negatived. The executive managers of Mitsubishi, in reality, ended up reforming themselves.

The Meiji government was quite enthusiastic about fostering the shipping business. The first reason was that as at the year 1867, Japan possessed 138 vessels including the Western-built steamships and sailers, a little more than 17,000 tons in tonnage, out of which the home-built ones were only 1 steamer and 20 sailers. The second reason was that Japan was a very appealing market then for foreign steamship companies which, in reality, occupied Japanese coastal routes as well as ocean navigation. For the reasons above, the Meiji government founded the 'Japanese Mail Steamer Co.' in August 1873 and commenced its business with 16 ships which they had expropriated from the feudal clans. In those days, there were many small and medium shipping firms and foreign steamship companies acting in the market so that the competition was truly severe and relentless. Japanese Mail Steamer Co., however, pursued to dominate on the market through a considerable reduction in fares and freight with the government's support and its abundant capital. A number of small-and-medium shipping companies, therefore, went bankrupt and the House of Mitsubishi was also driven into a severe circumstance. It is to be noted, however, that Japanese Mail Steamer Co. was lacking a spirit of service to passengers and arrogant in the attitude towards them as a government-run firm is usually to be. Mitsubishi, thus, took a rollback policy from that weakness of the government-run firm. That is, it adopted a passengers-first principle. The Mitsubishi's thought of passengers first was duly accepted on the market so that it could compete with Japanese Mail Steamer Co. to its advantage. In 1873, on the other hand, Yataro got into trouble. In July the same year, having been informed his father Yajiro's death, he immediately returned home to Tosa. However, he was then the person concerned in a lawsuit due to a matter of foreign bonds. Since he went back home with no permission from the court, he was imprisoned in Osaka. On having received the report on the above, his younger brother Yanosuke, who was then in the United States for study, hastily came back home to take up the post of managing the House of Mitsubishi in place of Yataro.

The next year was the time when Mitsubishi made a fairly rapid progress in business. That is, in 1874, such big incidents occurred as the 'Rebellion in Saga' and the 'Subjugation of Taiwan' where Mitsubishi came to gain great opportunities for its development. The Rebellion in Saga was a revolt against the new Meiji government by Shinpei Etoh from the Saga clan and former samurais from other clans as well as from the clan of Saga who were disaffected with the government. To suppress the rebellion, the government needed to carry the national army and war supplies to Saga, a place in the southeast of Japan, and requested Mitsubishi to transport the war supplies. The Rebellion in Saga was soon settled. The government, next, proceeded to plan and execute the subjugation of Taiwan. At that time, however, the United States declined to transport the Japanese army and munitions to Taiwan since it was on neutral ground as to the strife between the Empire of China and Japan. Other countries also turned down Japan's request for transporting war supplies to Taiwan by reason that it might violate the public international law. Yet, the vessels owned by Japanese Mail Steamer Co., a government-run company, had become fairly obsolete and were not effectively usable primarily due to the antagonism between the officials from the Satsuma clan and those from the Chohshu clan within the government. Accordingly, the government carried the army personnel over there by employing two to three ships out of those lately purchased through its meager finance. On that occasion, Yataro approached and tried to gain the favor of Shigenobu Ohkuma and Toshimichi Ohkubo, and succeeded in gaining an order from the government to transport munitions to Taiwan. The government later subjugated Taiwan and entered into negotiations with the Empire of China with the United Kingdom as arbitrator. As a result, the Meiji government could claim an indemnity of 500,000 yen for the strife and receive it from China.

The government's preferential treatment

After the incident had been settled, the government contrived a plan of giving Mitsubishi a preferential treatment in return for its contribution. As has been mentioned, the Shanghai line, which was a most significant sea route for trade, was monopolized by an influential foreign steamship company. That is, it was occupied by Pacific Mail Steamer Co., a US firm. The Meiji government thought that it could be an obstacle to the national politics and security. In 1875, thus, Toshimichi Ohkubo, Minister of Home Affairs then, consulted with Shigenobu Ohkuma, Minister of Finance, and Hisoka Maejima, Minister of Transportation, about the matter and decided to request Mitsubishi to open a Shanghai line. Immediately after Mitsubishi had accepted the request, the government transferred 13 ships, which it had purchased for a little more than 1,560,000 yen, for nothing and granted further 250,000 yen of annual subsidy to the House of Mitsubishi. In addition, it dissolved Japanese Mail Steamer Co., whose business had turned unprofitable due to the competition with Mitsubishi, bought out 18 vessels from it for 325,000 yen and then transferred them to

117

Mitsubishi for all but free of charge. Under such protection of the government as above, the House of Mitsubishi pushed ahead with the mastery of the sea. A little earlier, in May 1875, the House of Mitsubishi was renamed 'Mitsubishi Steamer Co.' and its headquarters was moved from Osaka to Tokyo. Mitsubishi then laid down its company law, whose outlines are as follows.

Article 1   This commercial house is virtually a family's occupation although it has the name of a company and so it altogether differs from such organizations that raise funds outside to form a company. All the affairs of the house are to be submitted to the president for his judgment.

Article 2   Any profit of the house is to belong to the president and the loss of it is also to be ascribed to him.

Article 3   In spite of the Article 2, the house may raise the employees' salary if it increasingly gains profits and prospers. If it suffers considerable loss due to its business falling, it may reduce the employees' salary and discontinue their employment.

(Y. Irimajiri, 1960)

As can be imagined from the above articles, Mitsubishi then seems to have followed the thought of father's rule to operate its organization. In September 1875, after having enjoyed substantial support from the government, Mitsubishi changed the name of Mitsubishi Steamer Co. to 'Mail Steamer Mitsubishi Co.' Mail Steamer Mitsubishi Co. decided to open the Shanghai line to contend with Pacific Mail Steamer Co. for its mastery which had solely dominated it. Pacific Mail Steamer Co. took a series of policies of cutting fares and freight. In competing with it, Mitsubishi had no choice but to take a countermeasure of reducing fares and freight, having left its profitability completely out of account. The government's support was its last resort. The first-class fare was at last reduced from 30 yen to 8 yen from Yokohama to Nagasaki. The situation turned out to be beyond the management's capabilities for both Pacific Mail Steamer Co. and Mail Steamer Mitsubishi Co. The management at Pacific Mail Steamer Co., then, planned to sell their company. Yataro, on that occasion, sought to buy it out and so approached Shigenobu Ohkuma on that matter. He finally succeeded in managing to borrow money for its purchase from the government. The purchase price was 810,000 dollars, and the government loan of that amount was to be repaid in installments covering 15 years with 2 percent annual interest. In 1876, in this context, a British steamship company appeared around the Shanghai route. Mail Steamer Mitsubishi Co. was then exposed to its threat for a while, but it successfully went through that critical situation, being backed by the government, and finally became dominant in the Japanese home waters. At the end of 1876, Mail Steamer Mitsubishi Co. possessed 45 Western-built vessels with their total capacity of 26,698 tons and employed 1,846 personnel.

While it had gained the mastery of the shipping line, Mitsubishi's business was not limited to it. Mail Steamer Mitsubishi Co. was then regulated to enter into other lines of business since it was operated under the protection of the government. Accordingly, Yataro privately set up enterprises in a variety of fields. The largest among them was a mining business at Yoshioka mine. The Yoshioka mine had been owned by the former lord of Itakura's family, but since its management had fallen in trouble, they had decided to sell it to Yataro for 10,000 yen in 1873. Yoshioka mine had plenty of gold, silver and copper underground. To operate it, Renpei Kondoh, a young man of talent, was dispatched there. He brought in modern ways of management to run it. For instance, he changed the conventional piecework system into a new wage system. In the beginning, mineworkers displayed keen opposition to those reforms, but they gradually came to accept them. When they succeeded in striking a mineral vein of good quality, Renpei Kondoh and the mineworkers could really enjoy drinking a toast for its success. This mining business turned out to be a reliable source of funds when Mitsubishi was in competition with the powerful rival mentioned previously in the line of marine transport. In 1875, Yataro founded Mitsubishi Iron Works primarily for the repairment of ships and in 1876 initiated a money exchange business. In 1880, he set up Mitsubishi Money Exchange House and also entered into a warehouse business. He, on the other hand, made an investment in many enterprises such as Tokyo Marine Insurance, Meiji Life Insurance, Trade House, Yokohama Shohkin Bank and Tokyo Stock Exchange. Moreover, he set up and ran a commercial college and a mercantile marine school. In 1881, he purchased Takashima Coal Mine in Hizen (Kumamoto). In such a way as above, Mitsubishi launched into a number of lines of business with its broad policy of transplanting and constructing industries in Japan. This policy seems to have contradicted Yataro's position of a businessman affiliated with the government in the shipping line of business. The fact is, however, that the thought of adapting to market economy coexisted with that of a government-affiliated businessman.

Now, with the monopoly of Mitsubishi established in the line of marine transportation as above, who could rise up trying to break it down? The first one who rose up was the House of Mitsui. Mitsui employed Mail Steamer Mitsubishi Co. for the transport of almost all its goods. The total amount of the freight reached 700,000 yen yearly. Mitsui, thus, repeatedly negotiated Mitsubishi about the reduction in freight, but Yataro obstinately declined to accept Mitsui's request. As a result, Takashi Masuda, the highest executive manager at Mitsui, determined to set up another large shipping company. It was Eiichi Shibusawa, who was then in the top position at the Tokyo Stock Exchange as well as at the First Bank, that agreed to Masuda's intention. A number of small and medium shipping companies also participated in that plan. In 1880, in this way, 'Tokyo-style Sailing Vessel Co.' was founded and listed on the Tokyo Stock Exchange. Up against that undertaking, Yataro employed all kinds of obstructive tactics. He, for instance, hired a secret agent to collect the internal information of Tokyo-style Sailing Vessel Co., purchased a press agency to have news story of slanderous nature about it put on the press, and tried to win over other shipping companies with flattery. He further went to the length of buying up all the stocks of Tokyo-style Sailing Vessel Co. on the stock market. As a result, soon after it had been founded, Tokyo-style Sailing Vessel Co. was forced to be closed before setting out to do its business. Mitsubishi solidified in that way its really powerful position in the marine transport business.

Political Change of the year 1881

A great crisis, however, awaited it in the coming years. The crisis began in 1878 when Toshimichi Ohkubo, a high government official, was assassinated in Shimizudani, Tokyo. He had been the most influential official in the government, having been at the back of Yataro. His assassination meant the loss of a principal business foundation of Mail Steamer Mitsubishi Co. which had been doing business in league with the government. In 1881, moreover, a historic incident occurred which came out to render Mitsubishi literally isolated. Since Toshimichi Ohkubo was already gone, the only patron in the government for Yataro was Shigenobu Ohkuma. However, Shigenobu Ohkuma was soon to retire from the political circles. The cause of his retirement was related to an incident of unjust transfer plan to a commercial house of state-owned property at Hokkaido Land Development Bureau. The Meiji government had spent about 15,000,000 yen carrying out land development in Hokkaido from 1872 to 1881. After the land development had been terminated, the government intended to transfer the state-owned property there to Kansai Trade House for 390,000 yen whose payment was to be made in installments covering 30 years with no interest. Kansai Trade House had been founded by Tomoatsu Godai from the Satsuma clan, Goichi Nakano from the Chohshu clan and others. To that government's intention, Shigenobu Ohkuma and his followers were vehemently opposed. An antigovernment newspaper instigated public opinion against it. The government then was driven into a tight corner. The officials from the Satsuma clan, however, who had taken a leading part in the government, waited for an opportunity to take a countermeasure to get out of such difficulties. It so happened then that Shigenobu Ohkuma attended the Emperor on a journey to the northeast district of the country. While he was away, those officials spread an ill-willed rumor that what Ohkuma and his followers had criticized on their policy was part of a scheme of overthrowing the government that the liberal-

120

and-civil-rights party was making. Next, they tried to persuade other officials in the government of their position and finally succeeded in winning over them to their side. On the night of October 11, 1881 when the Emperor returned to Tokyo, an urgent council was held in the Imperial presence. In the council, the officials from the Satsuma clan adopted the opinions that Ohkuma and his followers had thus far expressed as if they were theirs. That is, the first item on the agenda then was the issue of canceling the transfer of the state-owned property to Kansai Trade House and the second was that of opening the Diet. They unanimously approved both of them. The next day, an Imperial edict was issued that the Diet was to be opened in 1890. His design having been altogether baffled, Ohkuma decided to tender his resignation to the government and retired from the political circles. This historic incident was generally called the 'Political Change of the year 1881' whereby Hirofumi Itoh from the Chohshu clan and his followers could prepare the enactment of the Imperial Constitution following the model of the Prussian constitution. Thus, the argument of Shigenobu Ohkuma and Taisuke Itagaki and his followers at the liberal-and-civil-rights party that Japan ought to follow the example of British and the United States laws were turned down.

Under those circumstances, Yataro Iwasaki's tie to the government was completely cut off. Since the incident of unjust transfer plan of state-owned property was an object of criticism on the unjust relation between the government and some specific concerns, the blame was now leveled at Mitsubishi which had solely received the government's support in the shipping line of business. The criticism against Mitsubishi was furious indeed. Up against that blame, Yataro followed a principle of nonintervention in politics and a business-first principle. He then delivered a notice to the personnel at Mitsubishi that they should devote themselves to the shipping trade, not talk about news of political issues of the day; that the Imperial edict of opening the Diet and the government's decision of canceling the transfer of state-owned property in Hokkaido were both right in judgment; and that merchants ought to be assured to attend to their work. On the other hand, the government contrived a new way of beating Mitsubishi. That is, they planned to set up a new shipping firm named 'Joint Transportation Co.' The purport of its foundation was first to prepare vessels of good quality to compete with foreign shipping firms to Japan's advantage. The second was to set up a gigantic shipping company in case of a probable strife between the Empire of China and Japan. The third was a need to found a large marine transport company since the ships were congested with goods and people's discontent with the shipping was expressed everywhere due to Mitsubishi's high freight and its neglect of maintenance of vessels. In July 1882, thus, Joint Transportation Co. was founded. Its sea routes included foreign service routes from Yokohama to Jinsen (Korea) and to Shanghai, and Japanese coastal routes between provincial ports which overlapped those of Mitsubishi. Since Joint Transportation Co. and Mitsubishi both employed whatever measures feasible to attract passengers, the competition was overly intensified. In particular, they made an inordinate reduction in fares and freight. The second-class fare between Kobe and Yokohama was at last reduced from 5.50 to 0.55 yen. It was an extreme competition disregarding an economic principle. On the other hand, the denunciation by the public was vehement indeed against Mitsubishi. Tokyo Economic Journal run by Ukichi Taguchi, among others, consecutively carried an editorial comment titled 'Discuss subsidy to Mitsubishi'. Having been forcefully attacked from both the government and the public, Yataro seems to have had the whole world against him. In such a plight, Mail Steamer Mitsubishi Co. had no choice but to fight against Joint Transportation Co. Both companies severely competed for dominance in 1883 and 1884, whereby their financial strength came to weaken considerably. As may be expected, the government, which initially fueled the race, began to fear that both would fall together. In January 1885, accordingly, it advised both companies to reach a compromise. There was another reason, in this context, behind the fact that the government positively proceeded to undertake a mediation between Joint Transportation Co. and Mitsubishi. It was that a military conflict occurred then between the Japanese army and the army of China on the Korean Peninsula. The government thus supposed such a grave situation that it would have to mobilize civil boats. The government's advice for their compromise was, however, broken in less than one year after they had agreed on it. The relentless competition between them further developed.

Mitsubishi's turn of business from the sea to the land

Amidst that competition, Yataro Iwasaki died of illness at the age of 52 after having struggled hard against the indisputable difficulties above. Just before the time of his death, he determined to transfer all the lines of business at Mitsubishi to his younger brother Yanosuke who had jointly run Mitsubishi's business with him. Soon enough, Yanosuke encouraged the personnel of Mitsubishi to fight against Joint Transportation Co. to the bitter end. Under such a circumstance, the government decided to make it their policy to recommend the merger of Mail Steamer Mitsubishi Co. and Joint Transportation Co. They dispatched Masazumi Morioka, vice minister at the Agriculture and Commerce Ministry, to Joint Transportation Co. to investigate the company's business conditions. Following his investigation, it was made clear that the company had incurred a yearly loss of more than 1,000,000 yen. Morioka reported to the government that there was no alternative for Joint Transportation Co. but a merger with Mitsubishi. In July 1885, the government finally issued an admonition for the merger between Mail Steamer Mitsubishi Co. and Joint Transportation Co., whereby a new firm named Japanese Mail Steamer Co. was established. Mitsubishi made an investment of 5,000,000 yen and Joint Transportation Co. invested 6,000,000 yen in the new firm. Out of the 6,000,000 yen invested by Joint Transportation Co., 3,400,000 yen was from the private sector and 2,600,000 yen was from the government. The vessels succeeded by the new firm were 29 ships with 36,000 tons in capacity from Mitsubishi and 29 ships with 28,010 tons from Joint Transportation Co. which totaled 58 ships with 64,010 tons in capacity. Thus, Japanese Mail Steamer Co., a gigantic shipping firm, came into existence. On this occasion, Mitsubishi transferred all the assets of marine transport business and a quarter of its employees to the new firm. It, therefore, lost its main business.

In 1884, one year before his death, in this connection, Yataro had entered into a lease contract of Nagasaki Shipbuilding Yard with the government and ran it as Mitsubishi's business. Yet, at the time of withdrawal from the shipping line of business, Yanosuke kept back Nagasaki Shipbuilding Yard at Mitsubishi. He, then, united it with the other enterprises which had been run as Iwasaki family's such as Takashima Coal Mine, Yoshioka Mine and others as well as the 119th national bank, which had been acquired just before Mitsubishi's withdrawal from shipping, to form a new firm named Mitsubishi Co. in 1886. The foundation of this new firm was Yanosuke's attempt at reviving Mitsubishi, which was called 'Mitsubishi's turn of business from the sea to the land'. We can see here the thought of Yomigaeri, an attribute of the Kami Way. Nagasaki Shipbuilding Yard, in this connection, was officially transferred to Mitsubishi by the government in 1893 and thereafter Mitsubishi was to be engaged in a shipbuilding line of business of its own.

In 1891, Hisaya Iwasaki, son of Yataro, who had been in the United States for study, came back home and took office as single vice president at Mitsubishi Co.. At that time, the company was all but complete with men of talent needed in expanding and developing into many fields of business. Such professional managers were actively engaged in business as Heigoro Sohda, who had been at the nucleus of management since Yataro's times, Renpei Kondoh, Ryohei Toyokawa, Michinari Suenobu and so forth. Under those circumstances, Yanosuke determined to transfer the position of president to Hisaya. In 1893, he founded Mitsubishi & Co., Ltd., transferred all the lines of business at Mitsubishi Co. to that new firm, appointed Hisaya as president and took the post of supreme advisor himself. Thereby, the enterprises at Mitsubishi Co. were all transferred into their corresponding departments at Mitsubishi & Co., Ltd.. As for the department of mining, among them, the amount of gold produced in 1907 reached 18 percent of the total production in the country. Also, the silver production was 15 percent, the production of copper 14 percent and that of coal 8 percent of the total. The department of shipbuilding acquired a large order of building Hitachi Maru in 1895 from the government. It later made a large-scale investment in plant and equipment and actively introduced technology from abroad. Around 1911, the department obtained a sizable order for constructing a capital ship from the navy. The department of banking was opened in 1895, and in 1897 it took over the 119th national bank and turned its business to industrial finance to develop further. As for the undertaking of land development, Mitsubishi initially received state-owned land in the district of Marunouchi in Tokyo. They later built there and possessed 13 buildings for lease around 1911. In that way, Mitsubishi's lines of business went on developing in its respective departments.

The first layer of Mitsubishi's culture

When Mitsubishi & Co., Ltd. was founded, in this context, the first layer of Mitusbishi's culture may have formed. The foundation of Mitsubishi dates back to 1873 when Yataro and his younger brother Yanosuke set out to evolve and develop their business with the object of transplanting and constructing modern industries in Japan. The ethos of civilization and enlightenment was generally prevalent in the beginning of the Meiji times. They were then firmly determined to introduce whatever new and superior things from abroad. We can perceive here Kanjo, an attribute of the Kami Way. The House of Mitsubishi was originally a group of people from samurai. Therefore, they were urged to bring a spirit of commerce in their mind to reform themselves. They managed to achieve it one way or the other. The motto was clearly put that 'an apron is a merchant's formal dress'. Mitsubishi attended to the shipping business as its main line. Although the market was severely competitive, it evolved and developed its business with the thought of customers-first, which later proved to be the right way. Early on, Yataro had been enthusiastic about introducing and fostering men of ability and paid special regard to it. He entrusted Renpei Kondoh, a young talent with the highest academic background, with a task of managing Yoshioka Mine. It may have meant that he put much value on drawing capabilities out of a university graduate employed by providing him a chance and promoting him to a higher and responsible position. Yet, Renpei Kondoh lived up to Yataro's expectation. Yataro had such ways of viewing, modes of thinking and state of being as above. On the other hand, he had a mentality of government-affiliated businessman as well. He intended to develop the marine transportation business in league with the state authorities. In fact, it was the business of munitions transportation commissioned by the government, in the incidents of Rebellion in Saga and Subjugation of Taiwan, that offered a great opportunity of development to Mitsubishi. Later, with such influential officials as Toshimichi Ohkubo and Shigenobu Ohkuma as his backer, Yataro was able to obtain a number of steamers for nothing or on some favorable conditions, and also gain subsidies and things of that kind from the government.

Thus, at the House of Mitsubishi there coexisted the thought of being adaptive to the market economy and that of a government-affiliated merchant. In the Political Change of the year 1881, however, Mitsubishi lost its backers in the government and it was literally isolated, having been subjected to roaring criticism both by the government and the public. Under those circumstances, Yataro decided to abolish his thought of a government-affiliated businessman and sincerely follow the principle of nonintervention in politics and the business-first principle. In 1885, after Yataro passed away, Yanosuke took over the keen competition with Joint Transportation Co. run by the government. Due to this strife, Mitsubishi's financial strength increasingly diminished. Later, the strife ended with the merger of Mail Steamer Mitsubishi Co. and Joint Transportation Co.. As a result, Mitsubishi completely lost its main business of shipping. On that occasion, Yanosuke combined Mitsubishi's other lines of business together and formed a new organization named Mitsubishi Co. to make a fresh start. It was called 'Mitsubishi's turn of business from the sea to the land', and by this turn, Mitsubishi's mentality of a government-affiliated businessman may have been altogether discarded. Instead, such ways of thinking as the business-first principle and the principle of nonintervention in politics may have been deeply imprinted in the minds of Mitsubishi people. That is, the thought of being adaptive to the market economy, as previously noted, and some other concepts of similar nature united to form the first layer of Mitsubishi's culture.

Koyata's thought and belief

In 1906, Koyata, the first son of Yanosuke, who had been in the United Kingdom for study, came back home and took office as single vice president at Mitsubishi & Co., Ltd.. From 1907 to 1912, Mitsubishi & Co., Ltd. drived its principle of decentralization forward. Its organization was transformed from a structure of departments such as of mining, banking, shipbuilding and so forth into that of their respective decentralized divisions. By 1912, Mitsubishi comprised six independent divisions. In 1910, Heigoro Shohda retired from office who had long been a key man in the management of Mitsubishi. Until then, he had been the only managing director at Mitsubishi. On that occasion, then, Mitsubishi decided to have two posts of managing director in the organization and appointed Ryohei Toyokawa and Kyuhgo Nanbu for the posts. In 1911, next, its decision-making body was reformed so that vice president Koyata and two managing directors were to hold a meeting every day discussing the affairs of significance to the company. Furthermore, a briefing session was to be held three times every week with the vice president as chairman and the general managers of all the divisions as members. That session, therefore, worked as a mechanism of facilitating the smooth flow of information between the divisions. In that way, Koyata virtually became the leader in running Mitsubishi. Koyata, as single vice president, attempted to help the personnel to be in harmony, highly motivated and cultivate their mind. In 1914 when the Mitsubishi Club was set up to enhance the mutual friendship among the personnel, he stated the following in its bulletin.

It is the time now for people to show their ability to the fullest. Whatever high ideal one holds, the prosperity of the nation can not be achieved or the national prestage would not be raised unless one can contribute to the growth of its power. There may be many ways in increasing the nation's strength. No one could deny the fact, however, that the promotion of business is the most vital way of all. Therefore, people, who are now engaged in business, ought to be aware of their significant responsibility for it...Yet, those who are responsible for achieving business goals need to enjoy working. One's work without his feeling of satisfaction would not produce any good results. How can Mitsubishi help a little more than 4,000 personnel to enjoy working? That is a matter of great concern for the Mitsubishi management. In addressing whatever things, next, what is most crucial is the mind of fairness, justice and openness. It is the most shameful conduct of all to win a success by relying on chance and employing a cunning plan. The real success is the one that a person wins after striving for his object with genuine efforts, taking pains and not yielding to whatever failure. It is said that Andrew Carnegie set it a necessary condition in employing people that they have not dabbled in speculation. It may have meant to keep out those relying on good fortune.

(T. Miyakawa, 1996, originally in Japanese)

Koyata's statement above represents Mitsubishi's philosophy. That is, it expresses first that the creation and development of business are vital in attaining the prosperity of the nation and raising the nation's prestige and that Mitsubishi has responsibility for such creation and development. The thought of service to the nation and the society, in fact, played a significant part in attracting men of talent and ability to the organization of Mitsubishi. Kikuo Aoki, who, having graduated from Tokyo Imperial University, had entered Mitsubishi & Co., Ltd. the next year and later become a managing director, said that Mitsubishi could make rapid advance from its initial small-scale undertaking because of its sustained ideal from the company's foundation of transplanting and constructing modern industries in Japan which could match those of the developed countries. The philosophy at Mitsubishi seems to have helped the personnel to contribute to the development of the company. Koyata, next, said that one ought to be fair, just and open in addressing whatever matters and a success achieved by relying on chance and employing a cunning plan is not the real one. He thought that the real success was the one attained with genuine efforts, not yielding to any failure. Here is expressed how a

126

businessman ought to be and think. It seems to have been expressed after having reflected on the previous ways of thinking and state of being prevalent when Mitsubishi had been engaged in the shipping line of business. It may also have been an expression of confirming Mitsubishi's Yomigaeri, i.e., its reviving at the time when it had switched its business from the sea to the land. In Koyata's statement, thus, there are apparently found expressions of solidifying the first layer of Mitsubishi's culture but also his own way of viewing and thinking. For instance, such a view is of his own that one ought to enjoy doing one's work. He said that without enjoying work, good results cannot be expected. He was convinced, on the other hand, that cultivating personnel is fundamental to the development of business. The Mitsubishi Club was defined, therefore, as an exercise hall to train its members' human nature. With his own thought that one ought to enjoy working and train their human nature, he set out to reorganize Mitsubishi & Co., Ltd. That is, he decided to separate each division from the Mitsubishi organization and render it an independent enterprise as a joint stock company. Accordingly, in 1917, Mitsubishi Steel Manufacturing Co. and Mitsubishi Shipbuilding Co. were set up as independent firms, in 1918 Mitsubishi Trading Co. and Mitsubishi Mining Co. were formed, and in 1919 Mitsubishi Marine Insurance Co. and Mitsubishi Bank Co. were established as independent concerns while Mitsubishi & Co., Ltd. was transformed into the holding company of those concerns. Mitsubishi, thus, became an organization comprising a group of self-controlled enterprises. If part of an organization can be separated to form an independent enterprise, in this context, it means that men of ability have already been fostered in the organization to run a newly formed enterprise. Conversely, it is also true that men of ability can be further cultivated in such a newly formed company. In fact, out of those concerns above, new firms were further created later. We can see here a good cycle that by dividing an organization men of talent can be cultivated, which enables further division of the divided one and then by dividing it men of ability can be fostered, and on and on. What made the division of the Mitsubishi organization feasible may have been the ways of thinking at Mitsubishi that one ought to enjoy working and train themself. To put it another way, it may have been the thought that one ought to have faith in their people and that a man of ability is a leading actor.

In 1916, Koyata took over the position of president at Mitsubishi & Co., Ltd. from Hisaya. The next year, 1917, an accident happened due to ignition of chloric soda at Ashiwake warehouse of Mitsubishi Warehouse Co. in Osaka. In that incident there were 43 persons dead and 583 persons injured, and 7 houses completely destroyed, 23 houses partially destroyed and so forth in the neighboring streets. Having been informed of the disaster, Koyata at once went off to Osaka and on arriving he decided to offer a sizable amount then of 1,000,000 yen to the city of Osaka to express regret for the accident. He sent a

127

letter to the mayor saying that he was shocked to find the sufferers in such a pitiful state in the disaster area and that he wished to offer 1,000,000 yen to be appropriated for their care and consolation, and so on. It was the most significant of all to give sincere and faithful treatment and care to the sufferers. He thus wished and tried to show his mind of integrity.

As mentioned previously, Mitsubishi Trading Co. was founded in 1918. A little afterwards, World War I came to an armistice. The next year, in 1919, due to the restoration demand after the war, exports increased so much that business became overheated, having stimulated a speculation boom. Immediately before such craze for speculation had occurred, Koyata sent a letter to all the executive managers at Mitsubishi Trading Co. saying that they ought to concentrate on their work, abolish any thought of speculation, render the mind of personnel strained, and follow the main principle of management of bringing results by raising the effectiveness of the organization and so on. He argued that he and the leading members at Mitsubishi should be careful not to take a wrong policy in such a circumstance. The collapse in stock prices the next year, in 1920, followed after the boom of speculation. Business abruptly became worse. As a result, Mitsubishi Trading Co., which had just been founded, incurred a net loss of 690,000 yen. In this grave situation, Koyata summoned the executive managers to the headoffice and held a meeting. He emphasized there the responsibility of a trading firm for producers and consumers, while having criticized the speculation. Later, in 1934, Momotaro Miyakegawa summarized what Koyata had stated then and formed the principle of Mitsubishi Trading Co. It comprised the following:

> Duty to the society,
> Be just and fair on everything and
> Take trade as our own business

The principle is now expressed in English with a little modification as follows :

> Corporate Responsibility to Society,
> Integrity and Fairness and
> International Understanding through Trade

Koyata argued for fair competition, rejection of speculation and strict observance of justice. In 1921, following his argument, a general rule was stipulated forbidding dealings on speculation in the Commodity Transaction Rules at Mitsubishi Trading Co. It seems that the first layer of Mitsubishi's culture was tried at the time of the crisis in 1920, and it was duly confirmed and further consolidated.

As stated above, due to the crash in stocks in March 1920 following the boom of speculation in 1919, the economy became gravely sluggish. In addition, because of the poor harvest of rice the same year, its price sharply rose, which in turn affected the prices of other food. As a result, labor strifes occurred demanding a wage increase and others at factories and mines in various parts of the country. In 1921, a huge labor strife happened both at Mitsubishi Shipbuilding Yard and Kawasaki Shipbuilding Yard in Kobe. That strife, which was backed up by Yuaikai, a countrywide labor union then, was the largest that Japan had ever had. The labor side demanded a right to organize, a standard of 8 hours-a-day work, a wage hike and so forth. The strife was so overheated that there was even a case where the army had to be dispatched there to calm it down. It lasted one year and a half, and terminated. After the end of it, Mitsubishi genuinely addressed the matter of improving the labor and management relations. Early on, in 1919, Mitsubishi & Co., Ltd. had already studied the factory committee system, a cooperative organization of workers and managers advocated by Whitley Council in the United Kingdom, for introduction into its factories. On the occasion of the above labor strife, therefore, it had decided to bring it in. That is, in September 1921, the factory committee system had been introduced into the Nagasaki Shipbuilding Yard, the Hiroshima Shipbuilding Yard and the Nagasaki Arms Works, and then in November of the same year into the Kobe Shipbuilding Yard. Under the system, a factory committee, consisting of representatives of both the workers and the management, was set up to promote mutual understanding between them and discuss such issues as production efficiency, promotion of personnel's welfare, conditions for working and so on. The thought on the factory committee system, in this connection, came to be united with the ways of viewing and thinking that Koyata and his followers had already evolved, i.e., of enjoying one's work, cultivating one's human nature, creating an autonomous organization through decentralization, trusting personnel, taking a man of talent as a leading actor and so forth. That is, the above lines of thought later formed the second layer of Mitsubishi's culture.

Mitsubishi's members' autonomous action

In 1914, Tokyo Station was opened. The demand for business offices since then was on the rise in the Marunouchi district around the station due to its convenient location. The shortage of buildings, therefore, became obvious. Due to that demand, the department of land development at Mitsubishi & Co., Ltd. set out to construct an American-style, steel-frame, multistoried office building, and in 1923 finished constructing it. It was named the Marunouchi Building which has lived up to this day. Half a year after its completion, however, i.e., in September 1923, there occurred the Great Earthquake of 1923. It was accompanied by the greatest earthquake disaster on record in Japan. At 11:58 a.m. on September 1st, 1923, the first earthquake arrived. Afterwards, three violent shocks of earthquake were felt in Tokyo. A number of apparatus, window glasses, glass bottles and so forth were destroyed at the department of land development of Mitsubishi & Co., Ltd. on the fourth floor of the Marunouchi Building. An aftershock of the earthquake continued, and 210 aftershocks were recorded on September 1st and 337 recorded on September 2nd. When the first earthquake came at 11:58 a.m., almost at noon, most homes were making preparations for lunch using fire, and having felt the earthquake, many people left of their homes without putting out the fire. Since many houses collapsed later, fire broke out in various parts of the city of Tokyo and spread fast so that 45 percent of the area of Tokyo city was burned up. Then, Ryuji Akaboshi, general manager of the land development department at Mitsubishi & Co., Ltd., instructed the members to take an active part of relief and protection for people in the Marunouchi district. They carried 50 to 60 tatami mats from the exercise hall of the Mitsubishi Club at the Marunouchi Building out to a large square located between the Building and Tokyo Station to form a place of relief. After having set it up, the medical doctors who belonged to Mitsubishi & Co., Ltd. and other doctors working at the Marunouchi Building set out to give first aid to injured persons there. On September 2nd, furthermore, they cooked dozens of bags of rice which had been saved for emergency at the Building and delivered them to the sufferers. On the 5th of September, an emergency organization was formed at Mitsubishi & Co., Ltd. and Kikuo Aoki, managing director, took the post of its head. In addition, such groups were formed as of general affairs, correspondence and relief. Kikuo Aoki, on the same day, i.e., on September 5, decided to offer a relief contribution of 5,000,000 yen to Minister of Home Affairs in the name of Koyata Iwasaki. That was a little more than half the amount of the construction cost 9,000,000 yen of the Marunouchi Building which is equivalent to 13 billion yen in current price. Kikuo Aoki offered the relief contribution of 9,000,000 yen on his own judgment, i.e., without the president's approval. Koyata was then staying in Hakone, and the communication service between Hakone and Tokyo was paralyzed. Two messengers from Mitsubishi & Co., Ltd., therefore, left for Hakone by bicycle to report the incident of the great earthquake to him. Having been informed of the destructive state of Tokyo on the night of September 5, Koyata handed the messengers leaving for Tokyo an instruction to Aoki. It read 'Will you arrange to offer to the government a relief contribution of ...yen for the disaster of the earthquake'. The space for the amount of money was blank. As mentioned above, Aoki had already done it before receiving that instruction from Koyata. On September 18 when Koyata returned back to Tokyo, Kikuo

130

Aoki asked Koyata to give him an ex post facto approval of the relief contribution. Koyata admired Aoki's decision on that matter.

As has been stated, at the time of the Great Earthquake of 1923, such leading members of Mitsubishi as Ryuji Akaboshi and Kikuo Aoki acted autonomously. Koyata, in turn, evaluated highly their autonomy and self-judgment and praised them. We can see here that the values of autonomy and self-judgment in the second layer of Mitsubishi's culture came to be shared among the members of Mitsubishi. As to the policy of land development, in this context, Ryuji Akaboshi stated in the journal Jitsugyo-no-Nihon in 1927 as follows.

> It could be said that landlords, house owners and those who have direct or indirect relation to land keep, as it were, part of the national land in trust. Their responsibility for it, therefore, is extremely heavy...They ought to follow the royal road in management policy in every way. They are not permitted to adopt something similar to the rule of might. If one continues to do a wrong management through the rule of might, he might prosper like an upstart for a while, but is certain to go to ruin in the end...
>
> (T. Miyagawa, 1996, originally in Japanese)

Management must follow the royal road, i.e., its own right way. They have to strictly observe justice, reject speculation, and achieve its object with genuine efforts through competition. Thus, Ryoji Akaboshi certainly held the same culture in common with Koyata.

On the other hand, the public offering of the Mitsubishi group's stocks started when Mitsubishi Mining Co. decided to increase its capital in 1920. Thereafter, the other companies of the group successively offered stocks to the public. To cover funds for investment in plant and equipment, in particular, each company turned active from 1937 on in offering stocks to the public to increase its capital. In May 1937, in this connection, the department of land development, which had only been kept as a department at Mitsubishi & Co., Ltd., was separated to set it up as a new independent firm, i.e., Mitsubishi Land Development Co. At the same time, Mitsubishi & Co., Ltd. was renamed Mitsubishi Co., Ltd. which was the holding company in charge of all Mitsubishi business concerns.

Mitsubishi's culture maintained

In 1939, World War II broke out, and the military authorities came to hold the reins of government. Under those circumstances, there appeared a number of zaibatsu which intended to develop their business in league with the government and military clique. Mitsubishi also could not but co-operate with the government, but it tenaciously and continually followed the principle of nonintervention in politics. In 1942, Yokusan Seiji-kai, a political organization, was formed to set people in mobilization for the war where a few persons from Mitsubishi Co., Ltd. and Mitsubishi business firms were listed as promoter. Having been informed of it, Koyata immediately issued a notice to the executive managers of the Mitsubishi group that the Mitsubishi members should hold on to the traditionally held principle of nonintervention in politics. Since Koyata exceedingly detested the personnel's approaching to the military clique, the relationship between the persons in charge at Mitsubishi Heavy Industries Co. and those in the military was aggravated at times. There happened even a case that their negotiations, which were about to reach an agreement, broke down due to the above principle of no partiality. To such a case, Koyata maintained that one need to pay no regard to any criticism from an impure mind and not to fear if negotiations were discontinued because of such a criticism. He fastidiously disliked the executive managers at Mitsubishi having anything to do with political affairs. In that respect, he apparently succeeded Mitsubishi's culture originated at the time of Mitsubishi's turn of business from the sea to the land. In 1945, Japan unconditionally surrendered to the Allies and the war was brought to an end. The dissolution of zaibatsu became one of the fundamental policies at GHQ, and in the case of Mitsubishi, its holding company Mitsubishi Co., Ltd. was dissolved. The culture of Mitsubishi was, however, succeeded by the member firms of the Mitsubishi group, and turned out to be fundamental to their development later. Thinking backward, the first layer of Mitsubishi's culture formed by 1893 when Mitsubishi & Co., Ltd. was founded. It was united later with the second layer formed by Koyata Iwasaki, the fourth president at Mitsubishi and his followers to bolster each other. Yet, it was acting still at the time of 1945. Since then, it has helped promote the Mitsubishi concerns to develop further on.

Mitsubishi's culture and the competitiveness elements

Now, then, let us see how the culture of Mitsubishi is adaptive to the 3-Layer Structure of Enterprise Competitiveness and the 7 Principles of Enterprise Competitiveness. We shall first look into its adaptability competitiveness element by competitiveness element.

Ethos originated in the early days of an enterprise, i.e., the spirit of denying, the spirit of negating the status quo, the spirit of creativity and the spirit of creating a vision, are maintained Since the days of its foundation, Mitsubishi aimed to transplant and construct modern industries in Japan. Its object was later established as Mitsubishi's philosophy of rendering service to the state and the society through production and commerce activities, which helped to attract

132

men of talent to it. Next, in 1886, by its conversion of business from the sea to the land, Mitsubishi altogether abolished the mentality of a government-affiliated businessman and revived. It followed the principle of justice in commerce and industry. Koyata later expressed that principle in his own way. That is, he said that one ought to be just, fair and open in addressing whatever matters, not yield to any failure and strive for one's object. The success thus attained is, he thought, the real one. Here, we can see an expression of Akaki-kokoro, an attribute of the Kami Way.

Every member is willing to grapple with any situation without hesitation and without worrying about failure Primarily due to the Political Change of the year 1881, the criticism from both the government and the public became furious indeed against Mitsubishi for the government-affiliated activities which it had done thus far. Mitsubishi was completely isolated. Under those circumstances, Yataro died of illness in February 1885. His younger brother Yanosuke, then, encouraged the members of Mitsubishi, and they in concert coped with the relentless competition against Joint Transportation Co. From despair and excitement, they at one time discussed a plan of bringing all the vessels together off the shore of Shinagawa to blow up, sink them and dissolve Mitsubishi. It was to such a bitter end that they intended to fight against Joint Transportation Co.. In the end, Mitusbishi turned its business from the sea to the land, having withdrawn from the shipping line of business, and revived.

Personnel have pride and confidence in upholding their enterprise's competitiveness and have a sense of representing their enterprise In 1923 when the Great Earthquake of 1923 occurred, Ryuji Akaboshi, general manager of the land development department, decided to conduct, in concert with the other members, activities of relief and protection for people in the Marunouchi district. Kikuo Aoki, managing director at Mitsubishi & Co., Ltd. also made a decision to offer a contribution of 5,000,000 yen on September 5 to Minister of Home Affairs. It seems that they autonomously acted with a sense of representing Mitsubishi.

Pride and confidence in one's own work Koyata said that when people are engaged in their work, assuming the responsibility of promoting business, it is of absolute necessity for them to enjoy working. Working without gratification does not lead to anything good. To put it conversely, one's pride and confidence in one's work may give rise to good results.

Self-reforming abilities In its foundation days, since Mitsubishi's members were samurai, they were required to reform themselves to be a merchant. With the motto 'an apron is a merchant's formal dress', Yataro intended the personnel to

133

follow the merchant way. Yet, the executive managers at Mitsubishi managed to live up to his expectation. Their spirit of self-reform revealed itself again when Mitsubishi turned its business from the sea to the land, having denied and discarded the mentality of a government-affiliated businessman. We can perceive here Yomigaeri, an attribute of the Kami Way.

Abolishment of practices restricting competition Yataro expanded and developed the marine transportation business in league with the state power. At the turn of the Political Change of the year 1881, however, he pronounced that he would truly follow the principle of nonintervention in politics and the business-first principle. This thought was succeeded from then on at Mitsubishi. In 1942, in reality, Koyata, the fourth president, admonished the executive managers that the principle of nonintervention in politics was the traditional value shared at Mitsubishi and that, therefore, they ought to adhere to it.

Constraints on speculative purchases of enterprises or assets Koyata said that it is most shameful for a person to succeed by relying on chance and employing a cunning plan. He also stated that there is an absolute difference between one's motive for speculation, i.e., planning to win a fortune with rare possibility at a stroke, and that of investment based on precise investigation and detailed analysis. Therefore, he duly evaluated those who did not go with the current of the times, having put a high value on one's autonomy and his right judgment.

Enterprise ethics (Sense of responsibility to the society) In March 1920 when stock prices collapsed, Koyata summoned the leading members of Mitsubishi Trading Co. to its head office to tell them the mission of a trading firm. Later on, Momotaro Miyakegawa, president of Mitsubishi Trading Co., summed up Koyata's admonitory lecture to form the company's principle. It comprised the following:

> Duty to the society
> Be just and fair on everything
> Take trade as our own business

It was rewritten later and is now expressed as

> Corporate Responsibility to Society
> Integrity and Fairness
> International Understanding through Trade

Human resources From the time of Yataro, special regard was given to introducing and fostering men of ability at Mitsubishi.

Investment in the training of personnel Early on, Yataro opened an English school within the estate of his private residence in Osaka and appointed Renpei Kondoh as the first director. The school played an important role in fostering personnel at Mitsubishi. Moreover, Mitsubishi opened a commercial college later.

Cooperation with and participation in a community and its activities On the occasion of the Great Earthquake of 1923 which occurred on September 1, 1923, the members of Mitsubishi at Marunouchi Building carried out relief and protection activities to people in the Marunouchi district, and cooked rice, which had been saved for emergency, to give to the sufferers. They formed an emergency organization at Mitsubishi & Co., Ltd. and executed a systematic activity of relief. Even at present, in this context, there are some food and others stocked for emergency at Mitsubishi Land Development Co. in the district of Marunouchi.

Have a close relationship with customers In the days of its foundation, Mitsubishi could not but compete squarely against the government-run Japanese Mail Steamer Co.. Having adopted the principle of customers-first, however, it was accepted on the market and succeeded.

Organizational techniques In 1917, Koyata set out to reorganize the organization of Mitsubishi & Co., Ltd. Its divisions were consecutively separated from it to be independent joint stock companies with Mitsubishi & Co., Ltd. being their holding company. The object of this reorganization was to transform the Mitsubishi into a group of autonomous organizations. What virtually made the division of Mitsubishi & Co., Ltd. possible was that it had already fostered professional managers needed to run an independent concern. Men of ability were, in turn, cultivated at the separated organizations. This good cycle of dividing the organization and cultivating men of talent was facilitated with Mitsubishi's thought of enjoying one's work and training one's human nature.

Develop personnel's abilities and continue their learning In 1914, the Mitsubishi Club was set up which was designed as an exercising hall to train the personnel's human nature. To train one's human nature is a necessary condition for their autonomy and self-judgment. Without its members' autonomy and self-judgment, the organization can not be autonomous and independent. Koyata was firmly convinced that the personnel's self-advancement was fundamental to the development of Mitsubishi's business.

135

Every member is a leading actor At Mitsubishi, there is the thought of enjoying one's work and cultivating one's human nature on the one hand and the way of thinking that every man of ability is a leading actor on the other hand. These two lines of thought are two sides of the same coin. Based on such thought, Mitsubishi pushed ahead with the division of its organization to create a number of autonomous firms.

Ethics of relations between management and workers The issue of labor and management relations in the history of Mitsubishi was first addressed by Renpei Kondoh at Yoshioka Mine. He introduced a number of modern management ways there. For instance, he changed the conventional way of piecework payment into a modern wage system. When having struck a deposit of good quality, in this context, he drank a toast for its success with the mineworkers. Later, on the occasion of the great labor strike at the Kobe shipbuilding yard in 1921, Mitsubishi decided to introduce into its factories the factory committee system advocated by the Whitley Council in the United Kingdom to promote communication between workers and management.

To sum up, Mitsubishi's culture is, as a whole, adapted to the 3-Layer Structure of Enterprise Competitiveness and the 7 Principles of Enterprise Competitiveness. It is shown in Table 7.1 and 7.2.

Table 7.1   The 3-Layer Structure of Enterprise Competitiveness

I   Enterprise Organismic Foundation

Enterprise ethos
- Ethos originated in the early days of an enterprise,   Adaptable
  i.e., the spirit of denying, the spirit of negating
  the status quo, the spirit of creativity and the spirit
  of creating a vision, are maintained.
- Every member is willing to grapple with any   Adaptable
  situation without hesitation and without worrying
  about failure.
- People in the workplace freely exchange
  their views and opinions.

Enhancement of initiative
- There is teamwork among personnel.
- Personnel have pride and confidence in   Adaptable
  upholding their enterprise's competitiveness
  and have a sense of representing their enterprise.

136

- Diligence and positive activities of personnel.
- Pride and confidence in one's own work.   Adaptable
- Self-reforming abilities.   Adaptable

Provision of norms
- Law (company regulations, etc.).
- Abolishment of practices restricting competition.   Adaptable

Preparation of investment conditions
- Allow a sufficiently long time frame
  for management.
- Promotion of R&D and production-process R&D.
- Constraints on speculative purchases of   Adaptable
  enterprises or assets.

Enterprise ethics   Adaptable
(Sense of responsibility to the society)

Education
(General learning as citizen of the society)

II   Enterprise Economic Base

Infrastructure
- Physical assets   facilities, machinery,
                         network.
- Human resources   executives, scientists,   Adaptable
                         engineers, workers.
- Employment of human resources and
  procurement of physical assets to build
  and stabilize infrastructure.
- Investment in the training of personnel.   Adaptable
- Education on practical business.

Environmental improvement and conservation
- Conservation of the natural environment.
- Cooperation with and participation in   Adaptable
  a community and its activities.
- Improvement of the physical environment of
  the workplace.
- Attention and care to human relations in the workplace.

Diffusion of new ideas, planning and others
- Create smooth communication lines.
- Discussion on the vision, policies and the state of affairs of the enterprise from management.
- Diffuse new ideas, reforms, improvements, and intelligence on new products both inside and outside the organization.

III   Management System

Effectiveness
- Maintain a free market principle throughout the enterprise.
- Encourage competitive spirit.
- Improve cost, quality and delivery terms simultaneously.
- Development, introduction and use of technology to gain strategic predominance.
- Commercialize technology.
- Activate communication throughout.

Tense balance between effectiveness and ethics
- Have a close relationship with customers.   Adaptable
- Have intimate contact with suppliers.
- Organizational techniques.   Adaptable
- Organization whose workers are barely conscious of organizational hierarchy.
- Recognition of quality as the end result of overall production and service activities.
- Generate many alternatives to a decision-making process.
- Demand and expect personnel to do their best.
- Cope with things flexibly.
- Develop personnel's abilities and   Adaptable
  continue their learning.
- Guarantee long-term employment.

Ethics
- Every member is a leading actor.   Adaptable
- A view of work in which diligence is highly esteemed.

138

- Improvement of ethics.
- Fair employment.
- Appropriate transfer of personnel from one post to another.
- Fair and just promotion of personnel.
- Ethics of relations between management and workers.   Adaptable

Table 7.2   The 7 Principles of Enterprise Competitiveness

1   Creativity
- Ethos originated in the early days of an enterprise,   Adaptable
  i.e., the spirit of denying, the spirit of negating
  the status quo, the spirit of creativity and the spirit
  of creating a vision, are maintained.
- Every member is willing to grapple with any   Adaptable
  situation without hesitation and without worrying
  about failure.
- Self-reforming abilities.   Adaptable

2   Righteousness
- Law (company regulations, etc.).
- Ethics of relations between management and   Adaptable
  workers.
- Abolishment of practices restricting competition.   Adaptable
- Constraints on speculative purchases of   Adaptable
  enterprises or assets.
- Enterprise ethics   Adaptable
  (Sense of responsibility to the society).
- A view of work in which diligence is
  highly esteemed.
- Improvement of ethics.

3   Fairness
- Maintain a free market principle throughout
  the enterprise.
- Encourage competitive spirit.
- Fair employment.
- Appropriate transfer of personnel from one
  post to another.
- Fair and just promotion of personnel.

139

4 Equality
- People in the workplace freely exchange
  their views and opinions.
- There is teamwork among personnel.
- Personnel have pride and confidence in   Adaptable
  upholding their enterprise's competitiveness
  and have a sense of representing their enterprise.
- Organization whose workers are barely
  conscious of organizational hierarchy.
- Recognition of quality as the end result
  of overall production or service activities.
- Guarantee long-term employment.
- Every member is a leading actor.   Adaptable

5 Sharing
- Conservation of the natural environment.
- Cooperation with and participation in   Adaptable
  a community and its activities.
- Improvement of the physical environment of
  the workplace.
- Attention and care to human relations in
  the workplace.
- Create smooth communication lines.
- Discussion on the vision, policies and the state of
  affairs of the enterprise from management.
- Diffuse new ideas, reforms, improvements, and
  intelligence on new products both inside and
  outside the organization.
- Activate communication throughout.
- Have a close relationship with customers.   Adaptable
- Have intimate contact with suppliers.

6 Self-Cultivation
- Diligence and positive activities of personnel.
- Pride and confidence in one's own work.   Adaptable
- Demand and expect personnel to do their best.

7 Learning and Knowledge-Accumulation

Technology
- Commercialize technology.

- Development, introduction and use of technology
  to gain strategic predominance.
- Promotion of R&D and production-process R&D.
- Employment of human resources and
  procurement of physical assets to build
  and stabilize infrastructure.
- Physical assets.
- Human resources.   Adaptable

Systems thinking
- Allow a sufficiently long time frame
  for management.
- Generate many alternatives to
  a decision-making process.
- Improve cost, quality and delivery terms
  simultaneously.
- Cope with things flexibly.
- Develop personnel's abilities and   Adaptable
  continue their learning.

People
- Education
  (General learning as citizen of the society).
- Investment in the training of personnel.   Adaptable
- Education on practical business.
- Organizational techniques.   Adaptable

7.2 The House of Ohkura

As has been seen in the previous section, Mitsubishi evolved in the Meiji times, expanded later and went through the transition after the end of World War II to continue to develop to this day. In its history, Mitsubishi met its single largest turn in the Meiji era. It started with the Political Change of the year 1881 and ended up with Mitsubishi's turn of business from the sea to the land in 1886. During this period, Mitsubishi abolished the mentality of a government-affiliated businessman, and followed the ways of viewing and modes of thinking adaptive to the market economy such as the business-first principle and the principle of nonintervention in politics. Those ways of viewing and thinking came out to form the first layer of its culture. Later, at the times of Koyata Iwasaki, the thought advocated by him and his followers formed the second layer which then helped to reinforce and consolidate the first layer. Mitsubishi's

141

culture was from then on succeeded up to the end of the war and was conducive to promoting Mitsubishi companies to develop further still. Putting it another way, it was an utterly healthy culture adaptive to the 3-Layer Structure of Enterprise Competitiveness and the 7 Principles of Enterprise Competitiveness. Now, then, how was the House of Ohkura taken which had similarly evolved in the Meiji era and occupied one of the positions of zaibatsu before the end of World War II? Ohkura failed in overcoming difficulties after the end of World War II and fell into obscurity in the end. There was obviously a difference between the culture of Mitsubishi and that of Ohkura. We shall, therefore, next see how the culture of Ohkura had evolved and developed and in what state it was as at the time of 1945.

Ohkura Firearms Shop

Kihachiro Ohkura, founder of the House of Ohkura, was born in Shibata, Echigo (Niigata, now) in 1837. In 1853, when Matthew Calbraith Perry arrived at Uraga, Japan, his father passed away. Kihachiro determined then to go up to Edo to do business. He was 16 years old. In the beginning, he entered a merchant house of salted food as a clerk. Afterwards, he retired from it to join a house of dried bonito at Azabu Iikura, Edo. In 1857, four years after he went to Edo, he at last rented a house with a frontage of about 12 feet to open a shop of dry goods. He was 20. The same year, Townsend Harris, consul general of the United States, met the shogun for the first time. In 1859, the Tokugawa shogunate government concluded a treaty of friendship and commerce with the United States, Netherland, Russia, the United Kingdom and France. In 1860, thus, the ports of Yokohama, Nagasaki and Hakodate were opened to those five countries with which Japan proceeded to trade. Later, then, the strife increasingly intensified between the Tokugawa shogunate government arguing for opening the country to have commercial intercourse with foreign countries and the Imperial Court and the influential clans in the southwest region advocating the closing of the country and the Restoration of the Imperial Rule. Around this time in history, Kihachiro was seeking a big business opportunity. One day he visited Yokohama whose port had been recently opened and saw for the first time a steamship belching columns of black smoke offshore. He was then convinced that Japan would change. When the times change, a disturbance is bound to occur and then a war breaks out. And there is a demand for arms among others. Having been so convinced, he closed his shop of dry goods in 1866 to enter a shop of firearms as probationer at Hatcho-bori, Edo. Having duly finished his training as probationer, Kihachiro opened Ohkura Firearms Shop at Kanda Izumicho, Edo in 1867 when he was 29 years of age. He had many orders for firearms, but the competition was quite intense because there were about 100 merchants of the same trade. Therefore, Kihachiro would go up, it is said, to a trading house at Yokohama much earlier in the morning than any other merchant so that he could favorably settle a negotiation with the house before the firearms rose in price. He promptly and precisely attended to all orders and followed a honest trade although there were many merchants selling guns of inferior quality at an inordinately high price.

In 1868, one year after the opening of Ohkura Firearms Shop, Kihachiro Ohkura was ordered by Prince Arisugawa, governor-general of the Imperial expeditionary force against the Tokugawa shogunate army, to procure arms and provisions for the Imperial army. Due to this order and his procurement activity then, in this context, he came to take a great opportunity of developing his business in league with the Meiji new government as a government-affiliated businessman. The same year, the Tokugawa shogunate government turned over the reins of government to the Imperial Court and the clans which had supported it. The Meiji Restoration thus arrived. On that occasion, Kihachiro decided to change his business. In 1871, having thought that Western clothes would come into fashion, he opened Western Clothes Tailor's Shop at Nihonbashi, Tokyo while the same year he set up Naigai Trading Shop at Yokohama to conduct trade with foreign countries. Furthermore, he took part in a railway project where he undertook part of the construction work of Shinagawa Station. The work was to recruit and supply carpenters and procure lumber. Since his participation in that railway project, Kihachiro came to be engaged in construction contracting business. Early on, in 1872, he contracted for the building of Ginza Brick-Building Street which was part of a reconstruction work after a big fire had occurred in Ginza, Tokyo. As he had no experience at all in construction work, however, he determined to commit the whole work to subcontractors, and go on a long-term trip abroad from April 1872 to August 1873.

Ohkura & Company

The primary object of his trip was to acquire knowledge on a full-dress trading house. Kihachiro at first sailed over to the United States to investigate the demand for raw silk and tea exported from Japan. He next went across the Atlantic Ocean to the United Kingdom and conducted research on industrial production and others, having stayed there about 10 months. Then, he moved to France seeing the state of industry and commerce and on to Italy. Just about that time, he was advised of the grand exhibition held in Vienna. What he saw there was a variety of equipment and facilities of advanced civilization, many applications of physics and chemistry, plans of production advancement and promotion of industry and so forth. He was evidently impressed with them.

Having returned from the long journey covering 1 year and 5 months, Kihachiro immediately founded Ohkura & Company after the model of

European and American company system in October 1873. Its business was primarily of exporting, and importing to meet the demand from the government offices and the public. Ohkura & Company increasingly thrived to pave the way for its development onto zaibatsu. Later on, in 1909, Chokyuro Kadono, who had entered Ohkura & Company and worked for it during the two generations of Kihachiro and his son Kishichiro, stated as follows.

> I would say that old Mr. Ohkura was not an enterprising man of production but a genuine merchant. I found his true value in it. It seemed that he considered himself as a great merchant in the world.
>
> (Y. Sunagawa, 1996, originally in Japanese)

Kihachiro Ohkura seemed to have a gift for commerce. He was consecutively engaged in the construction contracting business as well as the trading line of business. In 1874 when the government decided to dispatch troops to Taiwan, therefore, the Army Department requested Kihachiro to procure war supplies other than arms. He immediately took on that task. Due to bad storage conditions, however, the foodstuff delivered to Taiwan went rotten. Moreover, a number of craftsmen and laborers dispatched there died because of the shortage of food and the adverse living environment. As a result, Ohkura & Company incurred a great loss, but it already had economic strength sufficient to recover itself at that time. On the other hand, Eiichi Shibusawa, president of the First National Bank, prepared a proposal of founding the first large-scale spinning company in Japan named Osaka Spinning Co. By his request, Kihachiro became a promoter of that company. Denzaburo Fujita, president of Fujita & Company, became its promoter and took office as the first president of Osaka Spinning Co. It was opened in 1883. Since then, Kihachiro kept friendship with Denzaburo Fujita. Ohkura & Company and Fujita & Company were both a large construction contractor then.

In those days, the Meiji government enthusiastically designed a plan of expanding armaments and the navy authorities laid out a scheme of consecutively constructing three ports: Sasebo Port first, Yokosuka Port next and then Kure Port for exclusive use of the navy. The construction work necessary for building those ports was so enormous that the navy authorities determined to give their contracts to such influential contractors as Ohkura and Fujita. Yet, the navy further wished for Ohkura and Fujita being merged in executing such a grand work. The interim bureau of construction under the direct control of the Cabinet also advised Ohkura and Fujita to merge their operations. Both companies, finally, agreed to merge their civil engineering and construction divisions whereby Japan Civil Engineering Co., Ltd. was founded in 1887. In this connection, Ohkura and Fujita each had a division of procurement for the navy. They decided, therefore, to unite those divisions to form a new firm named Naigai Procurement Co. the same year. With the establishment of the two companies above, most of the employees of both Ohkura and Fujita were transferred to them while the carpet sales shop and the Hokkaido branch office remained at Ohkura & Company and the mining division was kept back at Fujita & Company. Those two mammoth enterprises which the government took the initiative in founding, however, were to be dissolved in 5 and a half years. Its direct cause was that after the Imperial assembly was set up in February 1889, the Public Accounts Act was promulgated, following the principle of fair administrative procedures, and enforced in April the next year. According to the Act, when the government enters into a contract with a private enterprise, the contract is to be concluded through an open, public tender whether it is for construction contracting or for dealing in goods. As a result, the conventional way of contracting through a special command from the government was not permitted. Thus, Japan Civil Engineering Co., Ltd. and Naigai Procurement Co. had no choice but to compete with others on the market to get an order from the government. After the enforcement of the Act, the performance of Japan Civil Engineering Co., Ltd. became worse. In 1892, having judged that it was exceedingly difficult to maintain its business under the severely competitive public tender system, Ohkura and Fujita determined to break it up. The next year, in 1893, Kihachiro founded a privately owned Ohkura Civil Engineering Co., which took over the business of Japan Civil Engineering Co., Ltd.. In November the same year, the Commercial Law Act was put in force. On that occasion, Ohkura and Fujita decided to dissolve Naigai Procurement Co.. Since Fujita & Company determined to withdraw from the procurement business for the navy, Kihachiro set up Ohkura & Co., Ltd., which succeeded the business of Naigai Procurement Co. and absorbed Ohkura & Company. Thus, he obtained the people and business from Fujita & Company except its mining division.

Two pillars of undertaking

Kihachiro now had two pillars of undertaking, i.e., Ohkura Civil Engineering Co. which was to carry out a construction contracting line of business, and Ohkura & Co., Ltd. which was to conduct a trading line of business and to manage investment in a group of affiliated concerns. With those two pillars, he actively drove his business forward. Kihachiro, during his life, took part in founding and investing in a number of manufacturing firms. The number of affiliated companies at Ohkura & Co., Ltd., remarkably increased at one time. It was primarily because he acted as mediator in the economic circles to help launch new enterprises. When those companies developed and needed further capital for expansion, however, Kihachiro did not subscribe for their new shares. Thus, many blue-chip firms parted from Ohkura & Co., Ltd. in the end. In other

145

words, he dared not take in those manufacturing firms so as to render their business part of the main line of business at Ohkura. His business activities were those of a trading house focussed on dealings in goods on one hand and the supply of manpower on the other. In that sense, he was not an enterprising man of production but a genuine merchant. At any rate, as in 1893 when Ohkura Civil Engineering Co. and Ohkura & Co., Ltd. were founded, the first layer of Ohkura's culture seems to have formed. In 1873 when Ohkura & Company was set up, Kihachiro evidently had an enterprising spirit. The industrial production in the United Kingdom, the prevailing commerce and industry in France, and the variety of equipment and facilities of advanced civilization, the applications of physics and chemistry and the schemes of promoting industry and production shown at the great exhibition in Vienna. With such information and knowledge above, he created a new business house, i.e., Ohkura & Company. Immediately before the Meiji Restoration, he had run Ohkura Firearms Shop where he conducted prompt and precise dealings with customers, having followed a principle of honest trade. In 1868, he attended to the procurement of arms and provisions for the Imperial army, thereby having established relations with the new Meiji government. At the time of Subjugation of Taiwan, Ohkura accepted the government's request to carry goods and manpower over to Taiwan but the result was a great loss. In 1887, further, Ohkura was merged with Fujita following the government's initiative. The fair and open tender system, however, became the rule of the day, and subjected to a severe competition on the market, the merged companies were broken up. The new firms were, instead, formed to start again. Accordingly, although he was a businessman of government-affiliated disposition, Kihachiro had an enterprising spirit for business. The culture of Ohkura at that time seems to have been, taken as a whole, healthy.

Kihachiro's connection with the military

With the Sino-Japanese War in 1894 and the Russo-Japanese War in 1904, however, its culture changed enormously. In 1894, the Sino-Japanese War broke out which was the first modern war that Japan staked her fate on. The Imperial headquarters was set up and the economic circles accepted and followed its principle of national unity. The Army department successively gave orders for supply of manpower, procurement of various materials, execution of urgent construction works with Ohkura & Co., Ltd. and Ohkura Civil Engineering Co. The war came to an end in only half a year and Japan won an overwhelming victory. In April 1895, the peace treaty was concluded at Shimonoseki, Japan whereby the government acquired the cession of Taiwan, the indemnity of 360 million yen and so forth from the Empire of China, which were an immense return. The government soon established the Governor-

146

General Office in Taiwan. Although there was still much risk for civilian people to sail over there, Ohkura & Co., Ltd. and Ohkura Civil Engineering Co. were the first to go across to Taiwan, having assumed a supply mission for the expeditionary force there. They installed a telegraphic line, laid out a military road, constructed a railway and so on. The contribution made by Ohkura & Co., Ltd. and Ohkura Civil Engineering Co. to the army was enormous and remarkable during and after the war. Kihachiro thus gained immense profits. Having been facilitated by the overwhelming victory in the Sino-Japanese War, the government proceeded with its policy of military expansion. Japan had obtained, in this connection, the Liaotung Peninsula from China together with Taiwan by the peace treaty above. However, due to the Triple Intervention of Russia, Germany and France, it was forced to return it to China, which gave Japan an excuse for its military expansion to counteract big powers. In 1904, Japan declared war against Russia whereby the Russo-Japanese War opened. To raise war funds, the government issued a war bond in the domestic market. Kihachiro then was the first in subscribing for it. Furthermore, he dispatched his men to the front line headquarters to investigate what the army there really needed. On receiving their report, he ordered them to set up an Ohkura sawmill near the front line and operate it even under a shower of bullets. He obtained a special command from the army of constructing military and other railways, which he consistently executed. The war came to an end in 1905. Through the mediation of Theodore Roosevelt, President of the United States, a peace treaty was concluded between Russia and Japan at Portsmouth in September the same year. In the Russo-Japanese War, Ohkura & Co., Ltd. and Ohkura Civil Engineering Co. showed their real ability, again, in performing the supply mission to the army. Kihachiro, therefore, gained a substantial return.

During the Sino-Japanese War and the Russo-Japanese War, Ohkura & Co., Ltd. and Ohkura Civil Engineering Co. were both Kihachiro's private organizations. The task of those organizations was to procure goods and manpower, and so they were not really required to accumulate technical knowledge usually needed for a private enterprise in the free market system. Kihachiro's private connection with the military was the largest asset of Ohkura, and there was little need of introducing and cultivating men of ability there. It may have been sufficient for his men to work for him as messenger. Ohkura's customer was only the military authorities. As has been put forth, Ohkura was at the zenith of its fortunes during the two wars and obtained an immense profit. Due to this great success, however, it may have lost a chance of establishing the foundation of its commercial and industrial undertaking as private enterprise within the country.

Through the Sino-Japanese War and the Russo-Japanese War, it seems that the second layer of Ohkura's culture formed. It may have been founded on Kihachiro's experience of success as a government-affiliated businessman. At this stage, however, the first layer of Ohkura's culture still remained. Although it considerably weakened, it seems to have coexisted with the second layer. In fact, Kihachiro Ohkura intended to launch new lines of business in Taiwan. The first was a plan to run a sugar plant. Around 1909 when the sugar-refining business was in a boom, he set up Niitaka Sugar-Refining Co. with a capital of 5,000,000 yen. At the time of its foundation, the Governor-General Office in Taiwan permitted him to employ part of the middle and southern areas of Taiwan as sugar-cane growing land, having broken the conventional principle of limiting the sugar-cane harvesting areas to the specific districts. During World War I, Niitaka Sugar-Refining Co. could gain profits due to a temporary boom, but thereafter went into difficulty. The primary reason was that its sugar-cane harvesting area, which the company was newly permitted to use, was located in the middle part of Taiwan that had conventionally been a paddy region. Since the land of a paddy region was of high quality, crops from such a region were expected to be of high value and of high price. In good times, the sugar price was sufficiently high for the sugar-cane from those regions to be used. In bad times, however, the price of sugar abruptly depreciated while the price of the sugar-cane material there remained high. Thus, the poor performance of Niitaka Sugar-Refining Co. was exacerbated. In 1927, in the end, Ohkura & Co., Ltd. sold its holdings of Niitaka Sugar-Refining Co. to Dai Nihon Sugar-Refining Co. and withdrew from this line of business. In 1917, Ohkura & Co., Ltd. also acquired a coal mining right in Taiwan from Kimura Mining Co., the initial holder, for 2,300,000 yen to set out to open a coal mining business on its own. Soon, however, it transferred its holding shares to Mitsui Mining Co. and withdrew from it. Ohkura's attempts above show an example of the recklessness that a company with no fundamental production and engineering technology at home initiates an undertaking of production overseas. They betrayed Ohkura's weak point.

At one time, however, Kihachiro intended to undertake a production line of business at home. Ohkura & Co., Ltd. was a large agent dealing in imported steel comparable to Mitsui Trading Co. at that time. It was also a large trading house having dealings with Yawata Iron Works. With Ohkura's above position, Kihachiro had a keen interest in the production of steel, and so for the first time in the private sector he aimed at the production of steel pipes. In 1908, he laid out a scheme of producing steel pipes out of band steel in collaboration with Lloyd & Co., Ltd. in the United Kingdom. He intended to purchase the band steel from Yawata Iron Works while he planned to import pig iron from Honkeikoh Coal & Steel Co., Ltd., a scheduled new joint concern in China, to deliver it Yawata Iron Works. For that purpose, he scouted Kaichiro Imaizumi, general manager of both the department of steel materials and the department of engineering works at Yawata Iron Works, and proceeded to promote the foundation of a steel pipe manufacturing company. In 1910, he floated its shares as the principal promoter but was not able to raise sufficient money as he had expected and could not receive an advance order from the navy which he had taken as the most reliable customer. He, therefore, decided to withdraw from the promotion of this undertaking. The people having followed him, however, succeeded its promotion activities. Two years later, in 1912, the first steel pipe manufacturing company in Japan was set up by their united efforts. It was Japan Steel Pipe Co. which has continued to exist up to this day. Kihachiro withdrew from the promotion of the steel pipe manufacturing company by reason that he could not secure an advance order from the navy. Such a behavior clearly shows the mentality of a businessman that succeeded in performing a business commissioned by the government and the military. Yet, later, he was to launch into the business of coal mining and steel manufacturing in China with no fundamental technology and knowledge on their production at home.

Ohkura's culture changed

It was around 1904 to 1905, i.e., amidst the Russo-Japanese War, that men from Ohkura & Co., Ltd. conducted an investigation of resources on the Chinese mainland. Around the end of their investigation, they confirmed that there was a promising area of resources, i.e., Honkeikoh Coal field and Miyaruko Iron Ore, on the railway from Shenyang to Tantung. On receiving their report, Kihachiro determined to undertake the business of coal and pig iron mining and that of steel manufacturing there. In 1907, he visited Shenyang Province authorities having jurisdiction over the area of resources above, proposed to set up a joint enterprise between Ohkura and Shenyang Province authorities and entered negotiations with them. In 1911, after many turns and twists, the joint enterprise was founded. It was named Honkeikoh Coal & Steel Co., Ltd. which was in possession of basic materials of iron ore, coal and limestone. The company was the first joint enterprise in the private sector between China and Japan. The same year, in 1911, in this connection, Ohkura & Co., Ltd. was merged with Ohkura Civil Engineering Co. whereby Ohkura Co., Ltd. was established. Its main line of business was composed of trading and of civil engineering as it had been. Accordingly, in the beginning, the joint enterprise in China seems to have been taken as one of the investment activities by Ohkura's trading division and operated and developed as linked up with its main line of trading and civil engineering. The undertaking in Honkeikoh, however, demanded immense funds and Ohkura, a trading house zaibatsu, was to go beyond the limit of that single investment activity and bring the coal mining and the steel production there into its main line. As previously stated, it had not run any manufacturing concern at home. Ohkura, despite that, went deeply into the undertaking at Honkeikoh. In 1915, the steel mill started kindling in a furnace at Honkeikoh. Earlier, in 1914, World War I had broken out. The war brought down a merciful rain on the Japanese economy which had been in a state of financial crisis since the Russo-Japanese War came to an end in 1905. Ohkura Co., Ltd. turned out a substantial profit by expanding its volume of construction work. The dividend on its shares was 8 percent in 1915, 12 percent in 1916, and reached 25 percent in 1917. With the extension of its scale of business, the organization of Ohkura Co., Ltd. was reformed. In July 1918, all the lines of business were separated from it to form them as three business concerns, i.e., Ohkura Trading Co., Ohkura Mining Co. and Ohkura Civil Engineering Co., with Ohkura Co., Ltd. as their holding company. Thus, the mining business was then officially integrated into the main line at Ohkura with Honkeikoh Coal & Steel Co., Ltd. as its main part. Through World War I, in this connection, the second layer of Ohkura's culture had been strengthened and by 1918 when the above reorganization was conducted, it may have replaced the first layer which had unrecoverably weakened then. Around 1915, it is said, the organization of Ohkura was pretty disorderly and everything was determined through Kihachiro's exclusive right. As to the undertaking on the Chinese mainland, in particular, it was carried out with his personal enthusiasm so that Chokyuro Kadono, who had taken part in the management of Ohkura's business as the highest executive manager, came to dissociate himself from that enterprise. Moreover, many of the personnel engaged in business at Ohkura were wanting in talent and the branch office managers in various parts of the country were mostly a mediocre person and not a Ohkura man from the start (Ohkura Zaibatsu Kenkyu-Kai, 1982). For a government-affiliated businessman like Kihachiro Ohkura who lived on national finance, it was not really necessary to accumulate technological knowledge and consider the provision of corporate infrastructure as far as he was only engaged in the business commissioned from the government. His government-affiliated character, therefore, led to the shortage of talent at Ohkura. Or, to put it more precise, there was little room for cultivating and holding men of ability in that organization. Accordingly, men with the vigor of independence or men of talent were to depart from Ohkura. In this respect, the only exception was Chokyuro Kadono who was treated as the highest executive manager in the company. He had studied specially a railway engineering at Tokyo Imperial University and had practical training in railway technology for 4 years in the United States. After having returned to Japan, he entered Sanyo Railway Co. and attended to its railway construction work. At Kihachiro's request, he joined Ohkura & Co., Ltd. as the highest executive manager in 1897. He was 31 years old. Since then, he had displayed his ability in executing railway construction work whose order Ohkura had received from the government. With Chokyuro Kadono being the only exception, there was found no remarkable talent at Ohkura. In addition, no record of business strategy was left at Ohkura & Co., Ltd. (Ohkura Zaibatsu Kenkyu-Kai, 1982). It seems, therefore, that Ohkura & Co., Ltd. was not, in a real sense, a headquarters of the zaibatsu and that its three business concerns, Ohkura Trading Co., Ohkura Mining Co. and Ohkura Civil Engineering Co., were not essentially an independent company. Ohkura was a group composed of Kihachiro and those people who pledged loyalty to him and did not hesitate to serve him like a tool. Accordingly, there was no room for a capable person to demonstrate his managerial ability. Kihachiro's government-affiliated disposition and his great success by it kept him from taking a steady way of thinking that Ohkura should introduce and foster men of ability and establish the foundation of commerce and industry at home to meet, as a private enterprise, public demand.

Honkeikoh Coal & Steel Co., Ltd.

Around 1918 when World War I was brought to an end, there were few opportunities available at home for Ohkura to expand business in league with the government. In other words, the industrial revolution, led by private hands, had advanced in Japan. Ohkura found itself curbed at home by Mitsui and Mitsubishi which had already established the foundation of commerce and industry on their own. As its business came to a standstill, Ohkura chose to find a way out of the situation in the undertaking in China. Kihachiro thought that it was better to execute a new business on the Chinese mainland with no rival than to compete in vain at home. He thus got deeply into the business at Honkeikoh whereby the mining business was so enlarged as to impose restrictions on the development of trading and civil engineering activities. At Honkeikoh, there were a number of substantial problems at that time. Honkeikoh Coal & Steel Co., Ltd. was a company owning iron ore, coal and limestone as its 3 basic materials. Out of the three basic materials above, the coal was dug in the Honkeikoh coal field, part of which was delivered to the company's steel mill but part of which was exported to Yawata Iron Works, Tokuyama Briquette Manufactory and so forth in Japan. It was reported then that its coal mining business was very poorly managed. The following were listed as its main causes.

1 The way of mining is old-fashioned.
2 There are cliques among directors and technical workers, whereby the fair treatment and promotion of men of talent are not effected.
3 There are unjust and corrupt practices between directors and contractors.
4 Directors from Ohkura and Shenyang Province authorities have overlapping roles.

(Ohkura Zaibatsu Kenkyu-kai, 1982)

Although this joint undertaking was led by private hands, the other party was

151

the officials of Shenyang Province authorities. Yet, the undertaking covered the two countries although the area of Shenyang Province was part of Japanese colony then. As has been explained, it was also an enterprise launched by Ohkura which had no fundamental production and engineering technology at home. For the reasons above, it seems quite natural that there was a limit to the company's rational management. On the other hand, Kihachiro may have been able to display his ability to the full at Honkeikoh as far as he acted as a government-affiliated businessman. We can cite the matter of coal freight, for instance. While the railway had already been laid in the area of Honkeikoh by the Manchurian Railways, its freight of coal was markedly higher than that of Kyushu Chikuho Line or that of Hokkaido Railways at home. At the stockholders' meeting at Honkeikoh Coal & Steel Co., Ltd. in 1913, therefore, Kihachiro Ohkura was entrusted with the task of negotiating with the Manchurian Railways for the reduction in freight charges. Due to his efforts, the first cut in freight was realized in 1914. At the 4th stockholders' meeting held in January 1915, it was reported that the reduction in freight was not enough. Later, at the 6th stockholders' meeting in February 1917, it was reported that they had succeeded in cutting the freight charges. Kihachiro, then, had asked the navy's help and employed the authority of the Ministry of Foreign Affairs to approach the Manchurian Railways on that matter.

In 1924, Kihachiro Ohkura transferred the position of president at Ohkura & Co., Ltd. to his son Kishichiro. He was 87 years old then, and four years later, in 1928, he ended his days at the age of 91. Kishichiro, who had succeeded Ohkura & Co., Ltd., followed the business line Kihachiro had laid down to continue to make a partial and excessive investment in the business in China. In 1943, he reorganized the organization of Ohkura so that Ohkura & Co., Ltd., the folding company of Ohkura zaibatsu, was absorbed into Ohkura Mining Co. which then became the headquarters of the Ohkura group. The main reason for that reorganization had to do with Honkeikoh Coal & Steel Co., Ltd.. As World War II had broken out and the demand for steel had been on the rise, the military expected the company to be a reliable source of steel. To live up to their expectations, Honkeikoh Coal & Steel Co., Ltd. needed vast funds for investment. For the above reason, a plan was made of transforming Ohkura & Co., Ltd. to a business concern and converting its holdings in a number of affiliated companies to funds for investment at Honkeikoh Coal & Steel Co., Ltd.. Thus, it was decided that Ohkura & Co., Ltd. was to be absorbed into Ohkura Mining Co. with its holdings being disposed of.

Ohkura zaibatsu collapsed

In 1945, however, World War II came to an end and Japan was defeated. It lost all its colonies and the war industry became extinct. Ohkura Mining Co. was thus dissolved while Ohkura Trading Co. tried to reestablish itself but could not recover its performance as in the past. It was reduced then to a small trading house. As for Ohkura Civil Engineering Co., there had been no representative director from Ohkura family up to the end of the war since Tsuneo Tokumi, who was foreign to Ohkura family and an engineer from Tokyo University, for the first time took office as representative director in 1918. In 1946, the employees at Ohkura Civil Engineering Co. obtained its shares by transfer from Ohkura family. They took over the company completely disjoined from Ohkura family and changed its name to Taisei Construction Co. to start again. In such a way as above, Ohkura zaibatsu literally collapsed. It had been recognized as one of the eight zaibatsu in the Japanese economic circles before World War II. It had an influential power indeed. At the time of 1945, however, it was not in a position to change itself to revive and to make a fresh start.

Ohkura's culture and the competitiveness elements

Now, then, we shall see here how the culture of Ohkura is unadaptable to the 3-Layer Structure of Enterprise Competitiveness and the 7 Principles of Enterprise Competitiveness. We shall look into its unadaptability competitiveness element by competitiveness element.

Ethos originated in the early days of an enterprise, i.e., the spirit of denying, the spirit of negating the status quo, the spirit of creativity and the spirit of creating a vision, are maintained Immediately before the Meiji Restoration, Kihachiro Ohkura opened Ohkura Firearms Shop to seize a new business opportunity. Prince Arisugawa, governor-general of the Imperial expeditionary force against the Tokugawa shogunate army, ordered him then to procure arms and provisions for the Imperial army, which brought him later to establish an intimate relationship with the new Meiji government. On the occasion of the Meiji Restoration, Kihachiro decided to switch his business from that of firearms to a new one. He went on a long-term trip to the United States and European countries to get an idea of founding a full-dress trading house. Having returned home, he set up Ohkura & Company after the example of American and European companies in October 1873. The company's business consisted of two pillars, one being the dealings in goods and the other the supply of manpower. He thus started and succeeded in business as a merchant. In 1893, having dissolved the joint concern between Ohkura and Fujita which the government had taken the initiative in founding, he formed Ohkura Civil Engineering Co. and Ohkura & Co., Ltd. At this point in time, the culture of Ohkura was, taken as a whole, healthy. Later, through the two great wars, the Sino-Japanese War (1894-1895) and the Russo-Japanese War (1904-1905), the second layer of Ohkura's culture formed based on Kihachiro's experience of

153

success as a government-affiliated businessman. At this stage, the original first layer remained active at Ohkura although it considerably weakened. It attests to the existence of the first layer then that Kihachiro tried to initiate various manufacturing lines of business. For instance, he launched into the business of sugar-refining and coal mining in Taiwan while he tried to promote a steel pipe manufacturing company at home. The result was, however, that he withdrew from both the management and the promotion of those enterprises. Through World War I (1914-1918) when he had greatly succeeded in business as a government-affiliated businessman, the first layer of Ohkura's culture became extinct and the second layer instead took root at Ohkura. Since then, its culture had been succeeded to 1945 when World War II was brought to an end.

Personnel have pride and confidence in upholding their enterprise's competitiveness and have a sense of representing their enterprise There was no room for able men to display their ability at Ohkura. The Ohkura group was not such an organization that men of ability could identify themselves with.

Abolishment of practices restricting competition In 1910, Kihachiro made preparations for setting up the first Japanese steel pipe manufacturing company but later withdrew from its promotion because he could not secure an advance order from the navy which he had taken as the most reliable customer. Here is displayed the mentality of Kihachiro Ohkura who had succeeded by undertaking business commissioned from the government and the military.

Enterprise ethics (Sense of responsibility to the society) The report then on managerial conditions at Honkeikoh Coal & Steel Co., Ltd. said that there were unjust and corrupt practices between directors and contractors.

Physical assets and human resources During the two great wars, the Sino-Japanese War and the Russo-Japanese War, Ohkura was its zenith. While it gained enormous return and succeeded at the time, Ohkura zaibatsu lost an opportunity of establishing the foundation of commercial and industrial lines of business at home. Yet, with no fundamental production and engineering technology, it went over to China to launch into the lines of coal mining and steel manufacturing.

Employment of human resources and procurement of physical assets to build and stabilize infrastructure Around 1915, the personnel, who engaged in business work at Ohkura, were mostly men of little talent, and many of the branch managers were mediocre persons and not Ohkura men from the start.

Investment in the training of personnel In carrying out dealings with the military,

154

the largest asset to be used was Kihachiro's private connection to it. In other words, Ohkura had little need, as an organization, to foster men of ability and accumulate technical knowledge, and therefore paid little regard to the provision of corporate infrastructure. There was little room at Ohkura for fostering and holding men of talent.

Development, introduction and use of technology to gain strategic predominance It was reported then that the way of coal mining was fairly outdated at Honkeikoh Coal & Steel Co., Ltd. The importance of development and introduction of technology may not have been duly recognized there.

Organizational techniques It is said that around 1915, the organization of Ohkura was quite disorderly and everything was decided through Kihachiro's exclusive right. The undertaking on the Chinese mainland was, in particular, carried out with his personal enthusiasm so that even Chokyuro Kadono, who had taken part in the management of Ohkura as the highest executive manager, came to dissociate himself from Honkeikoh's business then. It is also said that there remained little record of business strategy at Ohkura & Co., Ltd., the headquarters of Ohkura zaibatsu, founded in 1918. Ohkura & Co., Ltd. may not have been, in its real sense, a headquarters of the zaibatsu, and the three business concerns, Ohkura Trading Co., Ohkura Mining Co. and Ohkura Civil Engineering Co., were not thought to be essentially independent companies.

Every member is a leading actor Ohkura was a group comprising Kihachiro and his followers who pledged loyalty to him and did not hesitate to serve him like a tool. There was no room, therefore, for capable persons to demonstrate their managerial ability.

Fair and just promotion of personnel There were cliques among directors and technical workers at Honkeikoh Coal & Steel Co., Ltd., due to which the able personnel were kept from being duly promoted.

Taken together, the culture of Ohkura shows, as a whole, its unadaptability to the 3-Layer Structure of Enterprise Competitiveness and the 7 Principles of Enterprise Competitiveness. It is shown as in Table 7.3 and Table 7.4.

Table 7.3   The 3-Layer Structure of Enterprise Competitiveness

I   Enterprise Organismic Foundation

Enterprise ethos
- Ethos originated in the early days of an enterprise,   Unadaptable
  i.e., the spirit of denying, the spirit of negating
  the status quo, the spirit of creativity and the spirit
  of creating a vision, are maintained.
- Every member is willing to grapple with any
  situation without hesitation and without worrying
  about failure.
- People in the workplace freely exchange
  their views and opinions.

Enhancement of initiative
- There is teamwork among personnel.
- Personnel have pride and confidence in   Unadaptable
  upholding their enterprise's competitiveness
  and have a sense of representing
  their enterprise.
- Diligence and positive activities of personnel.
- Pride and confidence in one's own work.
- Self-reforming abilities.

Provision of norms
- Law (company regulations, etc.).
- Abolishment of practices restricting competition.   Unadaptable

Preparation of investment conditions
- Allow a sufficiently long time frame
  for management.
- Promotion of R&D and production-process R&D.
- Constraints on speculative purchases of
  enterprises or assets.

Enterprise ethics   Unadaptable
  (Sense of responsibility to the society)

Education
  (General learning as citizen of the society)

156

II   Enterprise Economic Base

Infrastructure
- Physical assets   facilities, machinery,   Unadaptable
                       network.
- Human resources   executives, scientists,   Unadaptable
                       engineers, workers.
- Employment of human resources and   Unadaptable
  procurement of physical assets to build
  and stabilize infrastructure.
- Investment in the training of personnel.   Unadaptable
- Education on practical business.

Environmental improvement and conservation
- Conservation of the natural environment.
- Cooperation with and participation in
  a community and its activities.
- Improvement of the physical environment of
  the workplace.
- Attention and care to human relations in
  the workplace.

Diffusion of new ideas, planning and others
- Create smooth communication lines.
- Discussion on the vision, policies and the state of
  affairs of the enterprise from management.
- Diffuse new ideas, reforms, improvements, and
  intelligence on new products both inside and
  outside the organization.

III   Management System

Effectiveness
- Maintain a free market principle throughout
  the enterprise.
- Encourage competitive spirit.
- Improve cost, quality and delivery terms
  simultaneously.
- Development, introduction and use of technology   Unadaptable
  to gain strategic predominance.
- Commercialize technology.

157

- Activate communication throughout.

Tense balance between effectiveness and ethics
- Have a close relationship with customers.
- Have intimate contact with suppliers.
- Organizational techniques.   Unadaptable
- Organization whose workers are barely
  conscious of organizational hierarchy.
- Recognition of quality as the end result
  of overall production and service activities.
- Generate many alternatives to
  a decision-making process.
- Demand and expect personnel to do their best.
- Cope with things flexibly.
- Develop personnel's abilities and
  continue their learning.
- Guarantee long-term employment.

Ethics
- Every member is a leading actor.   Unadaptable
- A view of work in which diligence is
  highly esteemed.
- Improvement of ethics.
- Fair employment.
- Appropriate transfer of personnel from one
  post to another.
- Fair and just promotion of personnel.   Unadaptable
- Ethics of relations between management and
  workers.

Table 7.4   The 7 Principles of Enterprise Competitiveness

1   Creativity
- Ethos originated in the early days of an enterprise,   Unadaptable
  i.e., the spirit of denying, the spirit of negating
  the status quo, the spirit of creativity and the spirit
  of creating a vision, are maintained.
- Every member is willing to grapple with any
  situation without hesitation and without worrying
  about failure.
- Self-reforming abilities.

158

2 Righteousness
  · Law (company regulations, etc.).
  · Ethics of relations between management and
   workers.
  · Abolishment of practices restricting competition.   Unadaptable
  · Constraints on speculative purchases of
   enterprises or assets.
  · Enterprise ethics   Unadaptable
   (Sense of responsibility to the society).
  · A view of work in which diligence is
   highly esteemed.
  · Improvement of ethics.

3 Fairness
  · Maintain a free market principle throughout
   the enterprise.
  · Encourage competitive spirit.
  · Fair employment.
  · Appropriate transfer of personnel from one
   post to another.
  · Fair and just promotion of personnel.   Unadaptable

4 Equality
  · People in the workplace freely exchange
   their views and opinions.
  · There is teamwork among personnel.
  · Personnel have pride and confidence in   Unadaptable
   upholding their enterprise's competitiveness
   and have a sense of representing
   their enterprise.
  · Organization whose workers are barely
   conscious of organizational hierarchy.
  · Recognition of quality as the end result
   of overall production or service activities.
  · Guarantee long-term employment.
  · Every member is a leading actor.   Unadaptable

5 Sharing
  · Conservation of the natural environment.
  · Cooperation with and participation in
   a community and its activities.

- Improvement of the physical environment of the workplace.
- Attention and care to human relations in the workplace.
- Create smooth communication lines.
- Discussion on the vision, policies and the state of affairs of the enterprise from management.
- Diffuse new ideas, reforms, improvements, and intelligence on new products both inside and outside the organization.
- Activate communication throughout.
- Have a close relationship with customers.
- Have intimate contact with suppliers.

6   Self-Cultivation
- Diligence and positive activities of personnel.
- Pride and confidence in one's own work.
- Demand and expect personnel to do their best.

7   Learning and Knowledge-Accumulation

Technology
- Commercialize technology.
- Development, introduction and use of technology   Unadaptable
  to gain strategic predominance.
- Promotion of R&D and production-process R&D.
- Employment of human resources and   Unadaptable
  procurement of physical assets to build
  and stabilize infrastructure.
- Physical assets.   Unadaptable
- Human resources.   Unadaptable

Systems thinking
- Allow a sufficiently long time frame for management.
- Generate many alternatives to a decision-making process.
- Improve cost, quality and delivery terms simultaneously.
- Cope with things flexibly.
- Develop personnel's abilities and continue their learning.

160

People
- Education
  (General learning as citizen of the society).
- Investment in the training of personnel.   Unadaptable
- Education on practical business.
- Organizational techniques.   Unadaptable

7.3 Summary

The House of Mitsubishi and the House of Ohkura both started their business in the Meiji era. They had evolved and developed since then and formed large corporate groups as zaibatsu before World War II. Mitsubishi was a company founded by Yataro Iwasaki with the shipping as its main line of business. Through the Political Change of the year 1881, however, its business domain was changed from the sea to the land. The second president Yanosuke then united shipbuilding, mining and banking lines of business to start again, and laid down the foundation of Mitsubishi zaibatsu. On the other hand, Kihachiro Ohkura founded Ohkura & Company which was later reorganized to be two enterprises, i.e., Ohkura Civil Engineering Co. engaged in construction contracting business and Ohkura & Co., Ltd. conducting a trading line of business and managing investment in a group of affiliated companies. With these two pillars, Ohkura pushed ahead with its business. During the two war times, in particular, it showed its genuine ability of procurement for the military and increasingly grew. When World War II came to an end, however, Mitsubishi and Ohkura followed altogether a different route. That is, Mitsubishi continued to do its business and to grow further after the war while Ohkura collapsed with the end of the war and fell into obscurity.

Having pursued the primary cause of the difference between Mitsubishi's success and Ohkura's failure, we have traced historically how the cultures of Mitsubishi and Ohkura had evolved and developed respectively. It was found then that the culture of Mitsubishi was fully adaptive to the 3-Layer Structure of Enterprise Competitiveness and the 7 Principles of Enterprise Competitiveness as at the end of World War II while that of Ohkura showed its unadaptability to them. In Mitsubishi's culture, we can see Yomigaeri, an attribute of the Kami Way. It seems to have stemmed from Mitsubishi's reviving at the turn of its business from the sea to the land in 1886 when Mitsubishi completely discarded its government-affiliated disposition to follow the business-first principle and the principle of nonintervention in politics. Mitsubishi also had such a way of thinking that one is to observe justice in commerce and industry, be fair and win success with genuine efforts, not yielding to any failure. Here, Akaki-kokoro, an attribute of the Kami Way, can be recognized. The culture of Mitsubishi is fundamentally of two layers. The first layer formed by 1893 when Mitsubishi & Co., Ltd. was founded, and the second layer was created by the fourth president Koyata Iwasaki and his followers. Those two layers had been reinforced, consolidated and succeeded up to the end of World War II in 1945, when it was still acting. It could then continued to contribute to the development of Mitsubishi companies. On the other hand, the culture of Ohkura was generally healthy when it was primarily engaged in trading activities after having founded Ohkura & Company based on Kihachiro's knowledge of European and American commerce and industry. Later, through the two great wars of the Sino-Japanese War (1894-1895) and the Russo-Japanese War (1904-1905), Kihachiro achieved a substantial success as a government-affiliated businessman whereby the second layer of Ohkura's culture formed. At this stage, the initial first layer was still alive although it considerably weakened. Through World War I, however, he won a great success with his connection to the military, which in turn caused the first layer to be extinct and the second layer to replace it and deeply take root at Ohkura instead. The culture had been maintained until World War II was brought to an end, and Ohkura was ultimately dissolved as described before.

A government-affiliated businessperson carries out their business in league with the government officials and the military. They put themself in the government's position or the military's, but not in the public's position. That is, they do not try to learn from the general public. Accordingly, they are inevitably inclined to act arbitrarily on their own authority. The undertaking of Honkeikoh Coal & Steel Co., Ltd. was a good example. It is, in this context, the rule-by-virtue principle in Confucianism that was prevalently advocated by the government and the military. The rule-by-virtue principle by its nature underrates craftsmen and technology. There was, therefore, essentially a limit to rational management at Honkeikoh Coal & Steel Co., Ltd. since it was a joint concern of Ohkura with Shenyang Province authorities. To put it further, that limit is also the limit of Kihachiro Ohkura as a government-affiliated businessman.

8 Case Study:
W. L. Gore & Associates, Inc.

In Chapter 6 and Chapter 7, we have discussed the cases of healthy and unhealthy corporate culture and traced historically how they evolved and formed respectively. We have learned by that examination that a company with healthy culture may turn into that of unhealthy one, a company whose culture has turned unhealthy may revive or remain unhealthy, and so forth. Corporate culture takes many ways of formation and development. A firm is a living being and therefore it seems natural that its culture may change. Accordingly, a firm with a healthy culture ought to be modest and sincere while a company with an unhealthy one should understand that it could possibly transform its culture into the right one with genuine efforts. One can judge whether a company's culture is healthy or unhealthy by its adaptability to the 3-Layer Structure of Enterprise Competitiveness and the 7 Principles of Enterprise Competitiveness. It is of great consequence, therefore, for business leaders to see how their culture is adaptive or unadapted to the 3-Layer Structure of Enterprise Competitiveness and the 7 Principles of Enterprise Competitiveness.

Times change. Information technology, among others, has shown remarkable development recently. The future society, whose infrastructure will evidently be worked out with IT, is just around the corner. In that sense, it is meaningful to see what company can stay competitive and healthy in the coming years. In the author's opinion, it is the thought on the Internet that presents us a clue to the leading corporate culture in the 21st century. The ways of viewing, modes of thinking and state of being around the Internet give us a significant suggestion as to how a firm is to live in the next century. Along such a line of argument, we shall first take up the Internet and explain how to interpret it, and then, see W. L. Gore & Associates, Inc. as a typical example of corporate organization adapted to the lines of thought on the Internet.

8.1 Thought on the Internet

As is well known, the Internet is a large-scale network. It has so highly developed as to unite computers around the globe. What sustains such a scale is its setup of decentralization. The Internet is such big a network that any centralized setup, with its core somewhere to control the whole system, can not be appropriate for its operation. It is an open network that successively associates and aggregates a number of networks dispersed around the world into it. The Internet is not, however, in a state of no control. As S. E. Gillett and M. Kapor argue, the Internet is operated 99 percent in a decentralized way and 1 percent in an administered manner. In other words, it is by analogy an organization whose operation is 99 percent decentralized and 1 percent administered. It is like organization where the manager transfers 99 percent of work to qualified employees and carries out the remaining 1 percent on their own. That is, daily activities comprising 99 percent of the Internet organization's work are conducted by its qualified members while the exceptional 1 percent of work is done by the manager such as of initiating the system, integrating new activities when coming into the system and so on (S. E. Gillett and M. Kapor, 1997). Since 99 percent of its operation is decentralized, the Internet can be seen to run as a decentralized organization. The technical design that is embedded in the Internet makes such a decentralized operation feasible. On the other hand, the part analogous to the 1 percent of manager's work is carried out by several organizations as will be described later. To understand appropriately such a model of a decentralized organization, we shall first examine the decentralized operation and then the administered operation.

99 percent decentralized operation

The Internet stemmed from a network experiment conducted by the Advanced Research Project Agency (ARPA) in 1969. Later, in early 1970, ARPA set up a mutual networking program to thoroughly examine two basic network design alternatives. One had a central control function in the system like the telephone network where a number of networks are connected. The other had loosely united independently managed networks. ARPA selected the latter. By this selection, it was made a prerequisite for ARPA's setup that individual networks were to be autonomous and independent. In addition, a network design for the interoperability of individual networks was to be secured. That is, ARPA's selection was to achieve the interoperability of individual networks while sustaining their autonomy and independence. The above choice was made in anticipation of the expansion of the network scale. When its scale goes beyond a certain threshold point, the decentralized operation and autonomy of individual networks are certain to be indispensable. To put it another way, if the setup could not be designed to expand like cell division, it would not adapt itself to an ever-increasing size. How, then, was such a design developed and implanted?

It was initially developed by researchers who were offered funds for it by the government. They developed basic protocols such as Internet Protocol and Transmission Control Protocol. Those protocols later came to be employed by computer scientists all around the world and thus deeply implanted in the Internet. There are several reasons for TCP/IP above, which is an intermediary language commonly used by computers, to have become universally employed. The first reason is that the developers had no intention of marketing it. It was not a commercial product like IBM's SNA, Digital's DECENT and Xerox's XNS. The second is that the design of TCP/IP was not oriented towards specific vendors. The third is that whoever wished to employ TCP/IP was permitted to use it for nothing. This open standard of Internet Protocol has been accepted by almost all computer operators, and therefore, the interoperability among different computers has been realized. The Internet Protocol is designed not to curb the development of a newer, faster, better and cheaper physical network. On the basic layer of TCP/IP, HTTP forms a layer which assumes the role of delivering Web pages. HTTP is also an open standard. Every application developer can build a new application software on the layers of TCP/IP and HTTP. That is, the Internet Protocol is a fundamental building block, designed to be oriented to the needs of specific applications and to be supplemented by still higher levels of protocol. There is a business environment here which is open and has little barrier to the development of new applications. To put it another way, the Internet is so set up as to make competitive innovation and value creation much more feasible than the conventional, vertically integrated communication system. There is no central authority or authorities, here, to force the developers to use a specific protocol. There is no unified control or rule. Whoever participates in the Internet is esteemed as an individual. The Internet Protocol discriminates, in no way, users from providers, i.e., Internet connecting service providers. If a computer runs IP, it can render various application services working on IP. IP helps users choose whatever role they wish to take. It is at a user's disposal to decide whether they remain as a user or offer services of networking, applications or contents to others. Such individual's freedom in choosing a role has promoted entrepreneurial dynamism and made information on the Internet abundant and diverse.

Another aspect of Internet design, in addition to that of interoperability, is that the system has no single point which may lead to its overall defect. The system was to be set up so that if a component of it fails, others still work effectively. For that reason, the design of Internet Protocol keeps any 'chief' network from appearing. The Internet is positioned as a colleague network in contrast to a standard center-oriented system like the national telephone network. The linkage to the Internet is carried out by thousands of independent connecting providers in a decentralized fashion. The Internet is a mutually interconnected and decentralized network. Its customers have alternatives of how to use it. It also has a redundancy characteristic. There are a number of routes available in linking one point with another. There are roundabout routes as well as direct ones. This redundancy feature makes the Internet more dependable. If one line fails, a number of others can be employed.

Taken together, what renders the Internet 99 percent operated in a decentralized way is the interoperability founded on IP, colleague networking, and the redundancy characteristic which keeps the system working when a single component fails. Here, people participating in the Internet are respected as colleagues; the autonomy and individuality are sustained of linked networks; there is no control or rule; and everyone can be a leading actor. The Internet is, on the other hand, 1 percent operated in an administered fashion.

1 percent administered operation

As stated previously, the Internet started with the network experiment by ARPA. Since then, the network developed consistently for computer scientists to use. Once software has been developed, others can make use of it to develop other software. Therefore, if people hold some software products in common or exchange one software with another to develop new ones, it would be greatly conducive to their development work. In fact, computer scientists preferred to work under such an environment, and ARPA's network offered just that. Later, in 1989, ARPA was absorbed into the National Science Foundation and renamed the NSF network. The NSF network was composed of the core network of nationwide linkage named the 'backbone' and local networks. When the NFS network was set up, the principle was made that the local networks were to be successively privatized and the backbone was in the end to be discontinued. All the local networks came to be run by private firms while the NFS network ceased to exist in 1994. By abolishment of the NFS network, the remaining setup of networks, the Internet, had no core network and came to be an aggregate of decentralized networks. How, then, is the Internet operated?

As explained before, 99 percent of its operation is carried out in a decentralized way. Decentralization is the single largest attribute of the Internet. On the other hand, 1 percent of administered operation covers work such as making minimum rules, integrating new activities into the system when they come out, and so on. It is the Internet Engineering Task Force (IETF) that determines the principle and detailed matters of Internet technology at present. IETF now comprises about 3,000 engineers who mutually exchange information and opinions by e-mail. It holds meetings three times a year. IETF was founded as a non-profit, US government-funded research organization. Even now, it is granted $ 1.5 million annually by the National Science Foundation, a US government agency. That amount of money, however, is extremely small as compared with the working time and travel expenses spent by those who participate in IETF activities. IETF is assumed to be in charge of the development of Internet Protocol. It does not mean, however, that it is a kind of monopoly engaged in developing Internet standards. Whatever protocol can be a de facto standard if it is employed broadly. It is possible for any company to invent a new protocol on its own and render it a universal standard through its

166

marketing talent. Sun's development of NSF and Netscape's HTML are the good examples. Accordingly, IETF pays little regard to the foundation of standards on the levels of physical communication and software application. Instead, it concentrates its efforts on the affairs of interoperability between physical communication systems or software applications. IETF's concern is IP, routing protocols working with IP, utilities to translate users' names into IP addresses, functions needed between IP and dissimilar physical infrastructures (e.g., how to render IP working on ATM, mobile networks or a dial-up line), and so forth.

Another significant group in operating the Internet, along with IETF, is the Internet Assigned Numbers Authority (IANA). IANA refers to a group who work at Information Science Institute, University of Southern California, under the direction of Jon Postel. Their main function is to study networking for which a subsidy is granted by the US government. IANA has three Network Information Centers (NIC) as its subordinate organizations. They are APNIC in the Asia-Pacific region, RIPE NCC in Europe and the InterNIC in the United States. Those organizations make an allotment of protocol parameters. The protocol parameters are of 2 kinds. One is IP addresses for computers which are significant for connecting providers, and the other is a domain name which has a meaning to users like a trademark. Let us first explain the IP address. A user, who wants to link their network to the Internet, first applies to an Internet connecting provider to obtain a unique and guaranteed IP address for its linkage. Typically, a provider has one block of addresses out of which they can allot an address to a user. Such a block of addresses is, in turn, apportioned to the provider from Regional Internet Registries (RIRs). Accordingly, providers located in Europe apply to RIPE NCC for a block of addresses, those in the Asia-Pacific region to APNIC and those in the United States and other regions to the InterNIC. RIPE NCC and APNIC are Internet service organizations run and funded by a consortium of Internet connecting providers in their respective region. The InterNIC is operated with funds both from the National Science Foundation in the US and from the fee imposed on users for commercial domain names, i.e., '.com', which it administers. In this context, the ultimate supplier, which allocates a chunk of addresses to RIRs, is IANA. IANA makes its allotment to RIRs every two to three months. As can be imagined, the mechanism of IP address allotment is now founded on mutual confidence among people concerned. In fact, this trust-base mechanism has been efficient and effective. Since commercial networks rapidly increase on the Internet, a severe pressure is now imposed on the mechanism of allotting IP address resources. However, as far as Internet service providers collaborate with IANA/RIRs, the mechanism seems to continue to work well.

Now, let us next account for the domain name. To assign a domain name to users is technically simpler than allocating addresses to them. The domain

167

name is visible and has meaning to users. From users' point of view, to obtain a domain name is like getting an IP address. Most users apply for domain names through Internet connecting providers. However, domain names are not part of a limited space like IP addresses and providers have no fixed allotment. Users apply for a given domain name to providers who, in turn, only transfer their application to an appropriate Internet naming registry. The Top Level Domains, which are the most fundamental domains, are broadly classified into two lines. One line is of national domains like '.au' for Austria, and the other is of international domains such as '.com, .edu, .net, .org'. The national domains are administered by each nation's universities, telephone companies or government agencies. As to the international domains, RIPE NCC in Europe and APNIC in the Asia-Pacific region do not administer them, and when requested, they transfer them to appropriate registries although they run a naming server for the backup. In North America, however, they are administered by the InterNIC. Once it issues Top Level Domains (TLD) based on the Domain Name System to an organization outside, the InterNIC transfers their administrative responsibility to that organization. Due to the remarkable growth of the '.com' domain, however, the workload has become such that in 1995 the InterNIC began to levy $50 on '.com' users as an annual maintenance fee of their register to supplement NSF fund which it is officially granted.

As described above, IETF is primarily concerned in the technical interoperability of the Internet, and IANA and RIRs are engaged or concerned in the allotment of IP addresses and domain names. In that way, the 1 percent of Internet operation is administered. The agencies concerned are, however, not central authority figures but rather act as coordinators. Since they act as coordinators throughout, the diversity and openness of the Internet is sustained.

Summary

The Internet is a model of decentralized organization. The members of the Internet organization can collaborate with each other while sustaining their autonomy and individuality. Interoperability is assured among the members' computers by the Internet basic protocol of TCP/IP. That is, only with Internet Protocol in common, the members can freely develop new applications and create new values. The Internet, also, has no chief network acting as a foundation. There are a number of alternative routes in going from one point to another, and due to that redundancy characteristic, any defect occurring somewhere in the Internet does not affect the other parts. The Internet is referred to as colleague networking where everyone is provided an equal opportunity to play whatever role in it and can be a leading actor of communication. Thus, with the interoperability founded on TCP/IP, the colleague networking and the redundancy characteristic as given, the Internet is 99 percent operated in a decentralized fashion. On the other hand, there is IETF as a group technically supporting the present interoperability and devising still newer ways of interoperability for the future. There is also IANA and RIRs which are engaged or concerned in the allotment of IP addresses and domain names. Those agencies are positioned not as a monopoly of operating the Internet, but rather as a coordinating organ. They are coordinators of the decentralized organization of the Internet, and as previously stated, their work seems to be so small as to be about 1 percent of the whole operation. In that way, the Internet is 99 percent operated in a decentralized manner and 1 percent operated in an administered way (S. E. Gillett and M. Kapor, 1997).

8.2 W. L. Gore & Associates, Inc.

In this section, we shall take up W. L. Gore & Associates, Inc., a R&D-oriented firm in the United States. The reason that we take up this company is not only that it has a typical healthy corporate culture but that its culture has much in common with the thought on the Internet as described in the previous section. To put it another way, W. L. Gore & Associates, Inc. can be seen as a company that would be realized if we would follow the thought on the Internet and try to create a business organization. The thought on the Internet gives us many suggestions as to how a corporate organization is to be in the 21st century. Accordingly, we can learn much from such a firm that literally develops those suggestions into reality. In that sense, W. L. Gore & Associates, Inc. is taken as a forerunner of 21st century firms.

Foundation of W.L. Gore & Associates, Inc.

Wilbert L. Gore, founder of W. L. Gore & Associates, Inc., originally worked for Du Pont as a member of the R&D team on a new material PTFE (generally called Teflon). During his research and development work, he discovered that PTFE had insulator characteristics making it appropriate for computers and transistors. He then conducted several experiments, making ribbon cable coated with PTFE, but did not really succeed. He continued experiments at a private laboratory in the basement at home. One day, he mentioned the experiment to his son, Bob, who proposed trying a seamed tape of PTFE made by 3M. In the beginning, W. L. Gore adhered to the common sense then that a tape of PTFE could not be tied with another tape of PTFE, but at last tried to challenge that common sense. After a number of trials, he succeeded in his experiment and turned out a ribbon cable treated with PTFE. For about four months after the success of this experiment, W. L. Gore continued to ask Du Pont to develop a new product out of the ribbon cable treated with PTFE. Du Pont, however, firmly held on to the basic policy of staying in the domain of materials' supplier and had no intention of going beyond that domain to launch into any application field. As a result, W. L. Gore determined to start his own business. In January 1959, W. L. Gore and Genevieve Gore, his wife, founded a company named W. L. Gore & Associates, Inc. in the basement at home. For W. L. Gore, it was a change from a salaried man at Du Pont, where he had worked for 17 years, to an entrepreneur. For several years after its foundation, he had substantial difficulties trying to raise funds and developing products to be accepted on the market. At last, however, he won a contract for 100,000 dollars and thus got out of those difficulties in the days of the foundation of the company.

The lattice organization structure

Since then, the business at W. L. Gore & Associates, Inc. went on successfully. In 1965, the company had a factory with about 200 employees in Newark, Delaware. One day when W. L. Gore went around the factory, he realized that he did not know everyone there. If a group becomes too large, the unity of its members is inclined to weaken. Thus, he worked out a principle of growth saying 'Get big by staying small'. That is, the principle indicates that a new factory to be built from then on ought not to have more than 150 to 200 personnel. Also, when the number of personnel at the existing factory goes beyond that limit, it is to be divided into two factories.

W. L. Gore & Associates, Inc. is a firm of no organizational stratum. Although the president and the secretary and accountant are at the top of the organization, all the personnel are referred to as associate. It is taboo at W. L. Gore & Associates, Inc. to call the company's personnel employee, subordinate and administrator. W. L. Gore thought that hierarchy keeps an individual from showing their creativity. He was also convinced that everyone has a creative ability. Hence, the lattice organization structure was devised. It is shown as in Figure 8.1 (C. C. Mantz and H. P. Sims, Jr., 1993, p139).

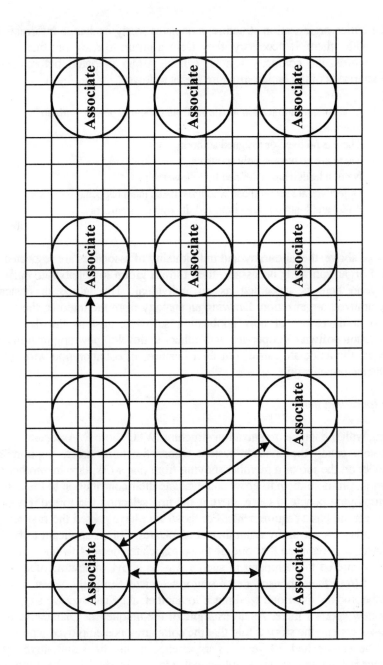

Figure 8.1 The Lattice Structure

In the lattice organization structure, associates freely exchange information and ideas with others. If necessary, they form a group to carry out their work. In other words, the company has no official group prepared beforehand. The characteristics of the lattice structure are as follows.

1　Lines of communication are direct from person to person, with no intermediary.
2　There is no fixed or assigned authority.
3　There are no bosses, only sponsors.
4　Natural leadership is defined by followership.
5　Objectives are set by those who must make them happen.
6　Tasks and functions are organized through commitments.

(Ibid. p138)

As seen above, the autonomy and individuality of associates are respected in the lattice organization. If necessary, they form a group to collaborate each other. Everyone here is esteemed as an individual. The lattice is basically a decentralized organization. Drawing an analogy from the Internet, the associate is like a developer of new application software. Just as the developer of application software cooperates with others to develop new applications on the Internet, the associate carries out their business in collaboration with others in the lattice organization.

The sponsor system

Along with the lattice organization structure, W. L. Gore & Associates, Inc. has a system called the sponsor system whose functions are to support a new member on the job or a member moving from one workplace to another on the new job, promote them to grow and evaluate their contribution to the company. In employing people at Gore, there is the first selection test to see if applicants can meet the basic requirements. For those who have passed the first test, there is an interview set up by a number of associates. For an applicant to be finally selected, it is required that one of those associates decides to undertake them. Having entered the company in such a way as above, a new member receives support from their sponsor, i.e., a senior associate. Similarly, when an existing member moves from one workplace to another, they can receive support from their new sponsor there. As an example of the uniqueness characteristic of the sponsor system, the story is told that the company once employed a person aged 84. The person had 30 years of experience in his field and there were no associates then against his employment. He had worked for the company for five years. In such a way, people of a variety of backgrounds are brought in at Gore. The sponsorship is of three kinds.

1   The sponsor who helps a new associate get started on the job or helps an associate get started on a new job (starting sponsor).
2   The sponsor who sees to it that the associate being sponsored gets credit and recognition for contributions and accomplishments (advocate sponsor).
3   The sponsor who sees to it that the associate being sponsored is fairly paid for their contributions to the success of the enterprise (compensation sponsor).

(Ibid. p136)

The three sponsor roles above are played either by three sponsors or all by one sponsor. Drawing an analogy from the Internet, here, the sponsor role 1 above is like the provider. Just as the provider gives support to a new participant in the Internet, the sponsor supports a new member of the company.

The compensation system

The compensation system at W. L. Gore & Associates, Inc. takes three forms. The first one is salary, the second is profit sharing and the third is an associates' stock option program (ASOP). The ASOP is legally almost the same as ESOP plan. An associate's salary is usually reviewed twice a year. The review is made by the compensation review committee consisting of some personnel from the factory where the associate works. The associate has a sponsor acting as their advocate during the review process. The sponsor collects data on the associate's performance on the basis of which they can support them. As to the profit sharing, the rule is set to make part of the company's profit shared among associates twice a year. It is awarded to each associate depending on their annual salary and years of service at the company. W. L. Gore & Associates, Inc. also makes it a rule to purchase its stocks equivalent in amount to 15 percent of each associate's annual income and hold them as a reserve for their retirement allowance. The ASOP is so designed that each associate may feel that they are an owner of the company and identify themselves with it.

The lattice organization structure and the support team

The lattice organization at Gore is truly effective as united with the sponsor system and the compensation system. W.L. Gore said,

Every successful organization has an underground lattice. It's where the news spreads like lightning, where people can go round the organization to get things done.

(Ibid. p138)

In the lattice organization, everyone can form a team with people from different

173

fields if it is necessary to accomplish their work. Each associate can form a group with people different in function, skill and knowledge. On the other hand, there is the support team of 30 to 40 people at Gore who facilitates the lattice organization to work well. The support team holds meetings periodically twice a year and plays the role of adjusting the company's marketing, sales and production plans. It is the minimum organ needed for the lattice organization to duly function. In other words, the support team corresponds to such co-ordination groups as IETF, IANA and RIRs of the Internet. Just as those co-ordination groups comprise the minimum organ for the decentralized organization to be effective, the support team at Gore works as the minimum adjusting mechanism. The support team is the co-ordinator in the decentralized organization of Gore.

Many leaders

As can be inferred from the characteristics of the lattice organization described so far, there are many leaders at Gore. According to W. L. Gore, there are 10 types of leaders there.

1 The Associate who is recognized by a team as having a special knowledge or experience (for example, this could be a chemist, computer expert, machine operator, salesman, engineer, lawyer). This kind of leader gives the team guidance in a special area.

2 The Associate the team looks to for coordination of individual activities in order to achieve the agreed-upon objects of the team. The role of this leader is to persuade team members to make the commitments necessary for success (commitment seeker).

3 The Associate who proposes necessary objectives and activities and seeks agreement and team consensus on objectives. This leader is perceived by the team members as having a good grasp of how the objectives of the team fit in with the broad objective of the enterprise. This kind of leader is often also the commitment seeking leader in 2 above.

4 The leader who evaluates relative contribution of team members (in consultation with other sponsors), and reports these contribution evaluations to a compensation committee. This leader may also participate in the compensation committee on relative contribution and pay and reports changes in compensation to individual Associates. This leader is then also a compensation sponsor.

5 The leader who coordinates the research, manufacturing and marketing of one product type within a business, interacting with team leaders and individual Associates who have commitments regarding the product type. These leaders

are usually called product specialists. They are respected for their knowledge and dedication to their products.

6 Plant leaders who help coordinate activities of people within a plant.
7 Business leaders who help coordinate activities of people in a business.
8 Functional leaders who help coordinate activities of people in a functional area.
9 Corporate leaders who help coordinate activities of people in different businesses and functions and who try to promote communication and cooperation among all Associates.
10 Intrapreneuring Associates who organize new teams for new businesses, new products, new processes, new devices, new marketing efforts, new or better methods of all kinds. These leaders invite other Associates to sign up for their project.

(Ibid. pp140-141)

The above types of leader roles are respectively undertaken by associates in the lattice organization. The associates undertaking leader roles, however, may change, and some associates perform more than one role. The types of leaders are of such a variety as above that associates have many alternative roles to play. The lattice organization, thus, promotes entrepreneurial dynamism at Gore, and, as W.L. Gore said, the communication among associates spreads like lightning and goes around the organization. It is just like the colleague networking characteristic of the Internet that everyone can be a leading actor of communication.

A crisis in 1975

The lattice organization structure has been tried a number of times in the history of Gore. The first large crisis occurred in 1975. The company's main line of product is 'Gore-Tex', a group of PTFE products used in such fields as of electronics, fiber, industrial equipment and medical treatment. As to the medical treatment, it was initially used as an arterial graft in patients at a hospital affiliated with the University of Pittsburgh. One day, however, Dr. Charles Cambell at the hospital discovered that it had an adverse side effect. That is, the Gore-Tex product caused one of the patients treated with it develop an aneurysm. The situation demanded, therefore, an urgent and timely solution. A few days after the report was made of such an adverse side effect, Dr. C. Cambell flew to Newark, and explained his discovery in more details to W. L. Gore, his son Bob Gore and a few associates. Then, Bill Hubis, one of the associates who listened to Dr. C. Cambell, hit upon a plan and left his seat. He and his colleagues tried new methods of its production. They spent three hours conducting 12 tests and finally found out a fundamental solution to that problem. The redesigned Gore-Tex arterial graft, having followed the fundamental solution then, is now broadly used among medical institutions. W. L. Gore stated.

> I'm told from time to time that a lattice organization can't meet a crisis well because it takes too long to reach a consensus when there are no bosses. But this isn't true. Actually, a lattice, by its name, works particularly well in a crisis. A lot of useless effort is avoided because there is no rigid management hierarchy to conquer before you can attack a problem.

(Ibid. pp146-147)

Having gone through the severe test above in 1975, people at Gore strengthened their confidence in the lattice. That is, the core thought around the lattice organization came to be deeply embedded in the mind of Gore people.

A crisis in 1978

At Gore there are 4 principles that associates abide by.

1 Try to be fair.
2 Use your freedom to grow.
3 Make your own commitments and keep them.
4 Consult with other associates prior to any action that may adversely affect the reputation or financial stability of the company.

(Ibid. p136)

The four principles above are referred to as fairness, freedom, commitment and waterline. Out of those principles, the waterline stems from the draft of a ship. If there is some hole above the waterline, the ship is in little danger. With a hole below that line, it is exposed to serious danger. As to a business organization, therefore, it would be put to a test when it goes below its waterline, i.e., its critical line of situation. In other words, associates at Gore can easily make their decision on whatever matters unless they are something critical for the organization. In fact, almost all of the daily work is of such a nature. The thing is, therefore, how associates can cope with a critical situation. W. L. Gore & Associates, Inc. suffered such a test in 1978. Gore-Tex was highly evaluated then for its good quality, and its sales were increasingly rising in the leisure and outdoor markets. It so happened, however, that some of the products shipped were leaking. That news immediately spread over the markets, and a large quantity of the products were returned. Since the success of Gore-Tex was primarily due to its waterproof nature, its reputation at once fell off. Peter W. Gilson, who led the fabric division at W. L. Gore & Associates, Inc. then, says.

176

It was an incredible crisis for us at that time. We were starting attract attention, we were taking off...and then this.

(Ibid. p137)

They spent a few months trying to find out the cause of such leakage. In the end, they determined that it was caused by certain oils in human sweat. They proposed, therefore, that the product ought to be washed well after its use. By good washing, they thought, the water proof nature can be restored. This solution is known as the 'Ivory Snow solution'. Later, however, a letter arrived from a mountain guide saying,

My parka leaked and my wife was in danger. (Ibid. p137)

The Ivory Snow solution proved to be useless. Having looked back on it, Peter W. Gilson says,

That scared the hell out of us. Clearly our solution was no solution at all to someone on a mountain top.

(Ibid. p137)

All the products were called back at Gore. The products on the shelf, in the manufacturing process and in the distribution channels were all called back. Then, a fundamental solution was pursued with every effort and, finally, the second generation Gore-Tex was developed. All the leaky parkas were exchanged with the new ones for which the outlay reached around 4 million dollars. Lessons drawn from this crisis were that one ought to earnestly listen to whatever voice from the market and sincerely deal with customers' claim. In addition to the above 4 principles, therefore, a principle of serving customers with sincerity and integrity may have taken root then in the mind of associates at W. L. Gore & Associates, Inc. To put it another way, this crisis taught them a lesson that they ought to pay due regard to the customers outside while they innovatively and effectively work on the lattice organization. It means much, therefore, that Gore weathered the crisis of 1978. Gore's culture, which gradually formed since its foundation, may have been further consolidated through the grave difficulties in 1978 and embedded deeply in its organization.

Innovation and Creativity

W. L. Gore passed away in 1986 when he was chairman and his son, Bob Gore, held office as president at the company. Since then, Bob has stayed in office as president and his mother Genevieve as secretary and accountant. All the other members of the company are associates. Therefore, there is no title other than

177

associate at Gore. Among outsiders, however, there are those who are particular about one's title. The story has been told at Gore, in this context, that Sarah Clifton, an associate at the Flagstaff factory, fixed her title 'Supreme Commander' and had it printed on business cards.

W. L. Gore & Associates, Inc. has successively developed PTFE-based products. It now consists of 4 lines of business, i.e., of electronics, medical instrument, fiber and industrial equipment, and manufactures a variety of products. In 1992, the company had 44 factories around the world where 5,300 associates were working. Out of the 44 factories, 27 were in the United States while 17 were scattered in Scotland, Germany, France, Japan and India. W. L. Gore & Associates, Inc. has no parking zone for directors' exclusive use as other firms although it has a parking lot for customers' and physically handicapped persons' use. At each factory, there is only one dining hall for everyone to use. As to the education, associates are offered diverse opportunities. Within the firm, there is a leadership development program as well as technical and engineering education. Outside it, there is an opportunity of education tied up with universities and other institutions whose expense is mostly born by the company. In case of a new member, they move from workplace to workplace until they find a job suited to them. During such a probationary period, they can gather information on the various jobs. When employed in sales, they take an education program prepared for sales people covering 6 months and then get to work. W. L. Gore & Associates, Inc. is a R&D-oriented firm with over 150 patents. The company does not have, however, any particular research and development department. Everyone can make experiments employing the PTFE material, and there is the belief that every associate has creative ability. It seems that the innovative and creative ability of each associate is displayed well at Gore. In 1985, W. L. Gore said.

> The creativity, the number of patent applications and innovative products is triple that of Du Pont.

(Ibid. p146)

As stated previously, how to display the leadership is the key to the effective operation of the lattice organization structure. Accordingly, the company helps an associate to think on their own and act in their own way to the utmost. Everyone is encouraged to work in a creative and innovative way at Gore.

Summary

The lattice organization structure is characteristic of W. L. Gore & Associates, Inc. It is a form of decentralized organization where its members can take any leadership role and act autonomously. On the other hand, there is the support team which works as co-ordinator for the organization to duly function. The team members hold meetings twice a year to adjust the company's marketing, sales and production plans. Here, we can see the same thought as that on the decentralized organization model of the Internet which is 99 percent operated in a decentralized manner and 1 percent operated in an administered fashion. That is, most activities at Gore are carried out in a decentralized and autonomous way and only the minimum function is left to the support team. How can, then, the associates comprising the lattice communicate and interchange information between them? It is the sponsor system that facilitates their communication and interchange. By analogy, the role of the sponsor corresponds to that of the provider or that of Internet Protocol. With the sponsor system as given, the lattice organization is 99 percent operated in a decentralized fashion. The lattice organization structure is a colleague network. It is taboo at Gore, therefore, to call its members employee, subordinate and administrator. Hierarchy is here thought to keep an individual from displaying their creativity. Associates are encouraged to work, like an application developer on the Internet, in a creative and innovative way in the open, barrierless work environment of the lattice organization. Everyone is a leading actor. Everyone can take the leadership in whatever matters, and the information among associates spreads like lightning on the lattice organization and goes around it. This organization is of no stratum, where everyone is respected as an individual. It works as a mechanism that promotes entrepreneurial dynamism and makes innovation and value creation feasible as in the Internet.

Taken together, W. L. Gore & Associates, Inc. is considered to be a form of enterprise realized out of virtually the same thought as that on the Internet. The company fundamentally has the ways of viewing, modes of thinking and state of being in common with the Internet. In that sense, it gives us many suggestions as to a corporate organization in the 21st century.

Gore's culture and the competitiveness elements

Finally, then, let us see how W. L. Gore & Associates, Inc. is adaptive to the 3-Layer Structure of Enterprise Competitiveness and the 7 Principles of Enterprise Competitiveness. We shall look into its adaptability competitiveness element by competitiveness element.

Ethos originated in the early days of an enterprise, i.e., the spirit of denying, the spirit of negating the status quo, the spirit of creativity and the spirit of creating a vision, are maintained W. L. Gore & Associates, Inc. is a firm founded by W. L. Gore in 1959. What made him decide to found this company is primarily that he had succeeded in producing the ribbon cable treated with PTFE. In the beginning, he adhered to the common sense that a tape of PTFE could not be

179

tied with another tape of PTFE. He was therefore hesitant to use a seamed tape of PTFE made by 3M, but at last tried to challenge that common sense and succeeded in the experiment to turn out a ribbon cable treated with PTFE. Since then, Gore's business went on successfully. In 1978, however, it was found out on the market that a line of Gore-Tex product had a defect of leakage, and a large quantity of the products were returned. They thought that the leakage was due to some oil in human sweat. Therefore, they proposed that the product ought to be washed well after its use. Later, however, that proved no solution to a mountain climber. Accordingly, they made all-out efforts to develop a completely waterproof product and finally created the second generation Gore-Tex by which they could fundamentally solved the problem. Thus, their spirit of creativity and innovation was confirmed then at Gore.

Every member is willing to grapple with any situation without hesitation and without worrying about failure The lattice organization structure has been tried a number of times in the history of W. L. Gore & Associates, Inc. It was put to a most severe test in 1975. At the hospital affiliated with the University of Pittsburgh, they employed Gore-Tex as an arterial graft to patients. It happened, however, that one of the patients treated with the arterial graft of Gore-Tex developed an aneurysm. The doctor in charge immediately came over to the Newark factory and held a meeting with W. L. Gore, his son Bob Gore and a few associates. In the middle of the meeting, an associate, who hit upon a plan, left his seat and with his colleagues tried to improve and rectify the method of Gore-Tex production. They spent three hours conducting 12 experiments on it, and finally found out a fundamental solution to the problem.

There is teamwork among personnel At Gore, associates work in collaboration with others on the lattice organization structure. How an associate displays the leadership is the key to the effective operation of the organization. Accordingly, there are many types of leadership roles at Gore out of which associates can choose to form a group.

Personnel have pride and confidence in upholding their enterprise's competitiveness and have a sense of representing their enterprise In the compensation system at Gore, there is the associates' stock option program (ASOP). It is the plan that the company periodically purchases its own stocks with funds equivalent in amount to 15 percent of each associate's annual income and keeps them as reserve for their retirement allowance. The ASOP is designed to heighten the workers' feeling that they are owners of the company and to help them have a sense of identity with it. On the other hand, the roles are so many for associates to perform that entrepreneurial dynamism can be facilitated.

Pride and confidence in one's own work As stated previously, there are many types of leaders at Gore. Out of the numerous leadership roles, an associate can choose one most suited to them. An associate finds out their job on their own. The job they choose is their own, not someone else's. There is no other person who can find out a job for them instead.

Self-reforming abilities As described previously, a large defect was discovered on the market in 1978. Until then, the Gore-Tex had been evaluated as a product of good quality and the associates had been very proud of it. Since the news on its defect at once spread over the market, however, the high evaluation of Gore-Tex fell off. Under such a circumstance, the associates did away with the conventional product, and concentrated on the development of a new impeccable product which the market truly demanded. The development work was tried a number of times, and at last the second generation Gore-Tex was successfully developed.

Promotion of R&D and production-process R&D W. L. Gore & Associates, Inc. is a R&D-oriented firm with over 150 patents. However, there is no particular department of research and development at Gore. Instead, opportunities are available to everyone who wishes to make experiments employing the PTFE material. There is the belief that every associate can be creative.

Investment in the training of personnel Associates are offered varied forms of education opportunities. Within the company, there is a leadership development program as well as technical and engineering education programs. The expenses needed for those programs are mostly born by the company.

Create smooth communication lines As W. L. Gore said, information spreads like lightning on the lattice organization structure, and thus the associates can immediately get the information needed to accomplish whatever matters to be done.

Diffuse new ideas, reforms, improvements, and intelligence on new products both inside and outside the organization On the lattice organization structure, information diffuses very quickly whereby entrepreneurial dynamism is facilitated. It is just like the colleague networking of the Internet where everyone can be a leading actor in communication.

Maintain a free market principle throughout the enterprise At Gore, an associate's salary is usually reviewed twice a year. The review is made by a compensation review committee consisting of some personnel from the factory the associate works for. The committee forms, as it were, the market for an appraisal of the associate's performance. During the review process, the associate has a sponsor acting as their advocate. The sponsor collects data on the associate's performance on the base of which to support them.

Have a close relationship with customers As stated before, it was made apparent in 1978 that the Gore-Tex had a large defect of leakage. In the beginning, the associates found that it was due to some oil in human sweat and therefore they proposed that the product was to be washed well after its use. However, a letter from a mountain guide came to smash that solution to pieces. The guide wrote, 'My parka leaked and my wife was in danger'. The initial solution proved useless for mountain climbers. At Gore, therefore, the new product development was tried over and again and at last the second generation Gore-Tex was materialized. Instructions drawn from this crisis were that the company ought to earnestly meet customers' claims and always serve them with sincerity and integrity.

Organizational techniques At Gore, there is a principle of growth saying 'Get big by staying small'. The principle means that the number of personnel at a factory is to be limited to 150 to 200 at the maximum. It is intended to keep the unity among personnel sustained at a factory. On the lattice organization structure, next, which is most characteristic of W. L. Gore & Associates, Inc., everyone can form a team with others in different fields. For any work to be carried out through such free group formation, there is the support team. As described before, the same thought can be recognized as that on the decentralized organization model of the Internet.

Organization whose workers are barely conscious of organizational hierarchy W. L. Gore & Associates, Inc. is an organization of no stratum. At the top of the organization there are president and his secretary, but all the other members are referred to as associate. There is no title but associate at Gore. Among outsiders, however, there are some who are particular about one's title. The story has been told, in this connection, that Sarah Clifton, an associate at the Flagstaff factory, fixed her title 'Supreme Commander' and had it printed on business cards. W. L. Gore & Associates, Inc. has no parking zone for directors' exclusive use as other companies. Instead, the company has a parking lot for customers' and physically handicapped persons' use. At each factory, there is only one dining hall for everyone's use.

Develop personnel's abilities and continue their learning Associates are offered diverse opportunities of education. Among them, there are opportunities of learning at universities or colleges tied up with the company. The expenses needed are almost all born by the firm.

182

Every member is a leading actor W. L. Gore thought that hierarchy keeps an individual from displaying their creative ability. He was also convinced that everyone can be creative. Hence, the lattice organization structure was contrived. Associates' autonomy and individuality are esteemed on the lattice organization structure. If necessary, they form a group to collaborate. Everyone here is respected as an individual.

Fair employment As a case typical of the sponsor system, the story has been told that a man aged 84 once worked for 5 years at Gore. He had 30 years' experience in his field and there was no associate against his employment. In such a way, people from diverse backgrounds are brought in at Gore.

Fair and just promotion of personnel The sponsor system consists of three kinds of sponsorship. The first is to help an associate start their job. The second is to appraise an associate's performance to back them up. The third is to see if an associate receives a compensation worth their contribution to the company. As stated previously, an associate's salary is reviewed twice a year. The review is made by a compensation review committee consisting of some personnel from the factory each associate works for. During the review process, an associate has the second kind of sponsor above who gathers data on the associate's performance to back them up.

In sum, the culture of W. L. Gore & Associates, Inc. is, as a whole, adapted to the 3-Layer Structure of Enterprise Competitiveness and the 7 Principles of Enterprise Competitiveness. It is shown in Table 8.1 and Table 8.2.

Table 8.1   The 3-Layer Structure of Enterprise Competitiveness

I   Enterprise Organismic Foundation

Enterprise ethos
- Ethos originated in the early days of an enterprise,   Adaptable
  i.e., the spirit of denying, the spirit of negating
  the status quo, the spirit of creativity and the spirit
  of creating a vision, are maintained.
- Every member is willing to grapple with any   Adaptable
  situation without hesitation and without worrying
  about failure.
- People in the workplace freely exchange
  their views and opinions.

Enhancement of initiative
- There is teamwork among personnel.   Adaptable

- Personnel have pride and confidence in   Adaptable
  upholding their enterprise's competitiveness
  and have a sense of representing
  their enterprise.
- Diligence and positive activities of personnel.
- Pride and confidence in one's own work.   Adaptable
- Self-reforming abilities.   Adaptable

Provision of norms
- Law (company regulations, etc.).
- Abolishment of practices restricting competition.

Preparation of investment conditions
- Allow a sufficiently long time frame
  for management.
- Promotion of R&D and production-process R&D.   Adaptable
- Constraints on speculative purchases of
  enterprises or assets.

Enterprise ethics
(Sense of responsibility to the society)

Education
(General learning as citizen of the society)

II   Enterprise Economic Base

Infrastructure
- Physical assets   facilities, machinery,
                        network.
- Human resources   executives, scientists,
                        engineers, workers.
- Employment of human resources and
  procurement of physical assets to build
  and stabilize infrastructure.
- Investment in the training of personnel.   Adaptable
- Education on practical business.

Environmental improvement and conservation
- Conservation of the natural environment.

- Cooperation with and participation in a community and its activities.
- Improvement of the physical environment of the workplace.
- Attention and care to human relations in the workplace.

Diffusion of new ideas, planning and others
- Create smooth communication lines.   Adaptable
- Discussion on the vision, policies and the state of affairs of the enterprise from management.
- Diffuse new ideas, reforms, improvements, and   Adaptable intelligence on new products both inside and outside the organization.

III   Management System

Effectiveness
- Maintain a free market principle throughout   Adaptable the enterprise.
- Encourage competitive spirit.
- Improve cost, quality and delivery terms simultaneously.
- Development, introduction and use of technology to gain strategic predominance.
- Commercialize technology.
- Activate communication throughout.

Tense balance between effectiveness and ethics
- Have a close relationship with customers.   Adaptable
- Have intimate contact with suppliers.
- Organizational techniques.   Adaptable
- Organization whose workers are barely   Adaptable conscious of organizational hierarchy.
- Recognition of quality as the end result of overall production and service activities.
- Generate many alternatives to a decision-making process.
- Demand and expect personnel to do their best.
- Cope with things flexibly.

185

- Develop personnel's abilities and continue their learning.   Adaptable
- Guarantee long-term employment.

Ethics
- Every member is a leading actor.   Adaptable
- A view of work in which diligence is highly esteemed.
- Improvement of ethics.
- Fair employment.   Adaptable
- Appropriate transfer of personnel from one post to another.
- Fair and just promotion of personnel.   Adaptable
- Ethics of relations between management and workers.

Table 8.2   The 7 Principles of Enterprise Competitiveness

1   Creativity
- Ethos originated in the early days of an enterprise,   Adaptable
  i.e., the spirit of denying, the spirit of negating
  the status quo, the spirit of creativity and the spirit
  of creating a vision, are maintained.
- Every member is willing to grapple with any   Adaptable
  situation without hesitation and without worrying
  about failure.
- Self-reforming abilities.   Adaptable

2   Righteousness
- Law (company regulations, etc.).
- Ethics of relations between management and workers.
- Abolishment of practices restricting competition.
- Constraints on speculative purchases of enterprises or assets.
- Enterprise ethics (Sense of responsibility to the society).
- A view of work in which diligence is highly esteemed.
- Improvement of ethics.

186

3 Fairness
   - Maintain a free market principle throughout
   the enterprise.   Adaptable
   - Encourage competitive spirit.
   - Fair employment.   Adaptable
   - Appropriate transfer of personnel from one
   post to another.
   - Fair and just promotion of personnel.   Adaptable

4 Equality
   - People in the workplace freely exchange
   their views and opinions.
   - There is teamwork among personnel.   Adaptable
   - Personnel have pride and confidence in   Adaptable
   upholding their enterprise's competitiveness
   and have a sense of representing their enterprise.
   - Organization whose workers are barely   Adaptable
   conscious of organizational hierarchy.
   - Recognition of quality as the end result
   of overall production or service activities.
   - Guarantee long-term employment.
   - Every member is a leading actor.   Adaptable

5 Sharing
   - Conservation of the natural environment.
   - Cooperation with and participation in
   a community and its activities.
   - Improvement of the physical environment of
   the workplace.
   - Attention and care to human relations in
   the workplace.
   - Create smooth communication lines.   Adaptable
   - Discussion on the vision, policies and the state of
   affairs of the enterprise from management.
   - Diffuse new ideas, reforms, improvements, and   Adaptable
   intelligence on new products both inside and
   outside the organization.
   - Activate communication throughout.
   - Have a close relationship with customers.   Adaptable
   - Have intimate contact with suppliers.

6   Self-Cultivation
     • Diligence and positive activities of personnel.
     • Pride and confidence in one's own work.   Adaptable
     • Demand and expect personnel to do their best.

7   Learning and Knowledge-Accumulation

Technology
     • Commercialize technology.
     • Development, introduction and use of technology
       to gain strategic predominance.
     • Promotion of R&D and production-process R&D.   Adaptable
     • Employment of human resources and
       procurement of physical assets to build
       and stabilize infrastructure.
     • Physical assets.
     • Human resources.

Systems thinking
     • Allow a sufficiently long time frame
       for management.
     • Generate many alternatives to
       a decision-making process.
     • Improve cost, quality and delivery terms
       simultaneously.
     • Cope with things flexibly.
     • Develop personnel's abilities and   Adaptable
       continue their learning.

People
     • Education
       (General learning as citizen of the society).
     • Investment in the training of personnel.   Adaptable
     • Education on practical business.
     • Organizational techniques.   Adaptable

9 Co-ordination Theory and Corporate Culture

Co-ordination science or co-ordination theory is propounded and advocated by Tom Malone and his colleagues at MIT. They address the following subjects and study them in an interdisciplinary approach.

- How can a firm employ computer networks which have increasingly high power?
- By those networks, can a firm change its organization structure and process so that it is able to compete much more effectively with others?

In other words, the co-ordination theory focuses on the subject of how the structure and process of an organization can be changed through the application of networks so that its essence of collaboration becomes the most effective. To realize how effectively people can collaborate by employing information technology, in turn, it is a prerequisite to know dependencies between their activities and ways of coordinating those dependencies. Co-ordination is defined here as managing dependencies. There are a number of different kinds of dependencies and their corresponding co-ordination processes. Tom Malone explains them as follows.

> But even there, our current hypothesis is that there are three elementary kinds of dependencies out of which all other important dependencies can be expressed, either by specialization or combination of these three elementary types. The three types of dependencies are flow, sharing, and fit. Flow means when one activity produces something that's used by another one, for example, when you write a report that someone else reads. Sharing occurs when multiple activities all need to use the same (limited) resource, like a machine on the factory floor or a fixed amount of money. Fit occurs when multiple activities produce things that have to fit together. For example, when multiple engineers are designing a car, there is a dependency between the engineer designing the engine and the engineer designing the body because the result of their work have to fit together in the same car. We define coordination as the management of dependencies among activities, and a key element of our approach is that, for each different kind of dependency, we identify a family of alternative coordination processes that can be used to manage dependencies of that type. For example, whenever there is a sharing dependency, you can, in principle, manage it with any of a variety of co-ordination mechanisms:

189

first come/first serve, priority order, managerial decision, market-like bidding, and others. And each of these co-ordination mechanisms can be specialized in many different ways for different kinds of situations.

(T. Malone, 1997, p15)

Now, let us suppose here that there are two types of organizations which set up the same objective, one being an organization whose activities are too many in number and too complex and the other being an organization whose activities are small in number and quite simple. By using Tom Malone's concepts, one is an organization with too many elementary kinds of dependencies, i.e., too numerous flow, sharing and fit dependencies, and a number of complex combination of those dependencies. The other is, on the contrary, an organization with not many elementary kinds of dependencies, i.e., not many flow, sharing and fit dependencies, and a small number of combination of those dependencies. The difference between the above two types of organizations is clearly manifest in their respective number of meetings, number of persons and places to report, number of telephone communication and others, and in the length of their decision-making process each. In the organization with two many and complex dependencies, there are seen an excessive number of meetings, too many persons or departments to report, too numerous contacts by telephone or other means, and a lengthy process of decision-making with too much time to reach a single decision. On the other hand, in the organization with not many and simple dependencies, the number of meetings, reports, telephone contacts and others is not many, and the decision-making process is short. In the organization with too numerous and complicated dependencies, both its decisions and actions are made too slow. In the organization with a small number of and simple dependencies, its decisions are made fast and its actions are taken quickly. Why, then, can the above two types of organizations be supposed and existing in reality although the object they set up to accomplish is the same?

Let us explain it here by using a key word of information. As is often argued, a corporate organization can be taken as a mechanism of getting information and processing it to make a decision. Accordingly, it can be recognized that the tardiness of decision-making and action is brought about by the following two phenomenal causes.

1   It takes an excessive amount of time to get information.
2   It takes an excessive amount of time to process information acquired.

Let us first see the (1) phenomenal cause that it takes an excessive amount of time to get information. What really produces that phenomenal cause? We can list the following fundamental causes behind it.

190

1-1 There is a barrier between the functional departments of an organization. Yet, there is no mechanism working to overcome such a barrier to smooth communication among personnel.

1-2 Seniors do not convey information to juniors, and juniors do not transfer information to seniors. We can see such a phenomenon above where there is no environment in the organization in which members freely exchange their views and opinion; where there is no care about human relations in the workplace so that the communication between managers and workers is deficient; where there is no or little mutual confidence between managers and workers; and so forth.

1-3 An organization is not open to the outside. Such a phenomenon can be seen where members of an organization are very much conscious of its stratum and therefore those positioned in the lower echelon, in particular, have no sense of representing their organization; where there is no setup prepared for diffusing new contrivances, improvement, knowledge on new products and others inside and outside the organization; and so forth.

1-4 A person who gets information is different from the one who makes a decision based on the information. Such a case can be found in an organization where first-hand information reaches a decision-maker only through layer after layer of management filtering; and so forth.

1-5 An organization has no intimate and close relationship with suppliers and customers. Accordingly, information on the supply and the demand sides does not appropriately flow into the organization.

Next, let us see the (2) phenomenal cause that it takes an excessive amount of time to process information acquired. What really produces that phenomenal cause? We can list the following fundamental causes behind it.

2-1 Members of an organization are scarcely offered opportunities of education and learning, or only a limited number of members are given such chances. It has to do with a matter of members' ability of understanding.

2-2 Members of an organization are offered few opportunities of education and learning on practical business. It has to do with a matter of members' ability of carrying out their work.

2-3 Members of an organization do not have most information in common. Such a phenomenon can be seen where an environment is not prepared for members to form a team in ad hoc manner; where a barrier is high between the functional departments of an organization; and so forth.

2-4 People and departments qualified to get information is limited. Such a case occurs where the thought is not accepted and shared by most members of an organization that every member is a leading actor; and so forth.

2-5 Many members of an organization can not determine which matters are to be given priority over others. Such a case occurs where mangers do not make it a practice to convey information fundamental to their company to workers; where there is no setup prepared of diffusing new contrivances, improvement, knowledge on new products and others inside and outside the organization; and so forth.

2-6 Unnecessary information is abundant. Such a case occurs where there are too many middle managers in the organization so that information indirect to decision-making is required for their intervenient role; where communication is not activated throughout the organization so that old and outdated information is liable to be accumulated.

Due to the fundamental causes above, i.e., 1-1 to 1-5 and 2-1 to 2-6, it takes an excessive amount of time to get information and it takes an excessive amount of time to process information acquired. As a result, the organization's decision-making and action are overly retarded. When we see the above fundamental causes very closely, in this connection, we can recognize that they represent certain kinds of attributes of an organization. It is understood, therefore, that those kinds of attributes are united or combined to produce the phenomena that (1) it takes an excessive amount of time to get information and that (2) it takes an excessive amount of time to process information acquired. That is, an organization with too many and complicated dependencies is regarded as that with many of the above kinds of attributes, while an organization with not many and simple dependencies is seen as that without or almost without the above kinds of attributes.

Now, then, how can those kinds of attributes be taken when viewed from the 3-Layer Structure of Enterprise Competitiveness and the 7 Principles of Enterprise Competitiveness? As can be imagined, they are considered to be unadaptive to the 3-Layer Structure of Enterprise Competitiveness and the 7 Principles of Enterprise Competitiveness. In particular, they may contradict the following competitiveness elements.

· People in the workplace freely exchange their views and opinions.
· There is teamwork among personnel.
· Personnel have pride and confidence in upholding their enterprise's competitiveness and have a sense of representing their enterprise.
· Education on practical business.
· Attention and care to human relations in the workplace.
· Create smooth communication lines.
· Discussion on the vision, policies and the state of affairs of the enterprise from management.

192

- Diffuse new ideas, reforms, improvements, and intelligence on new products both inside and outside the organization.
- Activate communication throughout.
- Have a close relationship with customers.
- Have intimate contact with suppliers.
- Organization whose workers are barely conscious of organizational hierarchy.
- Develop personnel's abilities and continue their learning.
- Every member is a leading actor.
- Ethics of relations between management and workers.

Taken together, the unadaptability of those attributes to the above elements can be seen as in Table 9.1 and Table 9.2.

Table 9.1   The 3-Layer Structure of Enterprise Competitiveness

I   Enterprise Organismic Foundation

Enterprise ethos
- Ethos originated in the early days of an enterprise, i.e., the spirit of denying, the spirit of negating the status quo, the spirit of creativity and the spirit of creating a vision, are maintained.
- Every member is willing to grapple with any situation without hesitation and without worrying about failure.
- People in the workplace freely exchange   Unadaptable
  their views and opinions.

Enhancement of initiative
- There is teamwork among personnel.   Unadaptable
- Personnel have pride and confidence in   Unadaptable
  upholding their enterprise's competitiveness
  and have a sense of representing their enterprise.
- Diligence and positive activities of personnel.
- Pride and confidence in one's own work.
- Self-reforming abilities.

Provision of norms
- Law (company regulations, etc.).
- Abolishment of practices restricting competition.

193

Preparation of investment conditions
- Allow a sufficiently long time frame for management.
- Promotion of R&D and production-process R&D.
- Constraints on speculative purchases of enterprises or assets.

Enterprise ethics
(Sense of responsibility to the society)

Education
(General learning as citizen of the society)

II Enterprise Economic Base

Infrastructure
- Physical assets   facilities, machinery, network.
- Human resources   executives, scientists, engineers, workers.
- Employment of human resources and procurement of physical assets to build and stabilize infrastructure.
- Investment in the training of personnel.
- Education on practical business.   Unadaptable

Environmental improvement and conservation
- Conservation of the natural environment.
- Cooperation with and participation in a community and its activities.
- Improvement of the physical environment of the workplace.
- Attention and care to human relations in the workplace.   Unadaptable

Diffusion of new ideas, planning and others
- Create smooth communication lines.   Unadaptable
- Discussion on the vision, policies and the state of affairs of the enterprise from management.   Unadaptable

194

- Diffuse new ideas, reforms, improvements, and intelligence on new products both inside and outside the organization.   Unadaptable

III   Management System

Effectiveness
- Maintain a free market principle throughout the enterprise.
- Encourage competitive spirit.
- Improve cost, quality and delivery terms simultaneously.
- Development, introduction and use of technology to gain strategic predominance.
- Commercialize technology.
- Activate communication throughout.   Unadaptable

Tense balance between effectiveness and ethics
- Have a close relationship with customers.   Unadaptable
- Have intimate contact with suppliers.   Unadaptable
- Organizational techniques.
- Organization whose workers are barely   Unadaptable
  conscious of organizational hierarchy.
- Recognition of quality as the end result of overall production and service activities.
- Generate many alternatives to a decision-making process.
- Demand and expect personnel to do their best.
- Cope with things flexibly.
- Develop personnel's abilities and   Unadaptable
  continue their learning.
- Guarantee long-term employment.

Ethics
- Every member is a leading actor.   Unadaptable
- A view of work in which diligence is highly esteemed.
- Improvement of ethics.
- Fair employment.
- Appropriate transfer of personnel from one post to another.

195

- Fair and just promotion of personnel.
- Ethics of relations between management and workers.   Unadaptable

Table 9.2   The 7 Principles of Enterprise Competitiveness

1 Creativity
- Ethos originated in the early days of an enterprise, i .e., the spirit of denying, the spirit of negating the status quo, the spirit of creativity and the spirit of creating a vision, are maintained.
- Every member is willing to grapple with any situation without hesitation and without worrying about failure.
- Self-reforming abilities.

2 Righteousness
- Law (company regulations, etc.).
- Ethics of relations between management and workers.   Unadaptable
- Abolishment of practices restricting competition.
- Constraints on speculative purchases of enterprises or assets.
- Enterprise ethics (Sense of responsibility to the society).
- A view of work in which diligence is highly esteemed.
- Improvement of ethics.

3 Fairness
- Maintain a free market principle throughout the enterprise.
- Encourage competitive spirit.
- Fair employment.
- Appropriate transfer of personnel from one post to another.
- Fair and just promotion of personnel.

4 Equality
- People in the workplace freely exchange their views and opinions.   Unadaptable

196

- There is teamwork among personnel.   Unadaptable
- Personnel have pride and confidence in   Unadaptable
  upholding their enterprise's competitiveness
  and have a sense of representing
  their enterprise.
- Organization whose workers are barely   Unadaptable
  conscious of organizational hierarchy.
- Recognition of quality as the end result
  of overall production or service activities.
- Guarantee long-term employment.
- Every member is a leading actor.   Unadaptable

5 Sharing
- Conservation of the natural environment.
- Cooperation with and participation in
  a community and its activities.
- Improvement of the physical environment of
  the workplace.
- Attention and care to human relations in   Unadaptable
  the workplace.
- Create smooth communication lines.   Unadaptable
- Discussion on the vision, policies and the state of   Unadaptable
  affairs of the enterprise from management.
- Diffuse new ideas, reforms, improvements, and   Unadaptable
  intelligence on new products both inside and
  outside the organization.
- Activate communication throughout.   Unadaptable
- Have a close relationship with customers.   Unadaptable
- Have intimate contact with suppliers.   Unadaptable

6 Self-Cultivation
- Diligence and positive activities of personnel.
- Pride and confidence in one's own work.
- Demand and expect personnel to do their best.

7 Learning and Knowledge-Accumulation

Technology
- Commercialize technology.
- Development, introduction and use of technology
  to gain strategic predominance.
- Promotion of R&D and production-process R&D.

197

- Employment of human resources and procurement of physical assets to build and stabilize infrastructure.
- Physical assets.
- Human resources.

Systems thinking
- Allow a sufficiently long time frame for management.
- Generate many alternatives to a decision-making process.
- Improve cost, quality and delivery terms simultaneously.
- Cope with things flexibly.
- Develop personnel's abilities and continue their learning.   Unadaptable

People
- Education (General learning as citizen of the society).
- Investment in the training of personnel.
- Education on practical business.   Unadaptable
- Organizational techniques.

Thus, out of the two types of organizations, that with an excessive number of and complex dependencies is considered to have many of the above attributes and, therefore, apparently unadaptive to the 3-Layer Structure of Enterprise Competitiveness and the 7 Principles of Enterprise Competitiveness. Accordingly, its culture is regarded as unhealthy. How, then, can an organization with few and simple dependencies be looked upon? We have already seen such an organization. W. L. Gore & Associates, Inc., as we have described in the previous chapter, is an organization typical of that with a small number of and simple dependencies. At Gore, information spreads like lightning on the lattice organization structure. Work is carried out by forming a group ad hoc. Accordingly, it does not take much time to get information, and it does not take excessive time to process information acquired. W. L. Gore & Associates, Inc. is a company with an utterly healthy corporate culture. Tom Malone cites, in this connection, McKinsey, a consulting firm in the United States.

McKinsey is one of the largest and most successful management consulting firms, and it already embodies some of these Internet-like principles. (In fact, many consulting firms do.) In McKinsey, for the most part, no one at the top of the organization tells their partners what to do. They don't tell partners which clients to go after or what kind of work to do. The partners are essentially independent, autonomous decision makers, like the people operating on the Internet. What the McKinsey organization does is establish the interaction protocols between these more or less autonomous entities or agents. For example, it establishes a lot of cultural expectations about what you do when another partner calls you on the phone. You answer, you return the call, you try to be helpful. The organization also establishes a set of protocols for the selection process at many stages in the organization. Then, because you know that anyone else at a certain level in the organization has gone through a certain rigorous selection process, you can make a whole lot of assumptions about what kind of person you're talking to, even if you've never met them before. The analogy I'm making is that, just as the Internet defines a set of interaction protocols, one of the most important things a consulting organization like McKinsey provides to its highly autonomous partners is a set of agreements about how to interact with each other. And within that communication framework, within those interaction protocols, there's very little centralized direction about what to do. The establishment of that framework for communicating can be a very powerful enabler for lots of very good emergent work.

(Ibid. pp17-18)

At McKinsey, as in Gore, the organization is formed with a thought which has much in common with the decentralized organization model of the Internet. Here, speedy acquisition of information and its timely processing is realized. In that sense, the dependencies of McKinsey seem to be small in number and simple in nature.

Now, we have described so far two types of organizations. One is an organization with too many and complex dependencies, and the other is an organization with not many and simple dependencies. Let us next see what solution the present information technology can come up with to the former organization, i.e., an organization with too numerous and complicated dependencies.

It is said that an age of new organizations has arrived. New forms of organizations seem to be made feasible by IT. When having carried out a collaborative work, for instance, it had conventionally to be done in a locationally limited area. With the present development level of IT, however, the collaborative work can be conducted in a decentralized fashion. Yet, it can be more effectively done than in the past. That is, IT helps to create a new form of collaboration and thus make a new form of organization feasible. It is technically possible. To elaborate on it further, IT has promising possibilities of turning the organization with too numerous and complicated dependencies into

199

that with not many and simple dependencies. It seems to be a fact, in this context, that the transformation of an organization has historically coincided with IT development. While hierarchical organizations have tended to move to flat forms of organizations, the centralized form of mainframe has mostly been replaced by the decentralized form of client server. It contains some truth, also, that IT revolution is both the cause and result of changes in organization. As alterations in the structure of an organization may promote a new technology development, changes in IT can affect the nature of an organization. For instance, dividing an organization to form small ones or forming ad hoc and project teams may have facilitated the development of IT. Conversely, changes in IT such as networking and development of client server may have transformed the nature of an organization, having promoted the division of an organization to form small ones and the formation of ad hoc and project teams. E. Brynjolfsson and H. Mendelson states the following.

> In our view, the growing use of IT and the trend towards networking and client-server computing are both a cause and effect of the organization transition. Lowering the costs of horizontal communications, facilitating teamwork, enabling flexible manufacturing and providing information support for time management and quality control are key enablers on the supply side. It is equally clear that the new organizational paradigm demands new information systems: nothing can be more devastating for cross-functional teamwork than a rigid information system that inhibits cross-functional information flows. We can unify these perspectives by noting that the structure of the organization's information system is a key element of organizational transformation. Changes in IT change the nature of organizations just as changes in organizational structure drive the development of new technologies...Client-server computing technology lowers cross-functional (as well as geographic) barriers. IT (when applied properly) streamlines the types of information that used to be the raison d'etre of middle management — quantitative control information — and turns it into general knowledge that can be readily transmitted to, and processed by, people other than those who originally gathered the data. A reduction in the number of management layers and the thinning out of middle management ranks is the predictable result.
>
> (E. Brynjolfsson and H. Mendelson, 1993)

It seems still true, in this context, that the development of IT is a necessary condition but not a sufficient condition for changes in organization. An organization has diverse kinds of attributes. Take, for instance, workers' sense of identity. It represents that workers are culturally committed to their organization. As described previously, in the thought on the Internet, technical characteristics are closely united with cultural traits. The characteristics of IT are combined with cultural traits to form the thought on the Internet. There is a clue here to the development and application of IT. That is, the new IT could be applied with some solid cultural traits to simplify the dependencies of an organization. Then, it would be recognized to be a match for the past industrial revolutions. It is the previously mentioned kinds of attributes of an organization that render the organization's dependencies too numerous and complicated. By introducing and employing IT in such a way as to eradicate those dependencies, the organization can be brought to a healthy state. Accordingly, how successfully the new IT has been introduced and employed in an organization can be judged by how much the organization's adaptability has been raised to the 3-Layer Structure of Enterprise Competitiveness and the 7 Principles of Enterprise Competitiveness. In other words, if and only if IT could virtually contribute to the creation of a new firm which is fully adaptive to the 3-Layer Structure of Enterprise Competitiveness and the 7 Principles of Enterprise Competitiveness, it would merit the name of IT revolution. It is no question that the thought on the Internet is a forerunner in that respect.

Epilogue

Corporate culture is to a corporate organization what personality is to an individual. Corporate culture is the personality of a company and its identity. As an individual's personality develops and forms while they grow, the company's corporate culture evolves and forms as it develops. While the corporate organization develops and forms, it continues to cope with the issues of external adaptation and internal integration, thereby learning from them. Through its development process, the members of the company learn how to view things, how to think of them and what state of being to comply with, whereby evolving and forming corporate culture. The way of viewing things here can be alternatively called 'a view of the world' or 'a paradigm', the mode of thinking 'a view of values' and the state of being 'an ethical norm'. While the company evolves and forms, its corporate culture comes to be shared among its members. It is the shared way of viewing, the shared mode of thinking and the shared state of being among its members. Corporate culture is a multi-level structure. It is said to consist of three levels in that it evolves and forms as a company develops and grows. According to Ed Shein, there are from the deepest 'Basic Assumptions', 'Values', and 'Artifacts and Creations'. Before the founding or before joining the company, however, each member of it has learned, as an individual member of the society they belong to, its prevailing culture. There are more than one culture in the society, but there is one leading culture prevailing among them. The leading culture has historically evolved and formed among the people of a nation. To be precise, the leitmotif of a nation's culture formed in its early days and then has been succeeded in its history through learning from generation to generation. In Japan's case, it is the leading culture formed early in its history, i.e., the Kami Way. The author thus argues that corporate culture is a four-level structure with the leading culture of the nation being in the deepest level.

A corporate organization is a being acting in an environment where competition goes on incessantly. Companies that win competition after competition can live long. What is of significance here is for a firm to maintain its competitiveness strength for a long time. There are elements indispensable to competitiveness, and corporate culture is duly related to those elements. Healthy corporate culture is appropriate to the elements of competitiveness while unhealthy culture is inappropriate to them. Companies with a culture unadaptable to the elements of competitiveness are not in a position to continue to win on the competitive market. If a firm survives due to the government's protective policies and regulations, the firm will, in time, be thrown out of the market because such policies and regulations can not be maintained for long. Regulated markets or regulated industries, where competition is unduly restricted, are a poison spreading over the national economy. They are the sources rendering the national economy unhealthy. The just and fair market principle is fundamental to the healthy state of the national economy. It is for this reason that a firm needs to form a healthy corporate culture adaptable to the competitiveness elements. The elements of competitiveness are, in turn, to be embraced in the 3-Layer Structure of Enterprise Competitiveness where the first layer is Enterprise Organismic Foundation, the second layer is Enterprise Economic Base and the third layer Management System. There are also the 7 Principles to which the elements of competitiveness belong. They are creativity, righteousness, fairness, equality, sharing, self-cultivation, and learning and knowledge-accumulation. Corporate cultures adaptable to the 7 Principles of Enterprise Competitiveness are healthy while those unadaptable are unhealthy.

The Kami Way is learned through tacit knowing. As Michael Polanyi said, a growing young mind tacitly absorbs and interiorizes the whole conceptual framework and the rules of reasoning out of the culture they belong to. The intellectual power obtained after they grow up is rooted in the knowledge tacitly absorbed in the above way. Their thoughts founded on that tacitly acquired knowledge gives meaning to all explicit knowledge. With informal recognition obtained through tacit knowing, one can formalize relations and make formal theories. In that sense, the basic part of culture tacitly absorbed is in the deepest level of one's mind and can have the capacity of acting as the principle of integrating. The core of the Kami Way is to practice the principles of life. It is to learn and adapt to nature. It is to learn human nature from the principles of nature. The Kami Way has only one criteria in judging things. It is to judge if things are healthy or unhealthy. Those adaptable to the principles of life and the principles of nature are taken as being healthy while those unadaptable to them are taken as being unhealthy. The Kami Way simply recognizes the state and phenomena of nature through 7 principles. The truth is always simple. The Kami Way strives to understand the principles of nature as simply as possible. As such, the attributes of the Kami Way are respectively adaptable to the 7 Principles of Enterprise Competitiveness.

Which firms in reality then, can we take up as a firm with healthy corporate culture or one with unhealthy corporate culture? In Chapter 6 and Chapter 7, we have respectively taken up a pair of companies, one as an example of healthy corporate culture and the other as that of unhealthy culture.

In Chapter 6, we have addressed the cultures of the House of Mitsui and the House of Kohnoike. The House of Mitsui and the House of Kohnoike were both representative merchant houses of the Tokugawa era (1603-1867). Mitsui

203

founded Echigoya drapery stores and Mitsui money exchange shops and laid the foundation of the Mitsui zaibatsu later on. Kohnoike started at first with the business of brewing sake and later the shipping line. When founder Masanari became its owner, furthermore, it initiated the money exchange line of business and afterwards closed its business of brewing. Later still, in the third generation Munetoshi, it abolished the line of marine transport and narrowed its business to the single line of money exchange. Mitsui and Kohnoike both evolved and developed in the Tokugawa times (1603-1867), having employed a number of employees and thrived. At the arrival of Meiji Restoration (1868), i.e., that of industrialization and modernization, however, they followed quite a different path respectively. That is, Mitsui successfully overcame the difficulties in this transition to develop further while Kohnoike failed and fell into obscurity.

To search for the main causes of Mitsui's success and Kohnoike's failure, we have traced historically how their cultures evolved and formed. And we came to understand that Mitsui's culture was fully adaptive to the 3-Layer Structure of Enterprise Competitiveness and the 7 Principles of Enterprise Competitiveness as at the beginning of Meiji era while Kohnoike's was altogether unadaptable to them.

In the culture of Mitsui, ways of thought similar to Baigan Ishida's can be found. For instance, thoughts in common were working hard, prudence, honesty and saving. Mitsui learned from the public what they demanded as Baigan Ishida learned from Yaoyorozu-No-Kami. It tried to expand sales of its silk fabrics to the general public, i.e., the craftsmen, merchants and farmers, although their selling had been conventionally limited to the samurai class and big merchant houses. In the latter half of the 17th century, the capital of Edo had a population of about one million. Out of the one million, 500,000 were samurai warriors, since, as well as direct retainers of the Tokugawa, lords around the country periodically lived in Edo with their retainers due to the alternate-year dwelling system. The remaining 500,000 were craftsmen and merchants. Into the 18th century, the population of craftsmen and merchants showed a rapid increase while that of the samurai remained unchanged. The economic strength of the craftsmen and merchants as well as farmers in the vicinity of Edo grew proportionately. It is understood that to learn from the public was vitally important. Moreover, the Tokugawa shogunate government and the lords adopted Confucianism as an official ideology whereas the general public's ways of viewing, modes of thinking and state of being are of the Kami Way. At times, merchant houses used the 'filial piety', a word from Confucianism. However, 'filial piety' was generally meant for merchants to maintain customers' confidence, cultivating such virtues as saving, endurance and honesty, and thereby becoming a wealthy merchant. Confucian thought was remodeled in their own way. It was Baigan Ishida that systematized those merchants' ways of viewing, modes of thinking and state of being. The House of Mitsui was, in this context, a typical performer of the merchant way advocated by Baigan Ishida.

On the other hand, the culture of Kohnoike was of a seniority system where classicism and the rule-by-virtue principle, i.e., attributes of Confucianism, were apparently recognized. Kohnoike's culture may have formed through its long acquaintance with lords and providing loans to them. The owners of the House of Kohnoike were permitted to use a surname and wear a sword like samurai, whereby they may also have been influenced by Confucianism. To put it another way, Kohnoike did not learn from the public, but learned from the samurai with whom it had so intimate a relation as to be a disadvantage to other competitors. It is in this fact where the seeds of Kohnoike's misfortune lay.

In Chapter 7, we have addressed the cultures of the House of Mitsubishi and the House of Ohkura. The House of Mitsubishi and the House of Ohkura both started their business in the Meiji era. They had evolved and developed since then and respectively formed a large corporate group as zaibatsu before World War II. Mitsubishi was a company founded by Yataro Iwasaki with shipping as its main line of business. Through the Political Change of the year 1881, however, its business focus changed from that of the sea to of land. The second president Yanosuke then united shipbuilding, mining and banking lines of business to start again, and laid down the foundation of Mitsubishi zaibatsu. On the other hand, Kihachiro Ohkura founded Ohkura & Company which was later reorganized to be two enterprises, i.e., Ohkura Civil Engineering Co. which was engaged in the construction contracting business and Ohkura & Co., Ltd. which conducted a trading line of business and managing investment in a group of affiliated companies. With these two pillars, Ohkura pushed ahead with its business. During the two wars, in particular, it showed its genuine ability for military procurement and increasingly grew. When World War II came to an end, however, Mitsubishi and Ohkura followed altogether a different route. Mitsubishi continued to grow business after the war while Ohkura collapsed with the end of the war and fell into obscurity.

Having pursued the primary cause of the difference between Mitsubishi's success and Ohkura's failure, we have historically traced how the cultures of Mitsubishi and Ohkura had evolved and developed respectively. Again, it was found that the culture of Mitsubishi was fully adaptive to the 3-Layer Structure of Enterprise Competitiveness and the 7 Principles of Enterprise Competitiveness as at the end of World War II while that of Ohkura showed its unadaptability to them. In Mitsubishi's culture, we can see Yomigaeri, an attribute of the Kami Way. It seems to have stemmed from Mitsubishi's reviving at the turn of its business from the sea to the land in 1886 when Mitsubishi completely discarded its government-affiliated disposition to follow the business-first principle and the principle of nonintervention in politics.

Mitsubishi also had a way of thinking that one is to observe justice in commerce and industry, be fair in addressing everything, and win a success with genuine efforts, not yielding to any failures. Here, Akaki-kokoro, an attribute of the Kami Way, can be recognized. The culture of Mitsubishi is fundamentally of two layers. The first layer formed by 1893 when Mitsubishi & Co., Ltd. was founded, and the second layer was created by the fourth president Koyata Iwasaki and his followers. Those two layers had been reinforced, consolidated and succeeded up to the end of World War II in 1945, when it was still strong. It then continued to contribute to the development of the Mitsubishi companies. On the other hand, the culture of Ohkura was generally healthy when it was primarily engaged in trading activities. Later, through the two great Sino-Japanese (1894-1895) and the Russo-Japanese Wars (1904-1905), Kihachiro achieved substantial success as a government-affiliated businessman whereby the second layer of Ohkura's culture formed. At this stage, the initial first layer was still alive although it was considerably weakened. When World War I commenced in 1914, he won great success through his connection to the military, which in turn caused the first layer become extinct, and allow the second layer to replace it completely and take root at Ohkura instead. That culture succeeded until World War II ended in 1945, and Ohkura was ultimately dissolved as described before.

A government-affiliated businessperson carries out their business in league with the government officials and the military. They put themself in the government's or military's position but not in the public's position. That is, they do not try to learn from the general public. Accordingly, they are inevitably inclined to act arbitrarily on their own authority. The undertaking of Honkeikoh Coal & Steel Co., Ltd. was its good example. The rule-by-virtue principle that was prevalently advocated by the government and the military. The rule-by-virtue principle by its nature underrates craftsmen and technology. There was, therefore, essentially a limit to rational management at Honkeikoh Coal & Steel Co., Ltd. since it was a joint concern of Ohkura with Shenyang Province authorities. To put it further, that limit is also the limit of Kihachiro Ohkura as a government-affiliated businessman.

In Chapter 8, we have examined the thinking behind the Internet, explained how to interpret it, and seen W. L. Gore & Associates, Inc. as a typical example of corporate organization adapted to that thinking. The Internet is a model of decentralized organization. The members of the Internet organization can collaborate each other while sustaining their autonomy and individuality. Interoperability is assured by the TCP/IP protocol. Even with only the Internet Protocol in common, the members can freely develop new applications and create new values. The Internet, also, has no chief network within it which can be its foundation or govern the whole system. There are a number of alternative routes in going from one point to another, and due to that redundancy, any defect occurring somewhere in the Internet does not affect the other parts. The Internet is referred to as the colleague network where everone is provided an equal opportunity to play whatever role in it and can be a leading actor of communication. Thus, with the interoperability founded on TCP/IP, colleague networking and redundancy characteristic, the Internet is 99 percent operated in a decentralized fashion. On the other hand, there is IETF as a group of technically supporting the present interoperability and devising a still newer way to interoperate for the future. There is also IANA and RIRs which are engaged or concerned in the allotment of IP addresses and domain names. Those agencies are positioned not as a monopoly operating the Internet, but rather as a coordinating organ. They are coordinators of a decentralized organization of the Internet, and as previously stated, their work seems to be so small as to be about 1 percent of the whole operation. In that way, the Internet is 99 percent operated in a decentralized manner and 1 percent operated in an administered way.

On the other hand, the lattice organization structure is characteristic of W. L. Gore & Associates, Inc.. It is a form of decentralized organization where its members can take any leadership role and act autonomously. There is the support team which works to coordinate functions within the organization. The team members hold meetings twice a year to adjust the company's marketing, sales and production plans. Here, we can see the same thought as that on the decentralized organization model of the Internet which is 99 percent operated in a decentralized manner and 1 percent operated in an administered fashion. That is, most activities at Gore are carried out in a decentralized and autonomous way and only a minimum function is left to the support team. How can the associates comprising the lattice communicate and interchange between them? It is the sponsor system that facilitates their communication and interchange. By analogy, the role of the sponsor corresponds to that of the provider or that of Internet Protocol. With the sponsor system as given, the lattice organization is 99 percent operated in a decentralized fashion. The lattice organization structure is a colleague network. Therefore, it is taboo at Gore to call its members an employee, subordinate and administrator. Hierarchy is thought to keep an individual from displaying their creativity. Associates are encouraged to work, like an application developer at the Internet, in a creative and innovative way in the open, barrierless work environment of the lattice organization. Everyone is a leading actor. Everyone can take the leadership in whatever matters, and the information among associates spreads like lightning on the lattice organization and goes around it. This organization is of no stratum, where everyone is respected as an individual. It works as a mechanism that promotes entrepreneurial dynamism and makes innovation and value creation feasible as in the Internet.

Taken together, W. L. Gore & Associates, Inc. is considered to be a form of enterprise realized out of virtually the same thought as that on the Internet. The company fundamentally has the ways of viewing, modes of thinking and state of being in common with the Internet. In that sense, it gives us many suggestions as to a corporate organization in the 21st century. It is evident, yet, that the culture of W. L. Gore & Associates, Inc. is fully adaptive to the 3-Layer Structure of Enterprise Competitiveness and the 7 Principles of Enterprise Competitiveness.

It is now an age of information technology. The development of IT advances with ever increasing speed. The technological development of the Internet, in particular, has been remarkable and its diffusion has been accelerating. It is often said that the advancement of the Internet well deserves the name of an information revolution or a new industrial revolution. It seems still true, in this context, that the development of IT is a necessary condition but not a sufficient condition for changes in organization. An organization has diverse kinds of attributes. For instance, take the workers' sense of identity. It shows that workers are culturally committed to their organization. As described previously on the Internet, technical characteristics are closely united with cultural traits. The characteristics of IT are combined with cultural traits to form on the Internet. There is a clue here to the development and application of IT. The new IT could be applied with some solid cultural traits to simplify the dependencies of an organization. Then, it would be recognized to be a match for the past industrial revolutions.

The history of corporate culture is as old as that of corporate organization. When a firm is founded, its corporate culture originates also. Accordingly, it means much to go back to examine past corporate cultures. On the other hand, the subject of corporate culture is that of the present and that of the future. It has much meaning, therefore, to examine corporate culture as associated with present information technology which may be the forerunner of the future. The author believes that the 3-Layer Structure of Enterprise Competitiveness and the 7 Principles of Enterprise Competitiveness can be a thread uniting corporate culture of the past, that of the present and that of the future. Competitiveness and corporate culture are unseparably united. Understanding this unseparable relationship in the correct fashion may be a large step forward for business leaders to create a genuinely healthy and creative company in the 21st century.

Bibliography

Arker, David A. (1984), *Strategic Market Management*, John Wiley & Sons, Inc: New York.

Barnard, Chester I. (1968), *The Functions of the Executive*, Harvard University Press: Boston, MA.

Brynjolfsson, Eric and Mendelson, Haim (1993), 'Information Systems and the Organization of Modern Enterprise', *Journal of Organizational Computing*, December issue, 1993.

Chandler, A.D., Jr. (1962), *Strategy and Structure: Chapters in the History of the American Industrial Enterprise*, MIT Press: Cambridge, MA.

Chimoto, Akiko (1998), 'Case 5' in Hiroyuki Itami, Tadao Kagono, Matao Miyamoto and Seiichiro Yonekura (eds.), *Nihonteki Keiei no Seisei to Hatten* [Evolvement and Development of Japanese Management], Yuhikaku: Tokyo.

Collins, James C. and Porras, Jerry I. (1998), *Built to Last*, Random House: London.

Crowston, Kevin (1994), *Electronic communication and new organizational forms: A coordination theory approach* (Technical Report #175), MIT Center for Coordination Science: Cambridge, MA.

Deal, Terrence E. and Kennedy, Allan A. (1982), *Corporate Cultures*, Addison-Wesley Longman, Inc.: Reading, MA.

Drucker, Peter F. (1993), *Innovation and Entrepreneurship*, Harper Business: New York.

Gillett, Sharon E. and Kaper, Mitchell (1997), 'The Self-governing Internet: Coordination by Design', in Brian Kahin and James Keller (eds.), *Coordination of the Internet*, MIT Press: Cambridge, MA.

Goldman, Steven L., Nagel, Roger N. and Preiss, Kenneth (1995), *Agile Competitors and Virtual Organizations: Strategies for Enriching the Customer*, Van Nostrand Reinhold: New York.

Hamuro, Yoriaki (1997), *Shinto no Kokoro* [The Essence of the Kami Way], Shunjyusha: Tokyo.

Hamuro, Yoriaki (1999), *Shinto to Nihonjin* [The Kami Way and the Japanese], Syunjyusha: Tokyo.

Hayashi, Shuhji (1984), *Keiei to Bunka* [Management and Culture], Chuo Koronsha: Tokyo.

Honda, Soichiro (1992), *Ete ni Ho agete* [Sail Before The Wind], Mikasa Shobo: Tokyo.

Iijima, Nobuko (1995), *Kankyo Shakaigaku no Susume* [Exhortation to Environment Sociology], Maruzen: Tokyo.

Irimajiri, Yoshinaga (1960), *Jinbutsu Sosho Iwasaki Yataro* [Pofile of Yataro Iwasaki], Yoshikawa Kobunkan: Tokyo.

Itami, Hiroyuki and Kagono, Tadao (1997), *Keieigaku Nyumon* [Introduction to Management Theory], Nihon Keizai Shimbunsha: Tokyo.

Itoh, Shuntaro (ed.) (1995), *Nihonjin no Shizenkan* [The Japanese View of Nature], Kawade-Shobo Shinsha: Tokyo.

Katoh, Hidetoshi (1969), *Ningen Kaihatsu* [Cultivation of the Mind], Chuo Koronsha: Tokyo.

Katoh, Hidetoshi (1970), *Ikigai no Shuhen* [Something about One's Life Worth Living], Bungei Shunjyu: Tokyo.

Katoh, Hidetoshi (1991), *Shuzoku no Shakaigaku* [Sociology of Folkways], PHP Kenkyujyo: Tokyo.

Kiplinger, A.H. and Kiplinger, K.A. (1989), *America in the Global '90*, Kiplinger Books: Washington D.C.

Koike, Kazuo (1997), *Nihon Kigyo no Jinzai Keisei* [Cultivation of Talents by Japanese Companies], Chuo Koronsha: Tokyo.

Kotter, John P. and Heskett, James L. (1992), *Corporate Culture and Performance*, The Free Press: New York.

Lawrence, Paul R. and Lorsh, Jay W. (1967), *Organization and Environment*, Harvard University Press: Boston, MA.

Leavitt, H.J. (1975), 'Suppose We Took Groups Seriously in E.L. Cass and F.G. Zimer (eds.), *Man and Work in Society*, Van Nostrand Reinhold: New York.

Malone, Thomas W. and Crowston, Kevin (1994), 'The Interdisciplinary Study of Coordination', ACM *Computing Surveys*, March issue, 1994.

Malone, Thomas W. (1997), 'Free On The Range', IEE *Internet Commmputing*, May/June issue, 1997.

Mantz, Charles C. and Sims, Henry P. Jr. (1993), *Business Without Bosses*, John Wiley & Sons, Inc.: New York.

Maslow, A.H. (1954), *Motivation and Personality*, Harper: New York.

McGregor, Douglas (1960), *The Human Side of Enterprise*, McGraw-Hill: New York.

McGregor, Douglas (1967), *The Professional Manager*, McGraw-Hill: New York.

Miyagawa, Takayasu (1996), *Iwasaki Koyata* [Koyata Iwasaki], Chuo Koronsha: Tokyo.

Miyamoto, Mataji (1958), *Jinbutsu Sosho Kohnoike Zenemon* [Profile of Zenemon Kohnoike], Yoshikawa Kobunkan: Tokyo.

Miyamoto, Matao (1998), 'Case 1' In Hiroyuki Itami, Tadao Kagono, Matao Miyamoto and Seiichiro Yonekura (eds.), *Nihonteki Keiei no Seisei to Hatten* [Evolvement and Development of Japanese Management], Yuhikaku: Tokyo.

Morita, Akio (1994), *Gakureki Muyo Ron* [No Use for School Career], Asahi Shinbun: Tokyo.

Murai, Jun (1995), *Intarnetto* [Internet], Iwanami Shoten: Tokyo.

Muramatsu, Ei (1994), *Jyukyo no Doku* [Poison of Confucianism], PHP Kenkyujyo: Tokyo.

Morton, Michael S. Scott and Allen, Thomas J. (eds.) (1994), *Information Technology and The Corporation of The 1990s*, Oxford University Press: New York.

Nakata, Yasunao (1959), *Jinbutsu Sosho Mitsui Takatoshi* [Profile of Takatoshi Mitsui], Yoshikawa Kobunkan: Tokyo.

Nishiyama, Kenichi (1985), *Kigyo no Tekioh Senryaku* [Corporate Adaptation Strategy], Chuo Koronsha: Tokyo.

Nonaka, Ikujiro and Konno, Noboru (1995), *Chiryoku Keiei* [Intellectualizing Capability], Nihon Keizai Shimbunsha: Tokyo.

Ohkura Zaibatsu Kenkyukai (eds.) (1982), *Ohkura Zaibatsu no Kenkyu* [Study of Ohkura Zaibatsu], Kondoh Shupansha: Tokyo.

Okuzumi, Masamichi (1997), *Kokyaku Shakai* [Customers' Society], Chuo Koronsha: Tokyo.

Ouchi, William (1981), *Theory Z*, Addison-Wesley: Reading, MA.

Pascal, Richard T. and Athos, Anthony G. (1981), *The Art of Japanese Management*, Simon & Schuster: New York.

Peters, Tom and Waterman, Robert H. Jr. (1995), *In Search of Excellence*, Harper Collins Publisher: New York.

Polanyi, Michael (1983), *THE TACIT DIMENSION*, Peter Smith: Gloucester, MA.

Porter, Michael (1989), *The Competitive Advantage of Nations*, Macmillan Press Ltd.: London.

Schein, Edgar H. (1985), *Organizational Culture and Leadership*, Jossey-Bass Inc., Publishers: San Francisco, CA.

Senge, Peter M. (1990), *The Fifth Discipline: The Art and Practice of the Learning Organization*, Doubleday: New York.

Shibata, Minoru (1962), *Jinbutsu Sosho Ishida Baigan* [Profile of Baigan Ishida], Yoshikawa Kobunkan: Tokyo.

Simon, Herbert A. (1976), *Administrative Behavior*, 3rd Edition, Free Press: New York.

Starr, M.K. (1988), *Global Competitiveness*, W. W. Norton & Co.: New York.

Sunagawa, Yukio (1996), *Ohkura Kihachiro no Gohkainaru Shohgai* [Kihachiro Ohkura's Exciting Life], Sohshisha: Tokyo.

Thurow, Lester (1996), *The Future of Capitalism*, William Morrow & Company: New York.

Walton, Richard E. (1989), *Up and Running*, the Harvard Business School Press: Boston, MA.

Yamashita, Hideo (1996), *Competitiveness and the Kami Way*, Ashgate Publishing Ltd.: Aldershot, U.K.

Yamashita, Hideo (1998), *Competitiveness and Corporate Culture*, Ashgate Publishing Ltd.: Aldershot, U.K.